IDENTITY THEFT
INVESTIGATIONS

CLIFF ROBERSON, LL.M., PH.D.

New York

This publication is designed to provide accurate and authoritative information in regard to the subject matter covered. It is sold with the understanding that the publisher is not engaged in rendering legal, accounting, or other professional service. If legal advice or other expert assistance is required, the services of a competent professional should be sought.

Published by Kaplan Publishing, a division of Kaplan, Inc.
1 Liberty Plaza, 24th Floor
New York, NY 10006

Printed in the United States of America

August 2008
10 9 8 7 6 5 4 3 2 1

ISBN-13: 978-1-4277-9743-8

Kaplan Publishing books are available at special quantity discounts to use for sales promotions, employee premiums, or educational pur-poses. Please email our Special Sales Department to order or for more information at kaplanpublishing@kaplan.com, or write to Kaplan Publishing, 1 Liberty Plaza, 24th Floor, New York, NY 10006.

TABLE OF CONTENTS

Restitution
Wrongful Arrest
Lawsuits Based on Negligence
Violation of Fair Credit Reporting Act
Need to Establish Monetary Damages
Recovery of Attorney Fees

Appendixes

FOREWORD

Identity theft is not a violent offense, but its victims will often feel as if their world is ending. It wreaks havoc on the lives of its victims, many of whom develop psychological issues that will take years to heal. In addition, because of the nature of identity theft, it is difficult to prosecute. This manual, *Identity Theft Investigations*, is for law-enforcement officers who investigate this kind of crime and prepare cases for prosecution, as well as for victims' rights advocates who assist in people's recovery from identity theft. This book is intended to assist in preventing and detecting identity theft, as well as apprehending and prosecuting individuals who commit identity theft. In addition, it is designed to provide self-defense against identity theft and guidance on how to help victims recover from this vicious crime. It also provides information that is highly useful to the individual who is either the victim of identity theft or wants to avoid becoming one.

Professionals assisting identity theft victims must remember to be compassionate. Normally, the victim is more frustrated and psychologically damaged than economically harmed. Chapter 1 contains a general discussion of identity theft, and chapter 2 discusses the types of theft and victimology issues. Chapter 3 focuses on preventing identity theft, and chapter 4 discusses the investigation of identity theft. Chapter 5 covers the prosecution aspects of the crime, and chapter 6 focuses on the victim's recovery. In Chapter 7, an experienced Los Angeles police officer and a veteran prosecutor provide practical guidance on investigating and filing identity theft incidents. Chapter 7 concludes with an article by an assistant U.S. attorney that provides a summary of the issues involved with identity theft incidents. Appendix A contains summaries of federal legislation on the crime, and appendix B focuses on state legislation. Appendix C provides an extensive list of resources available to law enforcement, victims, and victim advocates. Appendix D has a copy of an identity theft affidavit that may be used by the victim. Finally, appendix E has a copy of the Executive Summary of the President's Identity Theft Task Force Report.

Comments and any suggestions for improvement may be submitted to the author at *croberson@kaplan.edu.*

CHAPTER 1

IDENTITY THEFT: THE CRIME AND ITS MAGNITUDE

CHAPTER OUTLINE

- Introduction
- What Constitutes Identity Theft?
- Nature of the Crime
- Identity Theft Is Not New
- Magnitude of the Crime
- Laws Designed to Combat Identity Thieves
- Federal Trade Commission
- Role of Law Enforcement in Preventing and Handling Identity Theft
- Key Terms

INTRODUCTION

Although identity theft can be defined in many different ways, it is fundamentally the misuse of another individual's personal information to commit fraud or theft. According to the U.S. Postal Service, identity theft is America's fastest growing crime.[1] In this chapter, we will examine what constitutes identity theft, its nature, its history, and the legislation designed to combat it. This chapter is an introduction to the crime and its issues. In later chapters, the concepts introduced here will be explored in more depth.

On December 10, 2007, Byron Acohido reported in *U.S.A. Today* that the reports of personal data theft for 2007 were more than triple the number reported in 2006. He noted that over 162 million records were reported lost or stolen in 2007, more than triple the 49.7 million that went missing in 2006. According to Acohido, news stories in 2007 recounted data losses disclosed by 98 companies, 85 schools, 80 government agencies, and 39 hospitals and clinics. Yet arrests or prosecutions were reported in just 19 cases in that year.

Volunteers at *www.attrition.org* keep track of identity theft incidents, mostly in the U.S., and many of them are made public to meet new data loss–disclosure laws. Of more than 300 cases tracked in 2007, 261 were reported in the U.S., 16 were in Great Britain, 15 were in Canada, 6 were in Japan, 2 were in Australia, and 1 each were reported in Denmark, Ireland, Sweden, and Norway. Security experts consider the database a conservative indicator of the level of cybercrime. (Cybercrime is used to describe a crime in which a computer or network is an essential part of the crime.) The website states that names, birth dates, account numbers, and Social Security numbers have become very valuable in the cybercrime underground. Meanwhile, organizations expose rich veins of this kind of data as they convert paper documents into digital records. Benjamin Jun, vice president of technology at Cryptography Research Business, opines that as businesses "cram more and more data into a single place," companies and agencies present thieves with more opportunities for a big score. Data collected worldwide is expected to swell to 988 billion gigabytes by 2010, up from 161 billion gigabytes in 2006.

One victim of identity theft wrote:

> I was an identity theft victim. I spent hundreds of hours working on this but did succeed in getting a conviction. It is not easy to get a conviction, believe me. The felon received a slap on the wrist . . . probation and a $1,000 fine. I provided

the credit card company with everything, right down to a street address, and they "wrote off the charges" ($14,000) as "not cost-effective to pursue." So it is also the credit card companies that are at fault by not doing their part to curtail this scourge on the honest cardholders. They take the easy way out by covering their losses with higher interest rates.

While various reasons are given for the increase in identity theft in 2007, one victim gave a particularly unusual one: "Of course they have to steal more. Fewer people have credit and identities worth stealing, so they have to steal more to make up the difference."

WHAT CONSTITUTES IDENTITY THEFT?

The President's Identity Theft Task Force defined identity theft as "the misuse of another individual's personal information to commit fraud." Until the 1998 enactment of the Federal Identity Theft and Assumption Deterrence Act (Identity Theft Act), 18 U.S. Code 1028(a), there was no generally accepted definition of identity theft. The Identity Theft Act distinguishes identity theft offenders as anyone who:

> . . . knowingly transfers or uses, without lawful authority, any name or number that may be used, alone or in conjunction with any other information, to identify a specific individual with the intent to commit, or to aid or abet, any unlawful activity that constitutes a violation of federal law, or that constitutes a felony under any applicable state or local law.

The Identity Theft Act includes in its definition of identity theft the use of any name or number or data, including the following:

- Name, Social Security number, date of birth, official state- or government-issued driver's license or identification number, alien registration number, government passport number, employer or taxpayer identification number

- Unique biometric data, such as fingerprint, voice print, retina or iris image, or other unique physical representation

- Unique electronic identification number, address, or routing code

- Telecommunication-identifying information or access device

You will note from the above code definition that identity theft includes almost any situation where a person uses another person's personal information for any reason. In most cases, identity theft is nothing more than common theft or fraud. The primary value of the Identity Theft Act is that it makes prosecuting identity theft cases easier.

In 2004, Congress amended the Identity Theft Act and created the crime of aggravated identity theft. This amendment places minimum required prison sentences upon conviction of aggravated identity theft. This act is discussed in more detail in chapter 5.

State Definitions

All states have some form of identity theft legislation. This legislation gives a generic definition of identity theft, which may become a major concern when prosecuting under that statute. If an individual is being prosecuted in state court using a state statute, attention should be directed to the definition of identity theft in that statute.

Identity Fraud

Often, "identity fraud" and "identity theft" are used as interchangeable terms.[2] Many consider identity theft a type of identity fraud. From the legal point of view, there is a difference. Legislation generally distinguishes between fraud and theft by defining fraud as taking something from a victim by trickery or deception, and theft is the direct taking of something from a victim without authorization. Using these definitions, it is clear that in most cases what we call identity theft is actually identity fraud. For purposes of clarity, the popular use of identity theft will be retained in this book. Identity theft is rarely a stand-alone crime; it is generally composed of a wide array of related crimes.

Prosecution under the Identity Theft Act

One of the first cases tried under the Identity Theft Act was held in 1989 in U.S. District Court for the Southern District of California. The United States Naval Investigative Service (NIS) learned in late January 1989 that approximately 184 serialized, unissued, blank armed forces identification cards were stolen from a safe at the Marine Base at Camp Pendleton, California. Subsequently, the NIS was notified that Leslie Todd, the defendant, attempted to cash a check at the Marine Corps Exchange at Camp Pendleton using one of the stolen identification cards.

Later, the NIS was informed by the North County Transit District that a locker at the bus depot, which had unpaid rent due, was opened and a green camouflage bag found in the locker contained many items of United States Marine Corps property. Such property included 51 of the stolen identification cards. The NIS was informed that on March 8, 1989, a person who identified himself as Craig Armuth attempted to claim the camouflage bag. He was told to return the next day. On March 9, Leslie Todd (alias Craig Armuth) returned to claim the bag and was arrested. The district court sentenced Todd to 48 months imprisonment and a three-year period of supervised release.

In the case, the prosecution called a Marine Corps captain who testified on the gravity of the crime and the potential harm and security problems caused by the theft of the blank military identification cards. He testified that although it was not known whether or not Todd had planned to use these cards personally, military security would be greatly affected if these cards fell into the hands of subversives or terrorists. On the day that the trial started, 100 cards were still unaccounted for. The missing cards could have been used for entry onto military installations, and people using them would have had access to military equipment and classified information. On a lesser level, the captain related that the cards could be used to enter bases in order to steal and, most notably, to cash bad checks, causing severe financial losses.

The Identity Theft Prevention Act, New Jersey Statute C.56:11-44 Identity Theft, effective January 1, 2006 (Press release by New Jersey Division of Consumer Affairs)

It is estimated that identity theft is the fastest-growing financial crime in America and perhaps the fastest-growing crime of any kind in our society. It can happen in many different ways: a thief takes credit card receipts or bank statements from your wallet or garbage; you inadvertently provide personal financial information over the phone or Internet; or someone misuses your Social Security number or other confidential materials. But the results can be equally disastrous. Before you even realize your personal information has been compromised, your credit and good name can be damaged. But New Jersey has taken new and groundbreaking steps to prevent identity theft from happening and, if it does, helping you repair the damage that has been done. The Identity Theft Prevention Act, which took effect on January 1, 2006, is the most comprehensive and easy-to-use identity theft prevention law in the nation—it gives consumers the tools they need to protect their financial well-being.

Consumers may now:

- Request that a credit reporting agency place a security freeze on their consumer credit reports;

- File and receive a copy of police reports concerning his/her suspected identity theft;

- Require any company that lawfully collects and maintains computerized records containing personal information to notify him/her in the event that the personal data is compromised;

- Limit use of Social Security numbers as identifiers and prohibit public display and usage of their Social Security numbers on printed materials except where required by law; and

- Require businesses to destroy records containing personal information that is no longer needed.

NATURE OF THE CRIME

Identity theft has at least three stages in its "life cycle"[3]:

1. First, the identity thief acquires a victim's personal information.

2. Second, the thief attempts to misuse this information.

3. Third, an identity thief completes the crime and is enjoying its benefits, while the victim is experiencing the results of this crime.

Identity theft can happen in a variety of ways, but the basic stages are the same. First, offenders must gather personal information on the victims. Without the necessary personal information, it is almost impossible to commit identity theft. The information may be gathered either through low-tech methods such as stealing mail or workplace records, or "dumpster diving," or through complex and high-tech fraud such as computer hacking or the use of malicious computer code. Once the information is obtained, the offenders can either use the data themselves or sell it to others who specialize in using the information.

The data thieves, if they do not sell the information, use it themselves to open new credit accounts, take over existing ones, obtain government benefits and services, or even evade law enforcement by using a new identity. Often, individuals learn that they have become victims of identity theft only after their credit or employment is denied, or when a debt collector seeks payment for a debt the victim did not incur.

The stolen personal information is generally used in one of three broad categories: existing account fraud, new account fraud, and benefits fraud. The three types are discussed later in this section. The typology is a rough approximation; there is considerable overlap among the types, and one crime often covers two or all three categories.

Interacting Dimensions of Identity Theft

In "Identity Theft," Graeme Newman uses four interacting dimensions in discussing the types of ID theft. His dimensions are[4]:

1. Concealment

2. Financial gain

3. Commitment

4. Organization

With regard to concealment and financial gain, Newman notes that classifying identity theft into types is difficult, as it involves a wide variety of crimes and related problems. He states that the acknowledged motives for identity theft can be used to construct a simple typology. Research indicates that the two dominant motives for identity theft are financial gain and concealment (either of true identity or of a crime).

Newman's commitment category refers to offenders' levels of commitment to the task and the extent to which they are simply opportunists taking advantage of a situation.

His organization category suggests that offenders fall into two types:

1. Professionals—usually in gangs—who seek out targets and create their own opportunities; they have a high level of commitment. A lot of planning and organization is involved. Some lone offenders also display considerable commitment and planning, especially in regard to concealing personal history.

2. Offenders with low commitment who take advantage of identity theft opportunities that present themselves in order to solve an immediate problem; their identity thefts are "opportunistic."

Newman's four interacting dimensions of identity theft based on the combinations of commitment and motive.[5]

	Financial Gain	Concealment
High commitment (a lot of planning)	Organized: A fraud ring systematically steals personal information and uses it to generate bank accounts, obtain credit cards, etc. Individual: An offender establishes a look-alike Internet website for a major company; spams customers, luring them to the website by saying that account information is needed; steals the personal information provided; and uses it to commit identity theft.	Organized: Terrorists obtain false visas and passports to avoid being traced after committing terrorist acts. Individual: The offender assumes someone else's name to cover up past crimes and avoid capture.
"Opportunistic" (low commitment)	An apartment manager uses personal information from rental applications to open credit card accounts.	An offender uses his friend's name and identification when stopped by the police.

Existing Account Fraud

Crime in this category occurs when thieves use stolen information to profit from existing credit, brokerage, banking, or utility accounts. Existing account fraud is generally a less damaging form of identity theft, but it occurs more frequently than other forms.

In a common existing account fraud, a thief uses a stolen credit card to buy items. While fraudulent credit charges may amount to thousands of dollars, the cardholder will generally be liable for at most $50 because of credit card companies' policies and federal and state laws. In addition, a stolen credit card does not usually provide the thief with enough information to establish a false identity.

New Account Fraud

In new account fraud, thieves use personal information, such as Social Security numbers, birth dates, and home addresses, to open new accounts in the victim's name and obtain money or goods from these accounts. For example, one identity thief purchased two trucks valued at over $85,000 and a Harley-Davidson motorcycle for $25,000. The thief also rented a house and purchased a time share in Hilton Head, South Carolina, in the victim's name.

Eventually in these cases, the thief disappears, leaving the victim to deal with creditors and other problems. New account fraud occurs less frequently than existing account fraud, but it generally imposes much greater costs and hardships on victims.

Benefit and Document Fraud

Benefit fraud occurs when an identity thief uses someone else's identity to obtain government or other benefits to which that other person is entitled. For example, an individual needing medical attention, who lacks either the ability or desire to pay for the treatment, may steal someone's insurance card and use it to pay for that treatment. In one recent case, a military person with two children had a nephew who needed medical treatment. The soldier took his nephew to a military hospital and signed the nephew in to the hospital as his son. Since he was in the military, his children, but not his nephew, were entitled to medical care. In one case, a U.S. Marine major moved his girlfriend from Virginia to California at the government's expense by falsely stating that she was his wife.

Document fraud occurs when someone uses documents belonging to another to obtain a benefit. For example, the University of Houston hired a criminal justice professor, believing that the professor was a law school graduate. Only later did the university discover that the individual did not have a law degree and had used the law school transcript of a friend with a similar name to establish his credentials.

In 2006, Jerri Dunlap discovered that her sister Judy Dunlap had used Jerri's Social Security number to obtain employment in a school district. Judy had been convicted of a theft crime, and the school district would not have employed her if they were aware of the conviction. Jerri did not discover this fraud until she was arrested for a traffic ticket that her sister had received and failed to pay while using Jerri's name. Though benefit and document fraud is a problem, the extent of the loss is not as great as in the other categories.

Synthetic Identity Fraud

Adam Gregory, a Las Vegas, Nevada, resident, charged a $1,082 hotel bill to his American Express card while on a business trip to Phoenix. The problem was that Gregory never existed. He was a synthetic identity created by James Rose, a 46-year-old former credit-bureau employee. Rose had convinced the three major credit bureaus that Adam Gregory was a real person, obtaining over 200 credit cards in Gregory's name. There is evidence that Rose and his partner may have created over 500 fake identities during a two-year period. Rose's proceeds from the crimes exceeded $750,000.

Synthetic identity fraud, unlike traditional identity theft, does not normally affect consumers, but it does create significant issues for businesses such as banks and financial institutions. While no reliable figures on it exist, experts estimate that synthetic identity fraud accounts for about 20 percent of credit charge-offs and 80 percent of credit card fraud–related losses.

While attending credit-bureau seminars, Rose discovered that the credit bureaus maintain a file on every inquiry they receive. If a bureau cannot find an individual when it receives an inquiry, it establishes a "no-hit" file. Rose would generate no-hit files by applying for credit with phony credit-card applications. He then sent phony credit history reports from shell companies that he controlled to the credit bureaus' no-hit files; the identities in these files began to acquire histories and look like credit worthy customers. Rose paired the fake names with the Social Security numbers of real people. He rented offices in 14 different states to give his shell companies addresses.

The U.S. Secret Service first detected the scheme in 2003 when Rose's partner attempted to cash checks in Honolulu that were made out to some of the fake identities they had created. Secret Service agents raided Rose's home based on information provided by his partner. Rose was arrested in August 2006 and was sentenced to 70 months confinement in November 2007.

The Federal Trade Commission (FTC) estimates that the no-hit phenomenon has lead the credit bureaus to create millions of phony files. The FTC also noted that the credit bureaus do not routinely investigate these files because of the cost involved. The credit bureaus claim that they are required by law and regulation to create no-hit files. According to an October 22, 2007, *Wall Street Journal* report, the regulators are unsure of what, if anything, to do about the problem. Tweaking the system too much could slow down the credit-granting and economic activity, but the present approach invites fraud. The credit bureaus claim that their data-management procedures are adequate and legal and that they are constantly updating them. In addition, the bureaus market data-screening services to businesses, which are designed to weed out synthetic fraud.

IDENTITY THEFT IS NOT NEW

Born in Czechoslovakia in 1890 to middle-class parents, Victor Lustig (1890–1947) became famous as "the man who sold the Eiffel Tower." Lustig was considered the "king of the confidence men," could speak five different languages, and is known to have used 45 aliases. In the United States alone, he was arrested over 50 times.

One spring morning in 1925, while in Paris, France, Lustig read a newspaper article stating that the city was having problems maintaining the Eiffel Tower, and it might have to be dismantled. Lustig paid a forger to print some fake French government stationery for him. Using the stationery, he invited six of France's leading scrap-metal dealers to a meeting at the Hôtel de Crillon, one of Paris's most prestigious hotels. At the meeting, he introduced himself as a deputy director-general of the Ministry of Posts and Telegraphs. He invited the six dealers to bid on buying the tower for scrap metal. Not only did he sell the tower and receive funds for it, Lustig also collected a bribe from the buyer for giving him the inside track on the bids.

Often, there is the mistaken belief that identity theft is a product of the information age. But there are reports of identity theft in the earliest recorded history. For example, in the 14th century individuals tried to take the identity of Portugal's King Sebastian on at least four occasions, and in the 15th century there were individuals who claimed to be the pope. Identity theft incidents are simply theft and fraud enhanced by the robbery and use of personal information. While individuals and entities have always been vulnerable to identity theft, advances in technology have made it easier to collect personal information. This has significantly increased the opportunities for the crime.

Bill Rodman Henry, from Deer Park, Texas, pitched in the major leagues in the 1950s and the 1960s. He played for the Boston Red Sox, the Chicago Cubs, and the Cincinnati Reds. After retirement, he returned to his hometown and still resides there. In September 2007, Bill Henry was shocked to find out that a newspaper had reported that he had died in Lakeland, Florida. He discovered that the deceased, a Lakeland, Florida, resident, had used his identity for over 20 years without his knowledge.

When a baseball historian, David Lambert, saw an obituary stating that Bill Henry had died, he started to do some research on him. He noticed in the obituary that some things did not match up. When he found out that Bill Henry's last address on file with Major League Baseball was in Deer Park, Texas, he called to offer his condolences to Henry's wife. Her response to Lambert was that the real Bill Henry was sitting right next to her, alive and well.

MAGNITUDE OF THE CRIME

The Federal Trade Commission has reported that about ten million U.S. adults are victims of identity fraud each year. The FTC noted that the average loss is about $6,500 per victim, with a total loss of about $57 billion.[6]

Almost every governmental agency dealing with identity theft has published various estimations about the prevalence and cost of this crime in the United States. Numerous studies have unsuccessfully attempted to measure the annual cost of identity theft. While there is considerable debate as to the exact cost, all agree that billions of dollars are spent each year in recovering from the thefts. It addition, the victims' suffering is difficult to measure in monetary amounts.

Victims of Identity Theft

The Federal Trade Commission reports that 53 percent of all identity theft victims are between the ages of 18 and 39 years old. The largest number, 28 percent, are between 18 and 29 years old. Twenty-five percent of the victims are between 30 and 39 years old, and 23 percent are over the age of 50. Ten percent of the victims are age 60 and over.

Twenty-eight percent of the victims report that they knew how their identity was stolen. Fifteen percent report that they knew the offender. Forty-eight percent discovered that they were victims within one month of the first occurrence. Twenty-two percent discovered the loss between one month and six months, while 15 percent were not aware of the loss for more than two years after the first occurrence.

Direct Costs

Businesses suffer the most direct losses from existing and new account fraud because individual victims are not generally held responsible for fraudulent charges in excess of $50. The cost of identity theft to businesses is generally unknown.[7]

Indirect Costs

Indirect costs to businesses for fraud prevention and mitigation of the thefts are also estimated to be in the billions. Credit card companies sometimes publish information regarding their costs from lost or stolen credit cards, but they do not publish the costs associated with other aspects of identity theft, such as investigating cases and introducing new security procedures. Individual victims are required to spend time and money recovering from the thefts. In general, however individuals suffer more psychologically from the thefts.

To some extent, we all suffer indirect losses because businesses pass on the cost of combating identity theft to their customers in the form of higher costs for goods and larger fees for services. Individual victims suffer indirect financial costs from expenses involved in defending civil litigation initiated by creditors and in overcoming the many obstacles they face in obtaining or retaining credit. Victims of nonfinancial identity theft—for example, health-related or criminal-record fraud—face other types of harm and frustration. The California Privacy Rights Clearinghouse stated in one of its reports:

> Identity theft victims experience long-term and well-documented pain and suffering, such as harassment from debt collectors, banking problems, loan rejection, utility cut-offs, and even arrest for the identity thief's other crimes.[8]

Reporting of Identity Theft

The following issues have hampered the reporting of identity theft by local law-enforcement departments[9]:

- The difficulty of defining identity theft because of the extensive involvement of other crimes. Many police departments lack established mechanisms to record identity theft incidents as separate crimes. For example, the theft and use of a credit card may be prosecuted as credit-card fraud and theft without indicating that identity theft is involved.

- Identity theft crime may span many jurisdictions that are geographically far apart. For example, a credit card stolen in Los Angeles may be used in New York. The cross-jurisdictional aspects of identity theft crime may cause confusion as to which jurisdiction reports the crime. The International Chiefs of Police organization has been working on this issue.

- In many cases, the victim reports the crime not to the police but to his or her bank, credit card company, credit reporting agency, etc., and that organization writes off the debt and takes no further action in the case.

LAWS DESIGNED TO COMBAT IDENTITY THIEVES

Listed in this section are highlights of some of the more important legislation designed to deter identity theft. The relevant federal legislation is also discussed in appendix A.

Identity Theft and Assumption Deterrence Act of 1998

The Identity Theft and Assumption Deterrence Act of 1998 (Identity Theft Act), 18 U.S. Code 1028, criminalizes the unauthorized use or transfer of a means of identification with the intent to commit or to aid or abet any federal violation or state felony. Violations of the act may result in confinement for up to 25 years. The act was amended in 2004 to create the crime of aggravated identity theft with mandatory minimum prison sentences.

Reported Identity Theft Victims by State
(per 100,000 Population)
January 1 – December 31, 2006

Rank	Victim's State	Victims per 100,000 Population	Number of Victims	Rank	Victim's State	Victims per 100,000 Population	Number of Victims
1	Arizona	147.8	9,113	26	Tennessee	61.3	3,700
2	Nevada	120.0	2,994	27	Alabama	60.3	2,774
3	California	113.5	41,396	28	Ohio	59.9	6,878
4	Texas	110.6	26,006	29	Kansas	58.8	1,626
5	Florida	98.3	17,780	30	Rhode Island	57.6	615
6	Colorado	92.5	4,395	31	Alaska	57.3	384
7	Georgia	86.3	8,084	32	South Carolina	55.7	3,408
8	New York	85.2	16,452	33	Minnesota	55.6	2,872
9	Washington	83.4	5,336	34	Arkansas	54.7	1,537
10	New Mexico	82.9	1,621	35	Louisiana	52.6	2,256
11	Maryland	82.9	4,656	36	Mississippi	51.3	1,494
12	Illinois	78.6	10,080	37	Nebraska	49.1	868
13	Oregon	76.1	2,815	38	Idaho	49.0	718
14	New Jersey	73.3	6,394	39	Hawaii	47.8	615
15	Virginia	67.2	5,137	40	New Hampshire	46.1	606
16	Michigan	67.2	6,784	41	Montana	45.9	434
17	Delaware	66.7	569	42	Wisconsin	45.6	2,536
18	Connecticut	65.8	2,305	43	Wyoming	42.3	218
19	Pennsylvania	64.9	8,080	44	Kentucky	42.0	1,766
20	North Carolina	64.9	5,748	45	Maine	39.7	525
21	Missouri	64.2	3,753	46	West Virginia	39.3	715
22	Massachusetts	63.7	4,102	47	Iowa	34.9	1,041
23	Oklahoma	63.0	2,254	48	South Dakota	30.2	236
24	Indiana	62.2	3,928	49	North Dakota	29.7	189
25	Utah	61.8	1,577	50	Vermont	38.5	178

Based on data released by Federal Trade Commission on February 7, 2007.

Per 100,000 unit of population estimates are based on the 2006 U.S. Census population estimates.

The key impact of the act was to make the proscriptions of identity theft law applicable to a wide range of conduct that may also be prosecuted under numerous other statutes. The act also expanded the definition of identifiable victims of identity theft. The legislative history of the act makes it clear that its intent was to extend protection to any instance where identification means are misused to such an extent that it causes significant harm to an individual or entity. The identifiable harms are not limited to monetary losses. The losses can include harm to reputation and incontinences. Nonmonetary losses may include:

- An undeserved poor credit rating that impedes job opportunities

- The ability to obtain financing

- An unmerited arrest record or detention by law enforcement personnel

---

United States v. Hines, 472 F.3d 1038, 1039 (8th Cir. 2007)

The defendant left Arizona for California in an attempt to avoid prosecution for the state criminal charges in Arizona. After leaving Arizona, Hines conducted some research and obtained a birth certificate for one William Clorindo Bloom. William Clorindo Bloom had died of pneumonia when he was four months old. The defendant used the Bloom birth certificate and obtained a California identification card in the Bloom name. The defendant used the Bloom birth certificate and the Bloom ID to apply for a Social Security number in the Bloom name. The defendant received a Social Security number ending in the four digits 1447. The defendant also obtained a California driver's license in the name of William C. Bloom, which bore the same number as the previously issued Bloom ID.

Excerpt from Court's Opinion:

To convict defendant for violating the aggravated identity theft statute, that is, 18 U.S. Code § 1028A(a)(1), the government must prove that defendant: knowingly used the "means of identification" of another person, without lawful authority, during and in relation to a violation of a felony enumerated in 18 U.S. Code § 1028A(c).

Drivers Privacy Protection Act of 1994

The Drivers Privacy Protection Act of 1994 (DPPA), 18 U.S. Code Sections 2721-2725, prohibits the disclosure of a driver's personal information, including individual photograph, Social Security number, and driver identification number, obtained in connection with a motor vehicle record. The DPPA allows disclosure for use by an insurer or to provide notice to vehicle owners of towed or impounded vehicles. The DPPA prohibits an individual from knowingly obtaining a driver's personal information for a use not permitted by the act and from making false representations to obtain any of this information.

Violations of the DPPA may result in fines and civil penalties. In addition, an individual who is harmed or suffers damages from the violation of the DPPA may bring a private civil action against the offender.

Customer Identification Program Rules

Section 326 of the U.S. Patriot Act, 31 USC 5318(1), requires banks, savings associations, broker-dealers, mutual funds, and futures commission merchants to follow certain verification procedure rules issued by the U.S. Department of Treasury and other federal bank regulatory agencies. The rules require that covered entities call for and implement a customer identification program (CIP). While the CIP was designed to deter terrorist financing and money laundering, the rules also deter identity theft because of their required identification procedures.

Gramm-Leach-Bliley Act

Title V of the Gramm-Leach-Bliley Act (GLB Act), 15 U.S. Code, Sections 6801-6809, addresses the privacy and security obligations of financial institutions. The security provisions require federal regulatory agencies to write standards for financial institutions regarding appropriate physical, technical, and procedural safeguards to ensure the security and confidentiality of customer records and information, and to protect against anticipated threats and unauthorized access to such information. The privacy provisions require financial institutions to give notice to their customers of their information-sharing practices and to provide customers with an opportunity to opt out of sharing information with certain unaffiliated third parties.

The Federal Trade Commission, pursuant to its authority granted by the GLB Act, published the Privacy of Consumer Financial Information rule, Title 16 Code of Federal Regulations, Part 313, also known as the "Privacy Rule." The Privacy Rule limits financial institutions from disclosing nonpublic personal information to nonaffiliated third parties without first providing consumers with notice and opportunity to opt out of the disclosure. The notice must contain "a clear and conspicuous notice that accurately reflects the financial institution's privacy policies and practices," including those related to security.

Fair Credit Billing Act

The Fair Credit Billing Act, 15 U.S. Code § 1666, limits the liability of consumers for unauthorized charges to open-ended credit lines, including credit cards, to $50 if the consumer notifies the billing company "in a timely manner." As a general rule, within 60 days is considered a timely manner. The act also covers billing disputes and other credit account errors.

Fair and Accurate Credit Transaction Act

The Fair and Accurate Credit Transaction Act of 2003 (FACTA), 15 U.S. Code § 1681, has enhanced the accuracy and privacy of information in consumer credit reports. Recent amendments to the act have limited access to and the use of credit reports. The act requires the credit reporting agencies to comply with certain standards in maintaining their records. The act also gives consumers the right to review and protest entries in their credit records.

FACTA requires merchants to truncate account numbers on all credit card and debit card receipts. This restriction does not apply, however, to handwritten receipts or those made with an imprint of a card. FACTA provides that no person who accepts credit cards or debit cards for the transaction of business shall print more than the last five digits of the card number upon any receipt provided to the cardholder at the point of the sale or transaction.

FACTA provides identity theft victims with important new rights and remedies. The act requires that local law-enforcement agencies provide victims of identity theft with copies of the police reports involving their victimization. If a company extends credit to an offender using a victim's personal information, the victim can now obtain the identity theft–related transaction records, e.g., the false documents, at no charge from the company if the victim furnishes the company with a copy of the police report. In addition, police investigators may now obtain copies of these documents from the company without a subpoena if the victim provides written authorization.

Korman v. The Walking Company,
2007 U.S. Dist. LEXIS 63732
(Eastern Dist. PA August 2007)

Plaintiff Marlene Korman filed a civil action in U.S. District Court for Eastern Pennsylvania against defendant The Walking Company for alleged violations of the Fair and Accurate Credit Transactions Act of 2003 (FACTA). In relevant part, FACTA requires retailers, on the electronically printed receipts provided to customers, to eliminate specified portions of the customers' credit card information and the expiration date of the card. Plaintiff alleges that on March 25, 2007, she made a purchase using her Visa check card at defendant's store at the Oxford Valley Mall in Langhorne, Pennsylvania. She alleges defendant provided her with a receipt that contained four digits from her credit card account number and also contained her credit card's expiration date.

The trial court held that the customer adequately pled a violation of FACTA. [This means that if the facts stated in the civil action are established, the actions constituted a violation of FACTA.]

State Identity Theft Statutes

The state statutes on identity theft vary considerably. Two representative state statutes are included in this section. Appendix B contains a chart listing state statutes dealing with identity theft. Under most state statutes, stealing an identity is not itself a crime. But the obtaining, possessing, using, or transferring a means of identification or financial information of an entity or another individual, living or dead, with the intent to commit, aid, or abet any crime with intent to receive anything of value is a violation. For example, if I do not like my name, I can take another name and use it without violating the law. But if I use that identity with the intent to commit a crime, then it is a crime. Under most identity theft statutes, it is the obtaining, possessing, using, or transferring with the necessary criminal intent that is a crime. Actual use of the identity is not required. Generally, the grade of the crime or class of felony depends on the value received, or attempted to receive, from the theft.

FEDERAL TRADE COMMISSION

The Federal Trade Commission (FTC) was created in 1914. Its original purpose was to prevent unfair, anti-competition commerce methods as part of the battle to "bust the trusts." The FTC is presently the nation's consumer protection agency. The FTC's Bureau of Consumer Protection works for consumers to prevent fraud, deception, and unfair business practices in the marketplace.

In 1998, the Identity Theft Act established the FTC as the nationwide clearinghouse for information relating to identity theft. In accordance with that act, the FTC has established a number of central resources to provide information to law-enforcement agencies about identity theft and to provide guidance to victims of identity theft in order to help them defend themselves against the effects of the crime. Note that the FTC does not have any criminal investigation authority with respect to identity theft.

The FTC's website, *www.ftc.gov*, provides extensive information about the crime of identity theft. The site provides detailed information to help you deter, detect, and defend against identity theft. On the website, a consumer can download FTC's Identity Theft Consumer Education Kit. There is also an Identity Theft Affidavit that can be used to report identity theft to financial institutions and credit reporting agencies.

The FTC also maintains an information clearinghouse website for law-enforcement agencies, which is not available to the general public.

Code of Alabama § 13A-8-192
Identity Theft—Elements

(a) A person commits the crime of identity theft if, without the authorization, consent, or permission of the victim, and with the intent to defraud for his or her own benefit or the benefit of a third person, he or she does any of the following:

    (1) Obtains, records, or accesses identifying information that would assist in accessing financial resources, obtaining identification documents, or obtaining benefits of the victim.

    (2) Obtains goods or services through the use of identifying information of the victim.

    (3) Obtains identification documents in the victim's name.

(b) Identity theft is a Class C felony.

(c) This section shall not apply when a person obtains the identity of another person to misrepresent his or her age for the sole purpose of obtaining alcoholic beverages, tobacco, or another privilege denied to minors.

(d) Any prosecution brought pursuant to this article shall be commenced within seven years after the commission of the offense.

ROLE OF LAW ENFORCEMENT IN PREVENTING AND HANDLING IDENTITY THEFT

In recent years, identity theft has become a major problem in the United States. With the continuing development in technology, it has become widespread and more difficult to counteract. A strong law enforcement response is essential in order to arrest and prosecute perpetrators. [International Association of Chiefs of Police, Training Key #533, 2002]

According to the President's Identity Theft Task Force Strategic Plan (ID Task Force Report), strong criminal law enforcement is necessary to punish and deter identity thieves. The task force noted that the increasing sophistication of identity thieves in recent years has meant that law-enforcement agencies at all levels of government have had to increase the resources they devote to investigating related crimes. The investigations are labor intensive and generally require a staff of detectives, agents, and analysts with multiple skill sets. When a suspected theft involves a large number of potential victims, investigative agencies often need additional personnel to handle victim-witness coordination.

The U.S. Congressional hearings that resulted in the Identity Theft Act in 1998 concluded that many local law-enforcement agencies did not recognize individuals as victims because most of the actual financial loss, such as occurs when a credit card is stolen, is suffered by the card issuer, not the individuals. Only recently does it appear that local law-enforcement agencies are beginning to realize the psychological impact when an individual discovers that his or her credit has been stolen and the nuisance costs of restoring that individual's good name. Victim services or counseling should also be provided for these individuals. FACTA, discussed earlier, requires that local law-enforcement agencies provide police reports to victims of identity theft.

Excerpts from California Penal Code § 530.5 (2007)
Unauthorized Use of Personal Identifying Information

(a) Every person who willfully obtains personal identifying information, as defined in subdivision (b) of Section 530.55, of another person and uses that information for any unlawful purpose, including to obtain, or attempt to obtain, credit, goods, services, real property, or medical information without the consent of that person, is guilty of a public offense, and upon conviction therefore, shall be punished by a fine, by imprisonment in a county jail not to exceed one year, or by both a fine and imprisonment, or by imprisonment in the state prison.

(continued)

(b) In any case in which a person willfully obtains personal identifying information of another person, uses that information to
commit a crime in addition to a violation of subdivision (a), and
is convicted of that crime, the court records shall reflect that the
person whose identity was falsely used to commit the crime did
not commit the crime.

People v. Montoya, 373 Ill. App. 3d 78, (Ill. App. Ct. 2d Dist. 2007)

Defendant Montoya applied to work for Terra Harvest Foods using
Mona Cantu's name and Social Security number. From February
2000 to December 2003, defendant received $53,702.57 in wages at
Terra Harvest under the name and Social Security number of Cantu.
As part of her employment package, defendant was issued health
insurance from Blue Cross Blue Shield of Illinois (Blue Cross), also
under Cantu's name and Social Security number. Between December
2002 and August 2003, defendant received medical services at Swed-
ish American Hospital that involved the delivery of her baby. The
medical services totaled approximately $31,000.

Defendant was indicted on two counts of identity theft. The charges
arose after defendant, an undocumented immigrant, purchased a
Social Security card bearing Cantu's Social Security number and used
it to obtain a job. Defendant was charged with knowingly using personal identifying information of Mona Cantu to fraudulently obtain
employment and to obtain insurance benefits.

Defendant argued that she did not "fraudulently obtain" money and
services when she used Cantu's name and Social Security number to
obtain a job, because she earned her wages and the insurance benefits were part of her employment package. The trial court sentenced
defendant to 30 months' probation and 100 hours of public service
work and imposed a $500 fine.

> ### Court Opinion: Conviction Affirmed (Approved)
>
> Obviously, had defendant not used Cantu's name and Social Security number to obtain a job, she would not have been entitled to receive the wages and insurance benefits that flowed directly from her employment. While it is true that defendant did not actually steal money or services from her employer, she did obtain employment, compensation, and insurance benefits by misrepresenting herself as someone else. Contrary to defendant's assertion, the statute did not require her to "defraud" her employer by "stealing money" or by "being compensated for services not actually rendered" in order to be guilty of identity theft.

The Presidential Task Force recommended that United States attorneys designate an identity theft coordinator for each U.S. attorney's office and establish an identity theft program for each district. Similar coordinators are recommended for local prosecutors' offices. The local prosecutors should:

- Valuate monetary thresholds for prosecution
- Encourage prosecution of identity theft
- Create working groups and task forces
- Conduct targeted enforcement initiatives
- Conduct enforcement initiatives focused on using unfair or deceptive means to make Social Security numbers available for sale
- Conduct enforcement initiatives focused on identity theft related to the health-care system
- Conduct enforcement initiatives focused on identity theft by illegal aliens

Types of Identity Thefts Reported for Calendar Year 2006

How Information Is Misused	Percentage of Reported Identity Thefts
Credit card fraud	25%
Phone or utilities fraud	16%
Bank fraud (includes checking and savings accounts and electronic funds transfers)	16%
Employment-related fraud	14%
Government documents/benefits fraud	10%
Loan fraud	5%
Other types of identity thefts	24%
Attempted identity thefts	6%

Based on data released by the Federal Trade Commission on February 7, 2007.
Percentages were rounded to the nearest whole number.
Note: 18% of the cases include more than one type of identity theft.

Other types of identity thefts include nongovernment medical benefits, insurance fraud, property-rental fraud, securities fraud, child support, bankruptcy, and magazines.

Reported Complaints by Victim's Age for Calendar Year 2006

Age of Victim	Percentage of Total Reported
Under 18 years of age	5%
18–29	29%
30–39	23%
40–49	20%
50–59	13%
60–64	4%
65 and over	6%

Based on data released by the Federal Trade
Commission on February 7, 2007.
Percentages were rounded to the nearest
whole number.

IACP Model Law Enforcement Policy

The International Association of Chiefs of Police (IACP) has established a model law enforcement policy for dealing with identity theft. The IACP states that this policy is designed to enable police agencies to develop protocols for accepting, recording, and investigating identity thefts. Their model suggests the following:

- An identity theft report should not be taken when a related crime report has already been filed with any law-enforcement agency.

- An identity theft report should not be taken when a worthless-document report is more important.

- Forgery-related crimes should continue to be reported on a worthless-document report.

- The location of occurrence for an identity theft should be the victim's residence.

- Identity theft reports should not normally be taken telephonically. The victims should be directed to report to the nearest police station with the supporting documents.

- Officers conducting a preliminary investigation of an identity theft should include with the report the following:
  - All copies of documents supporting the allegations
  - Copies of victim's identification documents
  - Copies of all notifications made by the victim to any financial institution or credit reporting agency
  - Requirement that the reporting victim sign the report
  - Reports that will be reviewed by a supervisor for approval

- A review procedure, with any follow-up inquiries of the victim or others, as appropriate, should be in place.

- Procedures should be established to contact the FTC Consumer Sentinel Law enforcement network and database searches.

- Procedures should be created to contact other involved or potentially involved law-enforcement agencies for collaboration and avoidance of duplication.

Billings, Montana, Police Department's Identity Theft Program

The Billings Police Department was concerned with the identity theft problem and the need to establish a program that provided education and clear advice on this crime. The department collected information from various federal and state agencies and developed an information package of their own. The package addresses four distinct areas of identity theft prevention and assistance:

1. Detailed explanation of the scope and seriousness of identity theft and a list of the common methods used in the thefts

2. The notification process to be used, which was modeled after the FTC's Identity Theft Affidavit

3. A program to assist victims with the notification process, which includes a directory of the names, addresses, and telephone numbers of relevant agencies

4. Use of a proactive approach in the form of a synopsis of identity theft to attract the attention of potential victims[10]

Officer Training

The IACP contends that one of the most effective methods of preventing identity theft is to educate police officers on the latest techniques to recognize possible identity thefts during traffic and other detentions. The IACP notes that in many cases, identity thieves have been detected because the officers involved in traffic stops observed suspicious activities that provided probable cause to continue their investigations and to acquire search warrants.

The IACP states that an officer must be cognizant of the possession by an individual of the tools of trade for identity theft. These tools include:

- Blank checks and credit cards
- Laminating machines
- Skimming devices though which a user can swipe a card
- Color copying machines

The IACP states that the officers need to be cognizant of the types of crimes involved in identity theft. These crimes include:

- Mail theft and mail fraud
- Narcotics violations
- Money laundering
- Weapons trafficking
- Computer crimes
- Wire fraud
- Terrorism

United States v. Aguilar-Morales, 2007 U.S. Dist. LEXIS 73801 (N.D. Iowa Oct. 2, 2007)

Defendant moved to dismiss the Counts 2 and 4 of the indictment based on the argument that in order to be guilty of aggravated identity theft as charged in Counts 2 and 4, he must have known the means of identification he used were assigned to some other person. [Defendant had used a false Social Security number that he borrowed from a friend, but claimed he did not know that the number was assigned to another person.]

(continued)

The United States attorney countered that to be guilty of the offense, the Defendant only had to knowingly use the means of identification and did not have to know that the document he fraudulently used was assigned to another person.

Court's Holding: Apparently there was no question that Defendant knew the identification he used belonged to another person because his defense was that he had permission of that other person to use his name and Social Security number. In order to sustain a conviction for aggravated identity theft, the government must prove the defendant (1) knowingly used (2) the means of identification of another person (3) without lawful authority (4) during and in relation to a violation of [one of the enumerated crimes]. The "knowingly" requirement was satisfied by proof that defendant knew the identification he was using was not his. In order to be guilty of aggravated identity theft, the accused does not need to know that the fraudulent identification used belonged to a different person.

Special training in dealing with minority victims of identity theft is recommended. According to the IACP, 68 percent of the minority victims gave some part of their personal identification to an offender. It was also noted that minority victims are less likely to report identity thefts and that many minorities are afraid of reprisals if they report the crimes. In addition, possible language barriers can make the investigations more difficult.

Los Angeles County's Task Force on Identity Theft

Like the federal government, California passed its first identity theft statute in 1998. One of the problems the California law-enforcement agencies have in enforcing the California statute is the cross-jurisdictional issues involved in the crime. It is not unusual for the victim to live in one jurisdiction and the crime to occur in a different one. In 2000, the Los Angeles County Sheriff's Department formed a pilot program called the Identity Theft Task Force to provide a coordinated and localized effort to conduct investigations of identity theft. Los Angeles County contains 4,084 square miles of land, which is larger than the states of Delaware and Rhode Island combined. There are 88 independent cities located in the county. Forty-four of those cities contract with the sheriff's department for law enforcement coverage.

The original task force consisted of four full-time sheriff's investigators and one sergeant. In addition, there were representatives from the California Department of Motor Vehicles (DMV), the U.S. Secret Service, and the Office of the Inspector General for the Social Security Administration. The representatives were selected because of their specializations. The DMV maintains a database of California drivers and identification cards. The Social Security Administration provides the ability to access Social Security records and numbers. And the Secret Service, under the Identity Theft Act, has federal investigative responsibility and is allowed to cross state lines in investigating these kinds of crimes. A memorandum of understanding was signed by law-enforcement and federal agencies, which established clear guidelines regarding the investigation and prosecution of identity theft crimes.

By January 2008, the task force had three investigative teams. One team serves the northern part of the county and another serves the southern part. The third team serves nearby Ventura County. In addition to the investigators, the team has 36 staff members and now includes representatives from the Federal Bureau of Investigation, the U.S. Immigration and Customs Enforcement Agency, the Ventura County District Attorney's Office, the Glendale Police Department, and the Culver City Police Department. For more information, visit the website *www.lasd.org/sites/CCB_Internet/identity_theft.htm.*

KEY TERMS

Account takeover: A form of identity theft whereby the fraudster obtains full control over a consumer's existing account, such as by obtaining the PIN or changing the statement mailing address.

Application fraud: When a new credit application is submitted with fraudulent details. The fraud may be the true consumer misrepresenting details, or it may be identity fraud.

ATM fraud: Term used to describe fraud related to ATM-card accounts where a card is used to immediately withdraw funds from a consumer's account using a PIN-based transaction at an ATM.

Bank identification number: Often referred to as a BIN, this unique number consists of a two-part code that is assigned to banks and savings associations for identification. The first part shows the location and the second part identifies the bank itself.

Bust-out fraud: When fraud occurs on a credit account that has generally been open for a short time. The account appears to be a good one until the account's limit is raised, the limit is maxed out, and the account holder does not pay. This differs from account takeover since it is generally intended by and carried out by the original account holder.

Card-not-present (CNP): A transaction where the card is not present at the time of the purchase, such as for Internet, mail, or telephone orders.

Chargeback: A credit card transaction that is billed back to the merchant after the sale has been settled. Results when a cardholder disputes a transaction with the issuer, who then initiates the chargeback on the cardholder's behalf.

Check fraud: Term used to describe fraud related to checks, including kiting, counterfeiting, forgery, and paperhanging.

Credit card generators: Programs used by criminal organizations to generate valid credit card numbers that will successfully process for a transaction but are not actually issued card numbers.

Dumpster diving: The practice of rummaging through someone's trash to obtain personal information; often used to commit identity theft.

Money laundering: A process whereby the origin of funds generated by illegal means is concealed by making the funds appear to have derived from a legitimate source.

Phishing: A form of social engineering whereby fraudsters use "spoofed" emails and phony websites posing as legitimate and trusted organizations to fool recipients into divulging personal financial information that is then used to commit identity theft.

Point of fraud: Often referred to as a POF, this is a location where fraud occurs, generally through the use of stolen or counterfeit cards.

Profiles: Cardholder or merchant information that represents behavior patterns. These patterns compare historical behavior with recent patterns that correspond to legitimate and illegitimate behavior, which is then used by a neural network model to improve the detection and accuracy of the credit scoring.

Skimming: A common method used by fraudsters to obtain payment (credit or debit) card information. They use a small tool with a magnetic-stripe reader that stores the information on a payment card. Generally, the card is swiped through the skimmer when making an ATM withdrawal or a purchase at a location where the consumer provides their card but does not view the transaction process, such as at a restaurant. The information is then used to create counterfeit cards, or it is sold.

Third-party fraud: Any fraud scheme that occurs without the knowledge of the person whose information is used to commit the fraud. The first two parties of the transaction are the fraudster and the financial institution. The third party is the individual whose identity or credit has been compromised.

CHAPTER 2

IDENTITY THEFT FRAUD: TYPES AND WHO COMMITS THE CRIME

CHAPTER OUTLINE

- Introduction
- How Offenders Obtain and Use Stolen Identities
- Social Engineering
- Who Commits Identity Theft?
- Credit Card Fraud
- Brokering Stolen Data
- Telephone Records
- Notification of Data Breach
- Identity Theft Insurance

INTRODUCTION

Identity theft is a crime that victimizes people and businesses in every community, from major cities to small towns, and robs victims of their individual freedoms. [From press release by the U.S. Attorney General's Office, April 23, 2007.]

In this chapter, we will examine the various types of identity theft crimes and the people who commit them. Also included is a discussion of the victimization aspects of identity theft. A significant feature of identity theft is that offenders will often repeatedly victimize the same person. This may include repeatedly using a stolen credit card, taking over a card account, or using stolen personal information to open new accounts.

Victim characteristics are probably not related to identity theft vulnerability, though more research is needed in this area. The average age of victims is 42. They most often live in a large metropolitan area and typically do not notice the crime for about 14 months. Evidence suggests that seniors are less victimized by identity theft than the rest of the population, though they can be targeted in specific financial scams that may or may not involve identity theft. African-Americans may suffer more from check fraud and identity theft that is not credit card–related, especially theft of telephone and other utility services.[11] According to the Identity Theft Resource Center, the average victim spends about 600 hours trying to clear damaged credit or criminal records caused by a thief. According to the Minnesota Financial Crimes Task Force, the cost to law enforcement for each reported identity theft ranges from $15,000 to $25,000.

We tend to think of identity theft as a by-product of the Internet, but thieves get information online in less than 20 percent of cases, according to the Federal Trade Commission; most thieves obtain their information from paper documents.

Crimes committed to obtain personal information are all problems associated with identity theft. Those crimes include computer-related offenses, pick-pocketing, street robbery, counterfeiting, and forgery.

HOW OFFENDERS OBTAIN AND USE STOLEN IDENTITIES

Offenders use victims' personal information in countless ways. Some of the most common examples are as follows:

- They open a new credit card account using the victim's name. All this usually requires, apart from the applicant's address, are a few pieces of information: the victim's mother's maiden name, the victim's birth date, and sometimes the victim's Social Security number.

- They open a landline or cell phone account in the victim's name.

- They open a bank account in the victim's name. They often open multiple accounts in multiple places and write bad checks from each.

- They file for bankruptcy under the victim's name, to avoid paying their own debts or to avoid eviction.

- They steal the victim's identity, take over his or her insurance policies, and make false claims for "pain and suffering" resulting from auto accidents.

A Federal Trade Commission survey noted that 15 percent of identity theft victims had their personal information misused in nonfinancial ways. The most common such misuse was for the offender to give the victim's name and identifying information when stopped by law enforcement or when charged with a crime. Identity thieves also take out auto loans or mortgages under the victim's name and residence. They submit fraudulent tax returns using the victim's identity, and collect the refunds. They submit applications for Social Security using others' identities (often those of people who have died), and receive Social Security payments.

SOCIAL ENGINEERING

Another common method for obtaining personal information is to swindle an unwitting source into providing the information. Deception of this type is frequently referred to as "social engineering."

Phishing

One form social engineering may take is "phishing." Phishing is derived from the phrase "password harvesting or fishing." It consists of using email and websites that are designed to look like those of legitimate organizations to trick customers into divulging financial account information. The false email on the next page is an example of phishing.

Generally, a phishing email provides a link to a phony website. When the recipient accesses the site, he or she is then instructed to complete a form containing certain personal information, such as name, address, account number, bank card PIN number, and Social Security number. Often the link looks like the bank's or another organization's official website. For example, the link in the phony email from the IRS states that one must file a request for an income tax refund, which requires one's name, date of birth, address, and Social Security number, to receive that refund.

Malware

"Malware" is short for "malicious software," and is typically used as a catchall term to refer to any software designed to cause damage to a single computer, server, or computer network, whether it is a virus, "spyware," etc. Spyware is a program that runs on your computer and tracks your habits and tailors these patterns for advertisements, etc. Because it is a computer program rather than just a bit of text in a cookie, spyware can also do things to ensure that it keeps running and influencing what you see. Thieves can use malware to illegally gain access to Internet users' computers and data without the users' permission.

Pretexting

"Pretexting" is the practice of obtaining someone's personal information under false pretenses. Pretexters, the criminals practicing this scam, sell this information to others, who may use it to get credit in the victim's name, steal their assets, or investigate or sue them.

Cliff Roberson received the following email message from IRS.com in October 2007. Note the official Web address for the IRS is *www.irs.gov*. As a general rule, the IRS will never email you regarding your return unless there is a previous case and you have approved the use of email for contact.

From: Internal Revenue Service <refund@irs.com>
Sent: Thursday, November 29, 2007 5:43 am
To:
Cc:
Bcc:
Subject: Notification of Tax Refund on your Visa or MasterCard Now

> Notification of Tax Refund on your VISA or MasterCard Now,
> After the last annual calculations of your fiscal activity, we have determined that you are eligible to receive a tax refund of $329.30.
> A refund can be delayed for a variety of reasons. Fox example, submitting invalid records or applying after the deadline.
> Sorry for any inconvenience this may cause and thank you for your patience.
> To access the form for your tax refund please copy/paste the link below in your browser (or click the link below).
http://host217-36-235-101.in-addr.btopenworld.com:84/IRS.gov/refunds.php
> Note: For security reasons, we will record your IP address, the date, and time.
Deliberate wrong inputs are criminally pursued and indicated.
Regards,

Internal Revenue Service

© Copyright 2007, Internal Revenue Service U.S.A.
QJJTSCQUGERQZUSYDLVDLMLPWRKRIOBJLIQEQL

[When you log on, you are requested to provide your Social Security number, the name of your bank and account number, and your date of birth; everything that a thief needs to steal your identity.]

"Phishing" Schemes (*United States v. Dolan et al.,* District of Connecticut)

On September 20, 2006, a federal grand jury indicted six defendants for their participation in an elaborate Internet phishing scheme that targeted and victimized America Online (AOL) subscribers. According to the indictment, the defendants conspired to "harvest" the email addresses of AOL subscribers. The defendants then spammed thousands of AOL subscribers with counterfeit emails purporting, for example, to convey an electronic greeting card. If an AOL subscriber attempted to view the greeting card, the subscriber's computer would be infected with a software "trojan" that prevented the subscriber from accessing AOL without entering certain information, including the subscriber's name, address, Social Security number, credit-card number, bank account number, and personal identification number. The defendants then used the information to produce counterfeit debit cards, which they used at ATM machines, online, and at retail outlets to obtain money, goods, and services.

Pretexters may use a variety of tactics to get personal information. A pretexter may call a victim and claim to be conducting government research and ask a few questions. After getting the victim's personal information, the pretexter uses it to call companies with whom the victim does business, pretending to be the victim. The pretexter may claim that he or she cannot remember the account number or needs information about the account history. In this way, the pretexter may be able to obtain personal information about the victim, such as a Social Security number, bank and credit card account numbers, information in the victim's credit report, and the details of the victim's savings and investment portfolios. Note that some information about a person may be a matter of public record, such as whether the individual owns a home, pays real estate taxes, or has ever filed for bankruptcy. It is not pretexting for another person to collect this kind of information.

Skimming

An electronic credit card reader, or "skimmer," is a device designed for use with cash registers and credit card machines. The skimmer gathers information, including name, address, telephone number, credit card number, credit limit, and PIN, which is encoded in the magnetic stripe on the back of the card. When used legitimately, this information is collected and telephoned in for approval. When used illegitimately, the process is called skimming. According to the U.S. Secret Service, skimming is one of the fastest growing ploys used by criminals.

Skimming commonly occurs when a customer hands a waiter a credit card at a restaurant. During the skimming process, the card is swiped a second time using a small, handheld device, similar to a pager. The skimmer captures the card's information and re-encodes it on the magnetic stripe of a plain plastic card, or stores that information in the device itself so that it can be downloaded later for illegal purposes. With one swipe of a credit card, a criminal can take the information he or she has captured and make unauthorized purchases. Frequently, individuals doing the skimming are employees of the establishment— often gas stations or restaurants. They will pull the small skimming device out of their pocket, swipe the card, and hide it before any-one realizes what has happened. If they do not use the information themselves, they are often paid a flat fee or on a per-card basis for the information they steal.[12] At restaurants in many foreign countries, the waiter will bring the credit card reader to the table and allow customers to watch the credit card being charged for the meal. This procedure prevents the waiter from scanning the card a second time.

> ### *United States v. Carralero,*
> ### 2006 U.S. App. LEXIS 22888 (11th Cir. Fla. 2006)
>
> [Excerpt from plea hearing]Defendant Carralero admitted to the following facts. Beginning in December 2004, Carralero recruited and hired a number of individuals to swipe customers' credit cards using a credit card skimming device to capture the cards' account numbers and the customers' information. Carralero would then verify the authenticity of the credit card numbers, and after verification, would pay the individuals for each skimmed number he received. The numbers were skimmed from customers of restaurants located throughout the Southern District of Florida, and Carralero would use the unauthorized credit card numbers to produce a variety of fraudulent access devices, such as fraudulent credit cards and gift cards. In addition, Carralero personally used the unauthorized access devices to purchase merchandise and goods. From December 2004 until March 18, 2005, Carralero possessed 112,000 unauthorized credit cards, which he used or intended to use to produce unauthorized access devices. The government alleged that Carralero caused $56,020,000 of loss. His plea was accepted as knowing and voluntary.
>
> A presentence investigation report found that Carralero was responsible for 112,204 unauthorized access devices and identified at least 20 corporate victims. Each unauthorized device was assessed a loss value of $500. [Carralero was sentenced to serve 168 to 210 months' imprisonment.]

Stolen Media

Information is often obtained through the theft of data-containing devices. In March 2005, a laptop computer containing the Social Security numbers of more than 98,000 graduate students, graduate-school applicants, and other individuals was stolen from an unlocked office at the University of California. In October 2007, a laptop was stolen from a temporary employment agency in Texas. The computer contained the names, addresses, and Social Security numbers of about 160,000 individuals. In letters to these individuals, the company admitted that "personal information was not saved in an encrypted location, which was a clear violation of company policies."

Probably the biggest loss of personal information occurred in 2006, when the United States Department of Veterans Affairs (VA) reported that a laptop believed to have the personal records of 26.5 million former and current servicemen had been stolen. A VA contractor was robbed in his Maryland residence after taking the computer and an external hard drive out of the office to work at home. During the investigation, the VA employee revealed that he had been taking the personal information home routinely for at least three years and that he had been given permission to do so. The computer and the hard drive were recovered.

WHO COMMITS IDENTITY THEFT?

According to a July 19, 2006, press release by the U.S. attorney's office of the Southern District of Florida, identity thieves often have no prior criminal background and sometimes have preexisting relationships with their victims. Identity thieves may act alone or as part of a criminal enterprise, each way posing different threats to the public. Unlike murderers or other criminals, identity thieves cannot be readily classified. There are no reported surveys that provide comprehensive data on the thieves' personal or demographic characteristics.

Identity thieves who act alone commonly prey on coworkers, senior citizens for whom they are serving as caretakers, and family members. Often, the thieves rely on methods that take little sophistication, such as mail theft and searching trash cans for financial information.

According to the President's Task Force Report, the number of groups and organizations involved in identity theft has greatly increased in recent years. National gangs, such as the Hell's Angels and MS-13, are deeply involved in identity theft. Many foreign organized-crime groups are also involved, especially in Asia and Eastern Europe. Generally, the organized groups use high levels of sophistication and specialization in their crime efforts.

The organized groups often use identity theft to finance other criminal activity. For example, law enforcement officers in Salt Lake City suggested in 2006 that methamphetamine (meth) criminals in the western United States were using identity theft to serve as a major funding mechanism for their meth labs and raw-material purchases.[13] According to the United Nations Interregional Crime and Research Institute, studies have found that stolen identities and false documentation are essential to successful international trafficking in prostitution and other illegal labor markets.[14] Terrorist gangs frequently steal identities in order to conceal their illegal activities and to make tracking them more difficult. Nineteen of the September 11, 2001, terrorists were reported to be involved in some form of identity theft.[15]

Individual thieves also use identity theft to cover up past crimes by stealing the identities of others. Kathleen Soliah allegedly took part in the Crocker National Bank robbery in Carmichael, California, on April 21, 1975, during which a customer was shot to death. Four months later, she was reported to have planted bombs under two Los Angeles Police Department vehicles; the explosives, however, failed to detonate.

Soliah went underground, living in Minneapolis, Minnesota, under the alias "Sara Jane Olson." In 1980, she married Fred Peterson. Together they had three daughters. She became the quintessential "soccer mom," running her children to school activities and participating in many community-service projects and leftist causes. When the FBI finally found her in 1999, she was arrested and convicted of explosives possession and attempted murder. She was sentenced to serve 20 years to life in prison. In her years in Minneapolis, she protested apartheid, rallied against American policy in Central America, and helped organize a progressive bookstore. She campaigned for leftist candidates and for women's rights.[16]

CREDIT-CARD FRAUD

Credit and charge card fraud costs card issuers hundreds of millions of dollars each year. Credit card fraud is a crime under both state and federal law. The elements generally necessary to establish credit card fraud are exemplified in Iowa Code § 715A.6 (2006). According to that statute, a person commits a public offense by using a credit card for the purpose of obtaining property or services if he or she knows that:

- The credit card is stolen or forged.
- The credit card has been revoked or canceled.
- Use of the credit card is unauthorized for any other reason.

The Iowa statute, like most statutes, determines the degree of felony involved by the value received from the unauthorized use. As a general rule, the value of the property or services is the highest value determined by any reasonable standard at the time the violation occurred. Any reasonable standard includes, but is not limited to, market value within the community, actual value, or replacement value. If property or services are secured by two or more acts from the same person or location, or from different persons by two or more acts that are attributable to a single scheme, plan, or conspiracy, the acts may be considered as a single act and the value may be the total value of all property or services involved.

To establish the crime of credit card fraud, the prosecutor must establish that the person knowingly used a credit card without proper authority. This means that the offender must have known that the use of the card was not authorized. Generally, this element is established by circumstantial evidence; since the card was not the offender's, that offender must have known that he or she did not have the authority to use the card.

The offender may use an honest mistake as a defense. For example, Joan used her card at a local restaurant and was mistakenly given back someone else's card by the waiter, and then she attempted to use this card at a store without realizing that it was not her own card. In this case, the honest mistake would be an affirmative defense. Generally, the burden of proving an affirmative defense is with the person using that defense. Accordingly, in a court trial, Joan would have to establish the affirmative defense of her mistake to avoid a credit card fraud conviction.

In credit card fraud cases, establishing the fraud in court is usually not a difficult task. In most cases, the real task is in identifying, finding, and arresting the offender.

BROKERING STOLEN DATA

In testimony before Congress in 2005, the chairperson of the FTC testified that one of the commission's most recent concerns is "data brokers": companies that specialize in the collection and distribution of consumer data. According to the chairperson, data brokers epitomize the tension between the benefits of information flow and the risks of identity theft and other harms. Data brokers have emerged to meet the information needs of a broad spectrum of commercial and government users. The data broker industry is large and complex, and it includes companies of all sizes. Some of the information that they collect varies from company to company, and many data brokers offer a range of products tailored to different markets and uses. These uses include fraud prevention, debt collection, law enforcement, legal compliance, applicant authentication, market research, and almost any other function that requires the collection and aggregation of consumer data. Because these databases compile sensitive information, they are especially attractive targets for identity thieves. The commission recommended that Congress consider whether companies that hold sensitive consumer data, for whatever purpose, should be required to take reasonable measures to ensure its safety.

While the chairperson was referring to legal data brokers, there are numerous illegal data brokers who sell credit card numbers, Social Security numbers, and other personal information. For example, a waitress at a busy restaurant was arrested for selling credit card numbers to a data broker. The waitress received about $10 per card and made more money from this venture than from the tips she received from customers.

TELEPHONE RECORDS

In May 2006, the FTC filed lawsuits against five companies and their principals, alleging that they sold confidential consumer call records obtained through fraud or other illegal means. The FTC charged the defendants with violating Section 5 of the Federal Trade Commission Act (FTC Act) which prohibits "unfair or deceptive acts or practices in or affecting commerce." In each of these cases, the defendants had advertised on their websites that they could obtain confidential customer phone records from telecommunications carriers for fees ranging from $65 to $180. There was evidence that one data broker sold the home phone numbers and addresses of Los Angeles Police Department detectives to suspected mobsters, who then used the information in an apparent attempt to intimidate the officers and their families.

The FTC claims that the defendants, or the individuals they hired, obtained this information by using false pretenses, including posing as the phone carrier's customer to induce the phone company's employees to disclose the records. The FTC sought a permanent injunction to prohibit the future sale of phone records and requested that the courts disgorge any profits obtained through the defendants' alleged illegal operations.

The FTC's actions were in response to the development of an industry that offers to sell the general public's cellular and landline records to third parties. Earlier in 2006, news articles reported on the successful purchase of prominent figures' phone records. The FTC noted that the acquisition of telephone records does not carry the same risk of immediate financial harm as the acquisition of financial records, but it is a serious intrusion into consumers' privacy and could result in stalking, harassment, and embarrassment. Although there is no specific federal civil law that prohibits pretexting for consumer telephone records, the FTC has brought actions against telephone records pretexters for deceptive or unfair practices under Section 5 of the FTC Act.

NOTIFICATION OF DATA BREACH

When should a financial institution notify its customers that there has been an unauthorized disclosure of their personal information? Presently, there are two basic approaches, the bank regulatory agency standard and the California notice standard, to determine when notices should be required.

Bank Regulatory Agency Standard

Under the bank regulatory agency standard, notice is required as soon as possible when the institution becomes aware of an incident involving unauthorized access to or use of sensitive customer information. In addition, notice to consumers is required when, based on a reasonable investigation of an incident of unauthorized access to sensitive customer information, the financial institution determines that misuse of its information about a customer has occurred or is reasonably possible. This standard is described in "Interagency Guidance on Response Programs for Unauthorized Access to Customer Information and Customer Notice," 70 Fed. Reg. 15, 736–54 (Mar. 29, 2005).

California Notice Standard

The California notice standard is contained in Cal. Civ. Code § 1798.82. Under the California approach, all businesses are required to provide notices to their consumers when a defined set of sensitive data, in combination with information that can be used to identify the consumer, has been or is reasonably likely to have been acquired by an unauthorized person in a manner that "compromises the security, confidentiality, or integrity of personal information."

The California approach does not compel notice in every instance of improper access to a database. Instead, it allows businesses some flexibility to determine when a notice is necessary, while also providing an objective standard against which compliance can be measured by the broad range of businesses subject to the law. Under guidance issued by the California Office of Privacy Protection, a variety of factors should be considered in determining whether information has been acquired, such as:

- Indications that an unauthorized person is in the physical possession and control of protected data (such as from a lost or stolen computer, or other device)

- Indications that protected data has been downloaded or copied

- Indications that an unauthorized person has used protected data to open new accounts

These factors are discussed in the California Office of Privacy Protection's publication, "Recommended Practices on Notification of Security Breach Involving Personal Information," available at *www.privacy.ca.gov/recommendations/secbreach.pdf.*

IDENTITY THEFT INSURANCE

Identity theft has lead to the creation of the new identity theft insurance industry. At some point, anyone who presents classes on identity theft will be asked a question regarding the advisability of purchasing such insurance.

In some cases, companies who are responsible for the unauthorized disclosure of personal financial information offer individuals whose data they disclosed free identity theft insurance. For example, California Public Employees Retirement System, better known as CalPERS, is one of the world's largest retirement systems and controls billions of dollars in retirement assets for over 1.5 million retirees. In August 2007, CalPERS mailed a brochure to its members. Unfortunately, each brochure contained the addressee's Social Security number under his or her address. CalPERS notified its members of the data security breach and then offered each retiree one year of free identity theft insurance.

Identity theft insurance provides reimbursement to crime victims for the cost of restoring their identity and repairing credit reports. Some companies now include it as part of their homeowners' insurance policy. Others sell it as either a stand-alone policy or as an endorsement to a homeowners' or renters' insurance policy. Generally, these stand-alone policies cost about $50 to $75 a year for $25,000 worth of coverage. The insurance reimburses expenses, such as phone bills, lost wages, notary and certified mailing costs, and sometimes attorney fees. There is no reimbursement for the stress or psychological harassment, however.

The leading identity theft insurance programs offer more than reimbursement of losses from the crime. A program that only offers reimbursement is probably not cost-effective, because banks and other financial institutions cannot or do not charge the losses to consumers in most identity theft cases. Most programs offer credit monitoring as well as assistance when one of its subscribers suffers from identity theft. Some of the more common benefits of the insurance programs are discussed in the following sections.

Credit Monitoring

Credit monitoring generally includes regular monitoring of an individual's credit files in the three major credit bureaus. The subscriber receives alerts to any changes in his or her file, such as account inquiries, new account applications, delinquent accounts, bankruptcies, and notices of changes of address.

Internet Monitoring

Using technology such as Cyber Agent, the insurance company will search websites and chat rooms that thieves are likely to use to buy and sell information. If any of the subscriber's personal information appears in one of these places, a message is generated warning the subscriber. This provides a subscriber with an early warning of possible theft.

Criminal-Records Monitoring

When a subscriber enrolls in a program, an initial criminal-records report will be generated for the subscriber, and regular monitoring will continue during the policy period. This service lets you know when someone has used your identity and is caught committing a crime.

Initial Name and Aliases Report

An initial name and aliases report will alert you if someone has attached another name to your Social Security number. In one case, a schoolteacher in Houston, Texas, discovered that an individual in San Diego, California, was using her Social Security number. This report is usually generated only when the subscriber first registers, rather than daily or monthly, as with the other monitoring programs.

Initial Address History Report

An initial address history report, like the initial name and aliases report, is usually generated only when a person initially subscribes. The address report provides the subscriber with a list of all addresses associated with his or her name. If a strange address appears, this is probably a clue that one's identity may have been used.

Identity Restoration Service Specialist

This is an individual who is assigned to provide assistance to a subscriber whose identity has been stolen. Generally, the subscriber will receive a package of information on steps to take to recover from identity theft and a toll-free number to call for specialized help. In most cases, the same information may be obtained without cost from the FTC.

Economics of Identity Theft Insurance

There are three types of identity theft coverage generally offered to consumers:

1. Credit-monitoring service
2. Internet personal information–monitoring service
3. Reimbursement insurance

The first two are notification services rather than insurance and are designed to stop identity theft before it happens. The third type is like traditional theft insurance and covers costs incurred after a consumer's identity has been stolen.

The credit-monitoring service is generally offered through an individual's bank or credit card company. The service monitors a consumer's credit activity on a daily basis and provides the consumer with regular credit reports. While these services are not new, more companies are now offering them for less money, and consumer interest in them has grown. However, some of them do not monitor credit activity in all three major credit reporting agencies and could, therefore, fail to detect fraudulent activity. This service protects only against theft involving credit and would not protect an individual against someone using his or her name to commit a crime. A problem with this service is that it may give one a false sense of security of being totally protected from identity theft.

The Internet personal information–monitoring service generally monitors the Internet for any use of one's personal identifying information and credit card numbers. The service scans websites and chat rooms for the use of any personal information and checks against its own list of known merchant vulnerabilities. By searching areas where identity thieves commonly buy and sell personal and financial information, the service attempts to find a person's information before it can be used for fraudulent purchases, and it alerts the person while there is still time to block any accounts.

Reimbursement insurance is effective after an individual's information has been stolen and used. It provides reimbursement to a victim for the costs associated with restoring his or her credit and good name. Coverage normally includes lost wages, phone bills, notary services, and sometimes attorney's fees. Many companies are now including this as part of homeowners' insurance, others are offering it as a stand-alone or add-on policy, and some major banks are offering it to their account holders.

Gail Hillebrand, senior attorney at Consumers Union, the publisher of *Consumer Reports*, states that it is usually not a good idea to purchase any single-purpose insurance policy. She cautions consumers that if the insurance is advertised as free, to make sure that it is permanently free and that they are not signing up for an automatic renewal where they will be required to pay a fee down the road. Hillebrand also sees the risk of a false sense of security. Even if they have this kind of insurance, she says, people should still monitor their credit reports and bank statements. She points out that debit card problems only show up on bank statements, not credit reports. Hillebrand claims the banks are not terribly good at confirming the identities of applicants when they extend credit, and then they provide identity theft insurance. According to her, creditors should take more care on the front end to prevent thieves from stealing accounts.

Linda Foley, of the nonprofit Identity Theft Resource Center, says the credit monitoring is pretty much a waste of money. But if they do apply, applicants should make sure that the service is checking all three credit-reporting agencies on a daily basis. Some initially check all three and then monitor just one or two. If they're checking all three bureaus five days a week, the monitoring has some merit. But Foley believes that the insurance should be free since it is not the consumer that has allowed identity theft to grow so explosively.

Avivah Litan, of the research company Gartner, says consumer groups have a valid point when advising individuals against buying it, but that the insurance is a step in the right direction. According to Litan, banks need to be more proactive about closing security holes, but a lot of this is happening outside the bank's domain. Even if banks follow all the rules for preventing identity theft, there is no guarantee. The Federal Trade Commission says that people who have a legitimate reason to see the victim's personal information, such as waiters, health-insurance processors, car-rental companies, and employers carry out most of the identity theft.

It is important to keep in mind that most identity theft insurance only covers identity theft involving credit fraud. These policies will not help if an identity thief uses someone's name when getting a traffic ticket, or if the thief has taken over an identity and owes taxes in that person's name.

CHAPTER 3

IDENTITY THEFT PREVENTION

CHAPTER OUTLINE

- Introduction
- Public Awareness
- Social Security Numbers
- New Financial Accounts
- Data and Computer Protection
- Credit Freezes and Alerts
- Education

INTRODUCTION

People v. Andra,
156 Cal. App. 4th 638, (Cal. App. 3d Dist. 2007)

On December 23, 2005, Defendant Tiffany Andra opened a Citibank credit card account over the Internet using the name Brenda Baker. Two weeks later, on January 6, 2006, Defendant used that credit card to rent a Lincoln Navigator from Budget Rent A Car in Reno, Nevada. Defendant never returned the vehicle, which was to be returned on January 8, 2006, pursuant to the rental agreement. Nearly a month later, on January 24, police officers saw defendant driving the vehicle in Sacramento.

(continued)

When the officers approached Defendant and identified themselves, Defendant quickly drove away. She abandoned the vehicle behind a hair salon where it was found by the police officers. She was convicted of both theft of a motor vehicle and identity theft. She was sentenced to 15 years confinement. On appeal, Andra contended that sentencing her to consecutive terms on the two counts violated the prohibition against multiple punishments for the same offense. The court disagreed and stated that the identity theft and the theft of the vehicle were two separate offenses.

This chapter focuses on techniques to reduce the chance of becoming the victim of identity theft. Even if a person takes all the precautions discussed in this chapter, there is no guarantee that the person will not be a victim. The President's Identity Theft Task Force notes that the two keys to preventing identity theft are:

1. Preventing access to sensitive consumer information
2. Preventing misuse of any information obtained by the thieves

As noted by the President's Identity Theft Task Force, identity thieves can ply their trade only if they have access to a consumer's personal and financial data. While there is no such thing as perfect security, every preventive step removes one more opportunity for thieves to obtain data. In this chapter, we will focus on the two keys identified by the Task Force. In chapter 4, we will look at actions law enforcement should take when those keys fail, and in chapter 5, we will examine the prosecution of identity thieves.

PUBLIC AWARENESS

The FTC is conducting an ongoing national public awareness campaign using the theme of "Deter, Detect, and Defend" to help prevent identity theft. One of the campaign's goals is to cause behavioral changes in consumers to reduce their risk of becoming a victim (Deter). The FTC also recommends that consumers monitor their credit reports and credit accounts to alert themselves early to any possible issue (Detect). In addition, the FTC is publishing information designed to help consumers recover from any thefts (Defend). As part of this program, the federal regulatory agencies are providing extensive consumer-education materials intended to alert the public about identity theft crime. The FTC is also encouraging law-enforcement agencies to provide consumer education to their citizens. Notably, by 2007, over 500 local law-enforcement agencies in the United States have taken part in the FTC's Deter, Detect, and Defend campaign.

The FTC is also pushing to have a "Protect Your Identity Day" once a year. As part of the Protect Your Identity Day campaign, major financial institutions are holding community "shred-ins." For example, Wells Fargo Bank recently held their first community shred-in. Individuals were encouraged to bring old documents to the banks on a certain day, and the documents would be shredded by the local bank employees.

The FTC is also encouraging universities, colleges, and law-enforcement agencies serving high numbers of students to promote special programs for them. According to an August 1, 2006, *USA Today* report, one-third to one-half of all reported personal-information breaches occurred at colleges and universities.

The Need for Fast Action

An identity theft incident's cost is significantly lower if the misuse of the victim's personal information is discovered quickly. When the misuse was discovered within five months of its onset, the value obtained by the thief was less than $5,000 in 82 percent of cases (including all forms of identity theft). When victims took six months or more to discover that their information was being misused, the thief obtained $5,000 or more in 44 percent of cases. [FTC report from September 3, 2003]

SOCIAL SECURITY NUMBERS

One of the key items of information for a data thief is the victim's Social Security number (SSN). Using a victim's Social Security number, a thief can obtain sufficient other public information to successfully complete the crime. The Social Security Administration started using Social Security numbers in 1936 to track employees' wages. In 1961, the military services and the Federal Civil Service Employment Commission started using Social Security numbers as identification numbers. In 1962, the Internal Revenue Service began using Social Security numbers as Taxpayer Identification Numbers (TINs). In the 1960s and 1970s, many universities and states began to use Social Security numbers as identification numbers for students and employees. The simplicity and efficiency of using individual unique numbers resulted in its widespread use. By the 2000s, all military identification cards, Medicare cards, and Department of Defense insurance cards displayed an individual's entire Social Security number. Many student identification cards, state identification cards, insurance cards, and even private employees' cards displayed complete Social Security numbers. As late as 2001, 40 states and 75 percent of U.S. companies displayed Social Security numbers in records that were readily available to the public. Until 2005, checks issued by the federal government for income-tax refunds, benefit payments, and payment to companies doing business with the federal government displayed Social Security numbers on the checks.

Generally, court records are open to the public. In many states, you can see the Social Security numbers of individuals who have been divorced by going to the courthouse and checking out the court record of the divorce. In many civil cases, the parties' Social Security numbers may be obtained in the same manner. Other likely sources for Social Security numbers include property records, especially if a mortgage is recorded against the property. Many states, like California and New York, have removed documents containing Social Security numbers from court records that are publicly available.

Starting in the 2000s, organizations began to retreat from using Social Security numbers because of the potential liability and threat from identity thieves. In 2004, the Veterans Administration issued new health cards that did not contain the complete Social Security number. That year, many universities also reestablished old methods of issuing student numbers and stopped using Social Security numbers.

Individuals should be diligent in guarding their Social Security numbers; this is the first line of protection for the individual. In 2005, for a project with a major publishing company, I interviewed 17 police executives across the U.S. by telephone. I did not know any of these individuals prior to calling them. As part of the project, the individuals were paid a stipend for their time. The publishing company asked that I obtain the Social Security numbers of the executives for their tax records. Although they did not know me, all but one of the police chiefs disclosed his or her Social Security numbers to me. While this was a legitimate project, I later realized that I had obtained the Social Security numbers of 16 police executives who had never met me within a couple of days.

Is it a crime to publish another person's Social Security number in an attempt to harm that person or others? This question was addressed in a recent U.S. Court of Appeals case, *United States v. Sutcliffe*, U.S. App. LEXIS 23815 (9th Cir. Cal. Oct. 11, 2007). Defendant Sutcliffe, a computer technician, was hired by Global Crossing Development Company in August 2001. Shortly thereafter, however, his employment was terminated because he refused to provide the Human Resources Department with his Social Security number, Global Crossing discovered that he had failed to disclose past criminal convictions on his job application, and he threatened the director of Human Resources. After his termination, defendant began picketing outside the Global Crossing building with a sign referring to a website he had created. On this website, defendant displayed Global Crossing employees' personal information, including payroll information, Social Security numbers, birth dates, and residential addresses, with some of this information hyperlinked to an article about identity theft. Defendant was convicted of making interstate threats to injure in violation of 18 USC § 875(c) and transferring Social Security numbers with the intent to aid and abet unlawful activity in violation of 18 USC § 1028(a)(7). The United States District Court for the Central District of California sentenced him to 46 months of imprisonment and three years of supervised release. The Court of Appeals affirmed his conviction.

In addition to the federal laws restricting the use of Social Security numbers, at least 36 states have enacted additional protection. A copy of California's legislation is set forth below:

California Civil Code § 1798.85

Individuals and commercial entities and certain government entities, including public colleges and universities, may not:

- Publicly display or post Social Security numbers

- Print Social Security numbers on ID cards or badges

- Require people to transmit Social Security numbers over the Internet unless the connection is secure or the number is encrypted

- Require people to use their Social Security number to log on to the Internet without a password

- Print Social Security numbers on mailed documents, unless required by state or federal law

- Embed or encode a Social Security number on a card or document where it cannot otherwise be printed (this includes chips, magnetic technology, and bar coding)

- Mail Social Security numbers where the number is visible without opening the envelope (California Civil Code § 1798.85(a))

- Display a Social Security number that is part of a family court proceeding; it must be placed in a confidential portion of the court file. (California Family Code § 2024.5)

The case of *Thomas v. Smith*, 882 So. 2d 1037, 2004 Fla. App. LEXIS 11856, 29 Fla. L. Weekly D 1863 (Fla. Dist. Ct. App. 2d Dist. 2004), provides guidance on the requirement to provide Social Security numbers. In this case, Florida homeowners filed a timely application for ad valorem tax exemption. Under Florida state tax statutes, homeowners get a partial exemption for some of the property tax due on their homesteads (their primary place of residence). To obtain the exemption, homeowners must file an application, which requires them to list their Social Security numbers. A claim for an exemption is a property record that is filed in the courthouse and is subject to public examination.

The homeowners declined to make the required disclosure of their Social Security numbers. Their application was denied based on their refusal to make the required disclosure. As such, their property was assessed for that year and in each subsequent year without the homestead exemption. The taxpayers claimed that by reason of the assessment of taxes against their home without the benefit of the homestead tax exemption, they paid higher property taxes than they would have otherwise paid. In dismissing the claim, the trial court failed to determine whether a compelling state interest, rather than a legitimate state interest, had warranted the intrusion into the taxpayers' privacy.

The homeowners appealed, and the appellate court stated that the trial court should have first determined whether the taxpayers had a legitimate expectation of privacy in their Social Security numbers without regard to other considerations, such as the necessity to submit an application in order to obtain the benefit of the homestead tax exemption. The appellate court held that the trial court had erred in concluding that the taxpayers had no legitimate expectation for the privacy of their Social Security numbers.

The appellate court noted that the Florida Constitution, article I, § 23, affords individuals some protection against the increasing collection, retention, and use of information relating to all facets of that individual's life. The right to privacy in the Florida Constitution ensures that individuals are able to determine for themselves when, how, and to what extent information about them is communicated to others. Although the general concept of privacy encompasses an enormously broad and diverse field of personal action and belief, there can be no doubt that the Florida amendment was intended to protect the right to determine whether or not sensitive information about oneself will be disclosed to others. The court opined that against this background, it seemed obvious that private, sensitive, and confidential information regarding individuals is protected by the privacy clause in the Florida Constitution.

The appellate court stated that the right of privacy is not intended to provide an absolute guarantee against all governmental intrusion into the private life of an individual. The right of privacy does not confer a complete immunity from governmental regulation and will yield to compelling governmental interests. There is a test to be used in assessing a claim of unconstitutional governmental intrusion into privacy rights under the Constitution. Courts must first determine whether the individual possesses a legitimate expectation of privacy in the information or subject at issue. If so, then the burden shifts to the state to show that (a) there is a compelling state interest warranting the intrusion into the individual's privacy, and (b) the intrusion is accomplished by the least intrusive means. Legislation that infringes on the right to privacy will be invalidated unless it can survive the compelling state-interest test.

The court noted that the federal government, the State of Florida, and numerous other states have acknowledged individuals' expectation of privacy in terms of their Social Security numbers. The United States Congress recognized the sensitive and confidential nature of Social Security numbers more than 25 years ago when it enacted the Privacy Act. In 2002, the Florida Legislature enacted Section 119.0721 9, which makes Social Security numbers confidential and exempt from public disclosure under the public records law. As part of its findings in support of the law, the legislature noted the "sensitive personal nature" of Social Security numbers and their potential for misuse as "the link to an individual's personal, financial, medical, or familial records." The Supreme Court of Florida has amended the Florida Family Law Rules of Procedure to exclude documents containing Social Security numbers from court files in order to limit the possibility of identity theft. The Supreme Court has also approved amendments to the Florida Family Law Forms designed to delete unnecessary requests for Social Security numbers. The court noted that other district courts of appeal have recognized the confidential and sensitive nature of personal records containing employee Social Security numbers and protect such records from wholesale disclosure.

NEW FINANCIAL ACCOUNTS

National, state, and local financial institutions could help reduce identity theft by monitoring the opening of new accounts and by requiring positive identifications before opening these accounts. No verification system can prevent all identity theft because thieves often use false identification cards, and some employees are not properly trained or fail to properly follow established procedures.

Under Title 31, Code of Federal Regulations, Section 103.12 (31 CFR 103.12), banks, credit unions, and savings associations must have a reasonable belief that they know the true identity of each customer who opens an account. Many institutions consider that they have complied with this requirement when a new customer presents a government-issued photo identification card with a reasonable resemblance to the customer. Many institutions might hesitate to require additional identification procedures based on the fear of losing potential customers. Should these institutions be required to at least take the fingerprints of new customers? Most would balk at this regulation and counter that they are the ones who lose money, not the consumers, when there is an identity theft. But anyone who has suffered identity theft will attest that consumers are also the victims because of the time-consuming process and stress involved in recovering from the crime.

12 CFR 41.90 (Volume 12, Code of Federal Regulations, Section 41.90) provides that each financial institution or creditor that offers or maintains one or more covered accounts must develop and implement a written identity theft prevention program that is designed to detect, prevent, and mitigate identity theft in connection with the opening of the account or any existing covered account. The program must be appropriate to the size and complexity of the financial institution or creditor and the nature and scope of its activities.

DATA AND COMPUTER PROTECTION

According to the Institute for Information Infrastructure, the information infrastructure, taken as a whole, is not an engineered system. It is the result of the entrepreneurial efforts and the collective genius of the individuals and companies working to improve efficiency and provide new opportunities for themselves. "Information infrastructure" is used to indicate the structural elements that provide the framework supporting an entire collection of information. For example, the term would include the telecommunications and data network capabilities of a company. The institute states that security was not a significant consideration in its inception, and that even today security concerns do not override market pressures for new uses of technology or innovation, despite frequent incidents of hackers, criminals, and increasingly, terrorists and nations using or planning to use the information infrastructure as a criminal weapon.

The computer has changed the capability of management to store, retrieve, and use data. It also has provided new opportunities to misuse that information. The types of misconduct carried out by using a computer are little different from those committed without the use of a computer. The computer, however, enhances a person's ability to carry out misconduct a thousand fold. Most studies conclude that computer-assisted misconduct is the fastest growing white-collar crime in business. In addition, careless employees can significantly damage a business by accidental destruction or erroneous input of data.

Cracking

According to Kenn Roberson, a senior IT architect at IBM, the correct term to use is "cracking," not "hacking." According to Roberson, the media has latched on to hacking, but that is a different, non malicious way of getting the most out of a system. Roberson says that when thinking about security and computers, the following should be considered:

- Computers and equipment should be kept safe from malicious attacks and theft (both physical theft and theft of the information contained on the machine).

- The explosion of jump, flash, or thumb drives has made it easy to either infect or steal data from a computer system.

- With the increased use of laptop, tablet, and notebook computers, more care must be used to protect these from theft. Places with high people traffic and distractions are prime areas where portable devices are stolen. Airport security checkpoints are a good example: passengers must take out laptops and place them in a container to go through the X-ray machine. Very often, the computer will make it through the checkpoint before the passenger does, making it a prime target for theft. To help minimize this type of theft, Roberson suggests:

  - Putting the computer through the X-ray machine only when one is ready to go through the metal detector
  - Using boot and hard drive passwords (these can usually be set in the BIOS setup), which may not stop people from stealing the machine but will prevent the theft of the data from the machine once it is stolen
  - Using cable lock systems, which can help impede the theft of a machine by tying it to a larger physical device (for example, a table, bed post, or chair). These work on the same principle that bicycle locks do.

Sending machines out for repair can compromise the data contained in them. When a computer is sent out to be repaired or upgraded, one must be careful about giving a third party complete access to all of the information on the system. According to interviews done with people who work in the computer-repair field, there are people who do scan the hard drives to see what is there. For the most part pictures and movies or clips of an exhibitionist nature are the targets of such searches, but it would be easy to also pull financial information, credit-card numbers, proposals, and other confidential information. If sending out a machine, one should consider having the hard drive removed and, if available, replaced with a "clean" drive (one without sensitive information on it).

Passwords

Most computers use passwords for protection; the following steps should be followed when using a password:

- Passwords should be modified at frequent intervals, at least once every three months.

- Passwords should be easy to remember so that users will not have to write them down.

- The password should be short, and if possible, users should make up their own passwords so they mean something to them.

- Users should not use easily inferable words. They should never use first names, initials, or names spelled backward as a password.

- Curse words should not be used. Research has indicated that curse words are some of the first ones tried by someone trying to break a code. Microsoft has a site where one can check the strength of a password: *www.microsoft.com/ protect/yourself/password/checker.mspx.*

- Passwords should be entered without observation by unauthorized persons and should not be displayed on the terminal. Most computer software is designed to blank out passwords. If one's programs do not do this, one should adapt them or change software.

- If feasible, one should use different passwords for the computer system and the database. If different databases reside on the same computer, different passwords should be used for each one, thus restricting its use to the people who need to use it. If only one or two people enter data, but others need to view it, a special password should be used for those authorized to enter or modify the data.

- The computer should be programmed to record unsuccessful password attempts. This will alert one to possible unauthorized attempts to gain entry into the system. To prevent computer crackers from breaking the system with random attempts, the software should be programmed to shut down the computer after three unsuccessful attempts to enter the correct password.

- A password should be changed any time there is a question about whether or not it has been compromised.

- Passwords should not be taped to the sides of the terminals or in the back of the desk calendar.

- Passwords should have at least six characters. With only three characters, a professional computer criminal can solve the code in less than ten minutes. With six characters, the time required to try all possible combinations increases to five years. Alphanumeric characters, should be used for example: p8ssw4rd.

Locking devices are available for computer systems. These devices work like locks and require keys either to load a program or to modify one. The most popular one, Data Lock, can be set either to prevent a system from reading a program without the insertion of a special key or to prevent any entry of data without the key.

Identity Theft and the European Union

Until recently, the United States was considered the country most victimized by identity theft, and for many years, Europeans considered identity theft a U.S. problem. Now, according to Nicole van der Meulen, a researcher at the International Victimology Institute in Tilburg, the Netherlands, identity theft has spread and has become a problem for the European Union (EU) countries.[17] While identity theft has increased in Europe, it is still not as significant a problem as it is in the United States.

According to van der Meulen, identity theft has not been as significant a problem in Europe as is the U.S. because of the attitudes and actions by governments, businesses, and citizens. In particular, she notes that:

- Europeans are far less willing than Americans to provide personal information to others.

- EU countries have stricter laws governing the collection of personal data by businesses.

- Social insurance numbers, unlike U.S. Social Security numbers, are used only for their initial purpose, social security.

- Europeans tend to have fewer credit cards, and credit card applicants are subject to higher standards of verification and approval than U.S. citizens.

- Europeans tend to pay with cash and are less connected to their credit cards than people in the U.S.[18]

CREDIT FREEZES AND ALERTS

California, Florida, New York, New Jersey, Illinois, and a few other states now provide the option to put an "anti-identity theft freeze," or "security freeze," on a credit record to prevent others from looking at one's credit history and offering credit based on that record. As of 2007, 36 states had provisions in their state statutes for credit freezes and alerts.

The Fair and Accurate Credit Transactions Act (FACTA) provides identity theft victims with the ability to place a fraud alert on their credit accounts; this does not always prevent businesses from issuing on-the-spot credit for purchases. Accordingly, a security freeze provides greater protection by preventing anyone from accessing any part of a consumer's credit history. Without access to a person's credit record, a business will not offer credit.

The states allow the credit reporting agencies to charge for this service. For example, in California, this service is free for identity theft victims, but everyone else must generally pay a $10 fee for the initial freeze. It costs an additional fee of about $8 to temporarily lift the freeze. Accordingly, one would pay this fee to obtain a loan, to buy a car, or to rent an apartment. The fee must be paid to each of the three credit bureaus, so temporarily lifting the freeze costs about $24. The credit-freeze system uses a personal identification number (PIN) similar to the one used with an ATM card. To life the freeze, one must call each of the three credit bureaus and provide the PIN.

There is a lot of concern as to whether a credit-freeze system is overkill and unnecessarily prevents easy access to credit. In its first five years of existence, only about 2,000 people have used the California program. The low usage is attributed to the lack of publicity about the program and because it costs money and time to use it.

EDUCATION

An FTC Identity Theft Survey found that many identity theft victims opined that the most helpful tool they could have had in dealing with identity theft would have been "better awareness about how to prevent and respond to identity theft." The survey indicated that education and awareness were especially important for phishing attacks and may be the most effective strategies against traditional phishing at any of the three levels. Phishing is preventable if the victim is aware of what to look for unlike some forms of identity theft that occur without the victim's knowledge and which the victim could really do nothing to protect against. Phishers rely on a "hook," such as threat of account closure or unauthorized charges or even identity theft, to elicit an emotional reaction from a consumer. But if consumers are forewarned of this trick, they will critically examine any correspondence and will be less likely to step into a trap. Until an individual takes the bait and enters his or her personal information on the fraudulent site, the phisher cannot steal anything from him or her.

The following phishing email was received by Cliff Roberson:

> Dear Chase cardholder: It has come to our attention that your account information needs to be updated. If you could please take 5–10 minutes out of your online experience and renew your records, you will not run into any future problems. However, failure to update your records will result in account suspension. Please follow the link below and log in to your account and renew your account information.

[The link leads to a page that asks for an account number, Social Security number, and password. Then the user is informed that his or her account has been updated, and the thief has all the information necessary to use the victim's identity.]

Education may not be the entire answer for all potential phishing victims. Many consumers lack the experience to even know where to look for information on preventing identity theft and phishing and don't know what to do with the information once they learn of it. And education may not do much to prevent more sophisticated attacks that rely less on the victim's actions and more on technology, such as spyware and key-logging software.

CHAPTER 4

INVESTIGATING IDENTITY THEFT

CHAPTER OUTLINE

- Introduction
- Communication
- Victims' Assistance
- Police Resources
- Recommended Procedures for Handling Reports by Victims
- Standing Operating Procedures
- FTC's Identity Clearinghouse
- Investigation Steps
- Obtaining Identity Theft–Related Transaction Records from Creditors
- IACP Investigative Standards
- Handling Theft Reports
- Targeting
- Notice of Identity Theft Incident
- Crime Tracking
- Reports of Loss of Personal Financial Documents
- Federal Investigation Agencies
- National Organizations
- Interpol

INTRODUCTION

Identity Theft Is a Low-Risk and High-Return Crime

In Fresno, California, in 2006, Doris Shears noticed some unusual credit charges on her credit card statement. The charges were all under $50 each and were charged at a local bar with a questionable reputation. Doris, thinking that her husband was cheating on her, hired a private detective to check out the bar. After spending several afternoons in the bar, the detective assured Doris that her husband did not regularly frequent it. A subsequent investigation revealed that her neighbor had stolen one of her cards and was using it. The neighbor, after he was apprehended, stated that he used her card because he did not want his wife to know that he was a regular visitor to the bar.

After the passage of the 1998 federal Identity Theft Act and subsequent identity theft legislation, the issue of police response to victims has received a lot of attention. The act assigned prime responsibility to the FTC to assist consumers who had been victimized. Legislation now requires credit reporting agencies to respond quickly to correct victims' records. Since affidavits filed by victims with the credit agencies require a police report, victims are more likely to report the crime to the local police.

The investigating of identity thefts can be difficult because:

- Information concerning identity theft lies in many different places. There is the question of whether the police crime incident reporting systems have sufficient flexibility to collect such information, and if so, are line officers instructed to record it?

- The theft may be a combination of several common crimes. Often, the crime incident database structure used by police departments does not allow a crime analyst to check across many different crime types, making it more difficult to pick up on identity theft–related issues.

- As of December 2007, no research had been conducted on the effectiveness of police response to victim needs. Available evidence is mostly anecdotal, either collected by various interests or from victim testimony to congressional committees.

- Offenders' identities may be difficult to ascertain; an offender may use several identities or aliases, which can confuse investigations.

- A single piece of information may need to be obtained from several different sources, which is time-consuming and difficult for investigators to track.

- Offenders may commit crimes using a victim's identity, causing the victim to be arrested. One study reports that, on average, law officers surmised that only 11 percent of identity theft cases received by their departments are solved.

- In addition to providing anonymity, identity theft offers many offenders the advantage of physical distance, a serious problem for both victims and authorities attempting to bring offenders to justice.

- Jurisdictional issues complicate the reporting, investigation, and prosecution of identity theft cases, as well as the creation and effectiveness of related legislation.

Theft Survey Report

Federal Trade Commission, September 2003

Most victims of identity theft do not report the crime to the authorities. Only about 25 percent of victims who participated in the survey said that they had reported the crime to local police.

Even with the more serious "new accounts and other frauds" forms of identity theft, only 43 percent of victims said that they had reported their experiences to local police. Only 22 percent of identity theft victims said that they had notified one or more credit bureaus about their experiences. Even among those who suffered from the "new accounts and other frauds" types of identity theft, only 37 percent contacted a credit bureau. Of those victims who contacted credit bureaus, 62 percent asked to have a fraud alert placed on their credit reports.

Theft, including a lost or stolen wallet or pocket book or the theft of a victim's mail, was the most commonly mentioned way of obtaining a victim's personal information. Approximately 25 percent of identity theft victims reported that their information was obtained through such theft. Approximately one-half of identity theft victims said that they did not know how the person who misused their personal information had obtained it.

Most victims of identity theft must have a sense of these problems with law enforcement, and many never report their losses to the authorities. Of those who report, almost a third of the victims were "very dissatisfied" with the response they received from the police. Some victims felt law enforcement could improve the investigation of identity theft through a stronger commitment to catching the thief, better follow-up and communication, and increased assistance. A number of victims thought penalties for identity thieves should be stiffer.

Often, victims make the statement: "Why should I file a police report if it is unlikely that the thief will be caught?" A similar question is asked regarding the theft of property. With property theft, however, most people have insurance coverage, and the filing of a police report helps the insured recover money through his or her policy. Since far fewer individuals have identity theft insurance, that incentive is not present. The officer should be prepared to convince the victim that filing a police report is not a wasted effort. The officer may use the following justifications to encourage the reporting of the crime:

- "Your complaint could help stop an identity theft ring by providing information that may not have been noticed in other reports by victims of the same thieves."

- "If the thief or thieves are caught, you will have to have filed a report of the theft before you can recover anything."

- "Filing a report alerts the local police that an identity thief or thieves are operating in the area."

- "Agencies that track these crimes and formulate actions to prevent them need the information."

- "Providing a copy of a police report to your creditors and the credit reporting agencies makes it easier to clean up your accounts and credit files."

Identity Fraud Trends and Patterns: Building a Data-Based Foundation for Proactive Enforcement

The Center for Identity Management and Information Protection at Utica College completed a study in October 2006 regarding identity fraud trends and patterns. Findings of the study included the following:

- In approximately half of the cases, the Internet or other technological devices were used to commit the crime.

- Within the half of the cases with no use of the Internet or technology, methods such as change of address and dumpster diving were used in 20 percent of the cases.

- In 50 percent of those cases, a business provided the point of compromise or vulnerability for the stealing of personal identifying information or documents.

- A family member or friend was the point of compromise in approximately 16 percent of the cases.

- Approximately a third of the cases involved identity theft through employment.

- The most frequent type of employment from which personal identifying information or documents were stolen was retail (stores, car dealerships, gas stations, casinos, restaurants, hotels, hospitals, doctors offices), and it amounted to 43.8 percent.

- Private corporations were vulnerable to insider identity theft in about 20 percent of those cases.

- The most prevalent motive of the offenders was personal gain. This took several forms, including using fraudulently obtained personal identifying information to:
    - Obtain and use credit
    - Procure cash
    - Conceal actual identity
    - Apply for loans to purchase motor vehicles

- In most of the cases, the identity theft facilitated other offenses. The most frequent offense facilitated by identity theft was fraud. The next most frequent was larceny.

- Organized group activity was discerned in 42.4 percent of the cases, involving from 2 to 45 offenders.

(For a complete copy of the report, go to *www.cimip.org.*)

COMMUNICATION

The FTC reports that the most common complaint it receives is that "the police just do not care." According to the FTC, it is important during the course of the investigations to communicate to the victim that the police do care and for police to be constantly reminded that victims of identity theft have often been repeatedly victimized and that identity theft is an emotionally abusive crime. In responding to the victim's request for a report or investigation of the offence, the FTC urges police to adopt the victim as a partner. Anecdotal evidence suggests that victims are a major source of information in regard to investigations, both in terms of the financial records that the investigator may need to access and in terms of developing a list of possible suspects.

VICTIMS' ASSISTANCE

The FTC states that many victims do not know what to do once they discover that they are victims of identity theft, and they do not realize that swift action on their part may minimize the damage done. The police, as part of outreach programs, may help in educating consumers about these matters and teach them the steps they can take both to avoid victimization and to report any victimization that might occur. Many police departments now have information on their websites, and some offer online ways of reporting victimization. Directing victims to Internet resources or providing them written materials that explain how the recovery process works may help to reduce their suffering.

Victim's Profile

The director of the Georgia Bureau of Investigations, Vernon Keenan, recommends that victims' profile data be collected when victims report that their identity has been stolen. According to Keenan, the information needed for the file includes a victim's name, date of birth, Social Security number, and type of identity theft, which may include fraudulent use of credit cards, checking or savings accounts, loans, utilities, securities or investments, or government documents or benefits. He recommends that the victim select a password that can be readily recalled; this password is included in the victim's profile.

When there is any interaction between the police and the victim, such as when the victim is stopped by the police during a routine traffic stop, the use of the password can help the victim establish positive identification. Keenan recommends that the officer taking the initial victim report also obtain written consent from the victim so that the profile may be entered into a National Crime Information Center (NCIC) file. When an NCIC file is created, it will be available nationwide for law-enforcement officers whenever a question of an individual's identity is at issue.

As of 2007, only 29 states were involved in this program, and they had over 2,600 profiles at this time. Additional information on this system may be obtained from your state's NCIC Criminal Justice Information Services, or from the FBI's Law Enforcement Online System at *www.fbi.gov/hq/cjisd/leo.htm*.

POLICE RESOURCES

Consumer Sentinel Network

The FTC's Consumer Sentinel Network was created as a tool to coordinate law-enforcement investigations. Consumer Sentinel victim complaint data is made available to federal, state, and local law-enforcement agencies through a secure, encrypted website. Law-enforcement agencies, for example, can use clearinghouse data to coordinate investigations, isolate high-impact cases, or identify other patterns of identity theft. The Consumer Sentinel Network may be used by law-enforcement agencies free of charge; however, each agency must enter into a confidentiality agreement with the FTC. But out of an estimated 18,000 state and local law-enforcement agencies in the United States, only about 1,040 agencies have signed up for access to the network so far. Thus, both the FTC and local law enforcement have a long way to go to provide more benefits to the victim.

Joint Fraud Alert

The three major credit reporting agencies have launched a joint fraud alert. After receiving a request from a victim for the placement of a fraud alert on his or her credit report, the credit reporting agency will then share that request with the other two credit reporting agencies, thus eliminating the need for the victim to contact each company separately. Under this initiative, the FTC will also begin a program to refer victim complaints and requests for fraud alerts, received through the Sentinel Network, to the three credit reporting agencies.

Other Available Tools

Other tools used to facilitate coordination and cooperation among agencies include task forces, coordinating bodies (such as the U.S. Attorney General's Identity Theft Subcommittee), and national training seminars on the problem of identity theft. One of the most common means used by law-enforcement agencies to deal with multiple jurisdiction cases is the task force. Overall, task forces—both formal and informal—simplify all aspects of identity theft cases by increasing the advantages available to authorities through pooled resources, information, and expertise. The task force approach usually results in stronger and more thorough investigations, more seamless continuity for cases through the stages of the criminal justice process, and avoidance of duplicative efforts by various agencies. Also, since various federal, state, and local agencies have roles in investigating and prosecuting cases of identity theft, task forces can have participation from all levels of government and may include private-sector entities, such as banks or victim-advocacy groups.

The FTC has also launched an identity theft case referral program in cooperation with the U.S. Secret Service. A full-time special agent and an identity theft team develop case leads by examining patterns in the database and using other investigative resources. Significant patterns are then referred to one of the Service's Financial Crimes Task Forces located throughout the country for further investigation and prosecution.

RECOMMENDED PROCEDURES FOR HANDLING REPORTS BY VICTIMS

Listed in the following subparagraphs are steps that local law-enforcement agencies should use to deal with victims of identity theft.

Police Report

A report should be taken and classified under the department's identity theft or fraud code. A police report is critical in helping victims get rid of fraudulent debts and it helps them clear up their credit reports. If the state does not have an identity theft statute, a Miscellaneous Incident Report, or the jurisdiction's equivalent, should be filled out.

Advise Victims

Victims should be directed to call a toll-free fraud number at any of the three major credit bureaus to place a fraud alert on their credit report. Fraud alerts can help prevent an identity thief from opening additional accounts in victims' names. As soon as the credit bureau confirms the fraud alert, the other two credit bureaus will automatically be notified to place fraud alerts, and all three credit reports will be sent to the victim free of charge. The contact information for the bureaus is as follows:

Equifax

P.O. Box 740241
Atlanta, GA 30374
800-525-6285
www.equifax.com

Experian (TRW)

P.O. Box 9532
Allen, TX 75013
888-397-3742
www.experian.com

TransUnion Corp.

P.O. Box 6790
Fullerton, CA 92834
800-680-7289
www.transunion.com

The victim should be advised to close the accounts that they know or believe to have been tampered with or opened fraudulently. The victim should also be advised that when disputing new unauthorized accounts, many banks and creditors will accept the ID Theft Affidavit, which will save them valuable time in the recovery process.

The victim should be assisted in completing an ID Theft Affidavit using the online complaint form or the ID Theft Affidavit contained in appendix D. Note that the affidavit is not filed with the FTC. The victim should retain the original and make copies for the banks and creditors involved. More information can be obtained by calling the FTC's Identity Theft Hotline toll free at 877-ID-THEFT (438-

4338); TTY: 866-653-4261; going online at *http://www.consumer.gov/idtheft/pdf/affidacit.pdf*, or writing Identity Theft Clearinghouse, Federal Trade Commission, 600 Pennsylvania Avenue, N.W., Washington, DC 20580.

Identity Theft Reports

An identity theft report may have two parts:

Part one is a copy of a report filed with a local, state, or federal law-enforcement agency, like the local police department, the state Attorney General, the FBI, the U.S. Secret Service, the FTC, or the U.S. Postal Inspection Service. There is no federal law requiring a federal agency to take a report about identity theft; however, some state laws require local police departments to take reports. When an individual files a report, he or she should provide as much information as possible about the crime, including anything that is known about the dates of the identity theft, the fraudulent accounts opened, and the alleged identity thief.

Part two of an identity-theft report depends on the policies of the consumer reporting company and the information provider (the business that sent the information to the consumer reporting company). That is, they may ask the consumer to provide information or documentation in addition to that included in the law-enforcement report to verify the identity theft. They must make their request within 15 days of receiving the law-enforcement report or, if there is already an extended fraud alert on the credit report, withing 15 days of the date that the request was submitted to the consumer reporting company for information blocking. The consumer reporting company and information provider then have 15 more days to work with the consumer to make sure the identity theft report contains everything they need. They are entitled to take five days to review any information given to them. For example, if they are given the information 11 days after they request it, they do not have to make a final decision until 16 days after they asked for that information. If they receive the information after the 15-day deadline, they can reject the identity theft report as incomplete. In this case, the consumer will have to resubmit the identity theft report with the correct information.

FTC Booklet

Victims should be given a copy of the FTC's *Take Charge: Fighting Back Against Identity Theft*, which tells consumers how to minimize the risk of identity theft and how to recover from it. A free CD-ROM may be requested from the FTC, and it can be used to print copies of the publication with the department's logo on the cover. Not only is this good public relations for the department, it also helps people prevent or recover from identity theft.

Fraud Alerts

An initial alert stays on an individual's credit report for at least 90 days. Individuals may ask that an initial fraud alert be placed on their credit reports if they suspect they have been, or could be, victims of identity theft. An initial alert is appropriate if a wallet has been stolen or if an individual has been taken in by a phishing scam. When an initial fraud alert is placed on a credit report, the consumer is entitled to one free credit report from each of the three nationwide consumer reporting companies.

An extended alert stays on the credit report for seven years. An extended alert may be placed on a credit report if a person has been a victim of identity theft and he or she provides the consumer reporting company with an identity theft report. When an extended alert is placed on a credit report, the consumer is entitled to two free credit reports within 12 months from each of the three nationwide consumer reporting companies.

To place either of these alerts on a credit report or to have them removed, the consumer will be required to provide appropriate proof of his or her identity: that may include the SSN, name, address, and other personal information requested by the consumer reporting company.

STANDING OPERATING PROCEDURES

The President's Identity Theft Task Force and the International Association of Chiefs of Police (IACP) recommend that law-enforcement agencies take active steps to encourage victims to file police reports on actual or suspected identity theft crimes. The IACP states that a strong law-enforcement response is essential in order to arrest and prosecute perpetrators. It also notes that the involvement of local police departments in identity theft cases was typically minimal in earlier years. The IACP has adopted a resolution on the importance of local police involvement in the crime, which reads in part, "The International Association of Chiefs of Police calls upon all law-enforcement agencies in the United States to take more positive actions regarding incidents of identity theft . . . " (Posted on IACP website *www.theiacp. org/resolutions*, accessed Feb. 9, 2008.)

The IACP notes that when a victim is a resident of, or otherwise associated with, a police department's jurisdiction, the department has an obligation to assist the victim in every way possible. The IACP also notes that the victim of an identity theft is as much a victim as any other. The association states that a police department's first step in combating this crime is to ensure that its personnel have a comprehensive knowledge of what identity theft is, who commits it, and how it is committed. It recommends that police departments ensure that the handling of identity theft cases be included in the department's training curriculum, policies, and that standing operating procedures (SOPs) be developed for handling the cases.

Since most identity theft cases are multi-jurisdictional crimes, the SOP on identity theft should include guidelines for sharing information with other agencies. This sharing of information should also include the FTC's Identity Theft Clearinghouse, which acts as the national clearinghouse for identity theft victims.

THE FTC'S IDENTITY THEFT DATA CLEARINGHOUSE

The FTC's Identity Theft Data Clearinghouse is the national repository of identity theft complaints. All local, state, and federal law-enforcement officers can have free Internet access to this secure database. After their organization signs a confidentiality agreement with the FTC, the officers will receive a user ID and password. They can search the database for complaints relating to investigations they are working on or find clusters of reports detailing suspicious activity regarding locations or people in their communities. They can also receive email notifications each time a complaint that relates to their interests hits the database. To learn more about Consumer Sentinel, go to *www.ftc.gov/sentinel/*. To join Consumer Sentinel, go to *www.ftc.gov/sentinel/cssignup.pdf.*

INVESTIGATION STEPS

In a normal crime investigation, the investigation starts with an examination of the crime scene. In identity theft crimes, the investigation should start not where the information was stolen, but at the place where it was used. For example, if a check is involved, investigators should start at the address given on the check. If a credit card is used and the merchandise was delivered, they should start at the address where the merchandise was delivered. If the offender obtained a credit card, that card was mailed to a certain address. By working backwards, investigators may often catch identity theft rings and individuals because the address is the weakest link in the offender's crime. In most cases, the identity thief needs an address. Often the address will be a post office box or a vacant building, but generally there is some tie-in with the offender.

If a credit report was involved, the officer should know how to read a credit report and spot any critical information contained in that report. It is important to analyze credit reports from all three credit-reporting agencies, because each may contain different information.

If a false credit card application is involved, it should be examined carefully because it contains valuable information. While most of the information may be bogus, some of it may have a connection to the thief, especially telephone numbers. The bogus address can also help establish a pattern, because an identity thief often uses the same addresses in multiple crimes.

In investigating identity theft crimes, the use of the Internet can often be helpful. Michigan State University's Computer Science and Engineering Department has developed a program, OCTIS (online criminal tracking investigation system), that allows for deep-level searches in cases involving identity theft.

A "deep search" is the term used for a search of the Web that is narrower and more specific than a standard search. For example, bits of information contained on a false credit card application, in deep search, become queries that the system locates and compares to similar bits of information on other applications. The queries also generate other information and in many cases can lead to the location where identities were stolen. Information on OCTIS can be obtained by calling the Michigan State University Identity Theft Crime and Research Lab at 517-432-7170 or by sending an email to the CCI Administrator at *idtheft@msu.edu*.

OBTAINING IDENTITY THEFT–RELATED TRANSACTION RECORDS FROM CREDITORS

A law-enforcement officer can get a victim's identity theft–related transaction records from creditors without first obtaining a subpoena if the officer has authorization from the victim. This right was created by 2003 amendments to the Fair Credit Reporting Act, section 609(e) (*www.ftc.gov/os/statutes/031224fcra.pdf* (page 38).)

In order to request 609(e) documents, a request to the company must:

- Be in writing

- Show authorization from the victim

- Be sent to an address specified by the business, if any

- Allow the business 30 days to respond

If a creditor refuses the request for records under section 609(e), the FTC should be notified by email at *609erecords@ftc.gov.* Detailed information about the 609(e) request should be included, if possible.

Businesses can learn more about their responsibilities under section 609(e) by reading "Businesses Must Provide Victims and Law Enforcement with Transaction Records Relating to Identity Theft" (*www.ftc.gov/bcp/edu/pubs/business/idtheft/bus66.pdf*).

Frequently Asked Questions Regarding Section 609(e)

Q. Who must comply with Section 609(e) of the FCRA?

A. The law applies to a business that has provided credit, goods, or services to, accepted payment from, or otherwise entered into a transaction with someone who is believed to have fraudulently used another person's identification. For example, if a business opened a cell phone account in the victim's name or extended credit to someone misusing the victim's identity, the business may be required to provide the records relating to the transaction to the identity theft victim or the law enforcement officer acting on that victim's behalf.

Q. What documents must my business provide?

A. A business must provide applications and business transactions records, maintained either by the business or by another entity on behalf of the business, that support any transaction alleged to be a result of identity theft. Records like invoices, credit applications, or account statements may help victims document the fraudulent transaction and provide useful evidence about the identity thief.

Q. What are the procedures for requesting these materials?

A. Requests for documents must be submitted in writing. The business may specify an address to receive these requests. The business may ask the victim to provide relevant information, like the transaction date or account number, if known. The business can require that victims provide:

- Proof of identity, like a government-issued ID card, the same type of information the identity thief used to open the account, or the type of information currently requested from applicants

- Police report and completed affidavit. For the affidavit, victims can use the FTC's ID Theft Affidavit, available at *www.ftc.gov/idtheft*.

Q. Is it ever appropriate not to provide documents?

A. The business can refuse to provide the records if it determines in good faith that:

- It cannot verify the true identity of the person asking for the information.

- The request for the information is based on a misrepresentation.

- The information requested is Internet navigational data or similar information about a person's visit to a website or online service.

A business may not deny disclosure of these records based on the financial privacy provisions of the Gramm-Leach-Bliley Act (see Subtitle A of Title V of Public Law 106-102). However, the business may refuse to disclose them if a state or another federal law prohibits the business from doing so.

Q. Are there record-keeping requirements of Section 609(e)?

A. Section 609(e) does not require any new record-keeping procedures for a business.

IACP INVESTIGATIVE STANDARDS

The IACP states that at a minimum, each police department should do the following when an identity theft has been reported[19]:

- Develop a standardized procedure for taking identity theft reports. The online form provided by the FTC may be used as a guide to gather all pertinent information about the crime.

- Treat the victim's case seriously; victims should never be brushed off or arbitrarily referred to other agencies as a standard course of action. Also, the department should not merely refer the victim to prosecutor's offices or to private attorneys. The IACP states that it is a police department's obligation to take the complaint and to act on it.

- Initiate investigations of the theft reports just as they would for any other crime, since identity theft is also a crime. And unless it is determined that the report is unfounded for some reason, the police should investigate aggressively and fully.

- Prosecute violators. According to the IACP, identity theft is not a prank and should be prosecuted as a serious criminal offense.

- Cooperate with other agencies. Investigations of identity theft generally involve several jurisdictions and a number of agencies. Full cooperation should be given to departments in other jurisdictions, especially if those jurisdictions have a greater likelihood of successful prosecution.

- Assist the victim by providing him or her with helpful information.

HANDLING THEFT REPORTS

The officer or identity theft coordinator who takes the initial theft report from the victim should help start the emotional healing process when taking that report. With the victim's help, the officer should start developing a fraud file. The process of taking the report may be divided into three phases:

1. Taking the complaint and providing the victim with copies. This involves advising the victim to keep a copy of the document and a record of all contacts. A checklist is recommended. Generally, the victim will not have all the information needed to complete the checklist, so the victim should receive a copy of the document to complete at home and return. A sample checklist appears in this section.

2. Providing the victim with information regarding the steps to take to minimize the damage. If possible, the victim should be provided with a copy of the FTC's *Handbook for Victims of Identity Theft*. A CD of the booklet may be obtained free from the FTC and can be printed with the department's logo and address on it. The victims should be advised that it generally takes time to complete the process of notifying everyone who is affected, but that it is critical to do so.

3. Establishing a bond with the victim and informing him or her that you are available for any other questions the victim may have. It is important to explain the problems involved in investigating the case to the victim.

Social Security Administration

If the wrongful use of a Social Security number is involved, counsel the victim to report this fact to the Social Security Administration. This may be done by telephone to the Office of the Inspector General at 800-269-0271, by fax to 410-597-0118 , or online at *www.ssa.gov/oig/public_fraud_reporting/index.htm*.

The victim may also report by mail to:

SSA Fraud
P.O. Box 17768
Baltimore, MD 21235

In addition, the victim should be advised to obtain a Request for Earnings and Benefit Estimate Statement (Form SSA-7004) and examine it to determine if someone is using the victim's Social Security number. This form may be obtained online at *www.ssa.gov/online/ssa-7004. pdf.* If there are any discrepancies in the statement, they should be reported to the SSA Hotline for Fraud at 800-269-0271. The victim should also be advised that he or she can obtain an SSA publication 05-10064, *When Someone Misuses Your Number.* A copy of this booklet may be obtained online from *www.ssa.gov/pubs/10064.html.*

Obtaining Records

A law-enforcement officer may get a victim's identity theft–related transaction records from creditors without first obtaining a subpoena if the officer has authorization from the victim. This right is included in the Fair Credit Reporting Act, section 609c. A copy of this section may be obtained from *www.ftc.gov/os/statutes/031224fcra.pdf* (page 38).

Use the Clearinghouse Alert feature to coordinate with other law-enforcement agencies that may be investigating the same suspect from other jurisdictions or to determine if there is a crime pattern. The Identity Theft Data Clearinghouse has a database with over one million complaints, and it allows one to search for identity theft victims and/or suspect information across the country. Officers may use the Auto Query on the clearinghouse home page to receive automatic notifications of new complaints about a target address so they can eliminate the need for repeat searches. Note that the FTC does not have any criminal investigation authority with respect to identity theft, but its clearinghouse can provide useful information.

Sample Checklist for Taking Identity Theft Report

Identification Section

Date reported: _____

Citizen's name: _____

Officer taking report: _____

Officer contact number: _____

Complaint number assigned: _____

Contact Information

Citizen's full name: _____

Home telephone: _____

Work telephone: _____

Cell or pager number: _____

Home address: _____

Occupation: _____

Work address: _____

Best time to contact: _____

Best number to use: _____

Email address: _____

Date of birth: _____

Marital status: _____

Spouse or significant other: _____

Crime Information

Has an identity theft complaint been filed with the FTC? _____

    If so, attach a copy. If not when will one be filed? _____

When did the incident/crime occur: _____

Describe the specifics of the crime: _____

Was your Social Security number used? _____

Did the offender use your maiden or former name? _____

    If so, what name did offender use? _____

Do you have any idea who the offender is? _____

Do you know how the offender got your information? _____

Have you recently applied for credit? _____

    If so, explain: _____

Have you recently applied for new employment or an educational program? _____

    If so, explain: _____

Have you lost any documents recently that contained personal information? _____

Has anyone recently asked for your personal financial information?
    If so, explain: _____

When is the last time you checked your credit records? _____

Preventive Steps

Have you notified a credit-reporting agency of the incident and placed alerts on your records? _____

Have you cancelled any credit cards or financial accounts that were involved? _____

What other steps have you taken? _____

Whom have you discussed this theft with? _____

If theft involved a credit card or financial account:

Who issued the credit card and number? _____

Amount involved? _____

Date of transaction? _____

How was the merchandise or service obtained? _____

Was a cash advance obtained? _____

How did you discover it? _____

If a new card, how was the application submitted? _____

Address listed on the application: _____

References listed on the application: _____

If more than one card was involved, obtain information on other cards.

If medical-insurance fraud:

Name and address of insurance provider: _____

Type of insurance and policy number: _____

Have you been to a doctor recently? _____

When and what doctor? _____

Have you recently filled any prescriptions? _____

Where? _____

Have you applied for new insurance recently? _____

Check Fraud

Name of bank or credit-union involved: _____

Amount of check or checks: _____

Date cashed or presented: _____

Type of check (personal or business): _____

Payee on the check: _____

Identification used to cash check: _____

Use of Personal Financial Information:

Who has access to your Social Security number? _____

_____

List all recent occasions in which you have provided someone with your Social Security number:

_____

If a credit card was involved:

List all recent uses of the card: _____

_____

If a check was involved:

List who had access to your checkbook: _____

_____

Have you written a check recently to a new business or person that you are not familiar with? _____

Who has access to your driver's license number? _____

Who has access to your health-insurance card? _____

Detailed Statement

Write a detailed statement of everything you know about the crime, and describe any places or instances that someone could have obtained your personal financial information.

_____

_____

_____

_____

_____

_____

This report is true and correct to the best of my knowledge.

Date: _____ Signed: _____

Individual reporting the theft

TARGETING

One tactic a local police department may wish to consider is to focus at different times on particular aspects of the identity theft. For example, the department may wish to focus on how the financial information is obtained for a period of time and then at another time on how the information is used. Generally, identity theft occurs in conjunction with a variety of other crimes, and given the limited resources that may be available to a local agency, it may not be feasible to address all such crimes at once. It may be more effective to be on the lookout for rashes of specific types of identity theft, such as credit-card fraud or immigration fraud (if the department's jurisdiction is near a U. S. entry point). Focusing on a specific crime will make it easier to collect relevant information and to measure response effectiveness.

NOTICE OF IDENTITY THEFT INCIDENT

As noted earlier, it is essential that identity theft information be shared with adjoining jurisdictions and filed with the FTC's clearinghouse. The notice should be a stand-alone document and written in clear, concise, and easy to understand language. The notice should be suitable to be posted on the agency's website and other information sites. The following information should be included in the notice:

- Brief description of the circumstances of the theft

- Description of the types of personal information that were involved in the theft, e.g., bank account numbers, Social Security numbers, etc. (No actual personal information should be included in the notice.)

- List of agencies involved in the ongoing investigation or the case proceedings

- Contact procedures for individuals or agencies who need more detailed information

- Any special steps being taken to combat the risk involved in the crime

CRIME TRACKING

The Office of Community Oriented Policing Services, U.S. Department of Justice (COPS) recommends that police departments should strongly consider the following issues and practices in handling identity theft cases:

- Does the crime analyst (if the department has one) track crimes that relate to and facilitate identity theft? When victims report burglaries or thefts, tracking the use of stolen identity–related items such as credit cards may provide clues concerning offenders' activities, such as which stores they prefer. This practice will help officers work with the stores to improve security, if it is lax, and also to identify the thieves.

- Does the police department have an established procedure for verifying and recording the identities offenders give when they are stopped, questioned, or arrested? Do officers receive training in identity authentication?

- Does the police department have a crime-reporting system that facilitates making a police report for identity theft or fraud?

- Does the police department know how other local agencies respond to identity theft? Do they have established reporting procedures?

REPORTS OF LOSS OF PERSONAL FINANCIAL DOCUMENTS

When a citizen reports the loss of a wallet, credit card, medical identity card, etc., the citizen should be advised to immediately take the following actions to minimize the potential for identity theft:

- Financial accounts: Advise the individuals to close accounts, like credit card and bank accounts, immediately. When they open new accounts, they should place passwords on them. Individuals should avoid using their mother's maiden name, birth dates, the last four digits of Social Security numbers or phone numbers, or a series of consecutive numbers.

- Social Security number: Advise the individuals to call the toll-free fraud number of any of the three nationwide consumer-reporting companies and place an initial fraud alert on their credit reports. An alert can help stop someone from opening new credit accounts in another person's name.

- Driver's license/other government-issued identification: Instruct the individuals to contact the agencies that issued the license or other identification documents and follow their procedures to cancel the documents and get replacements. They should also request that the agencies flag their files so that no one else can get a license or any other identification documents in their names.

- Observation: Once individuals have taken these precautions, request that they watch for signs that their information is being misused or that their identities are being stolen.

FEDERAL INVESTIGATION AGENCIES

The United States Secret Service is the primary federal agency tasked with investigating identity theft and fraud and its related activities under Title 18, U. S. Code, Section 1028. The Secret Service is mandated by statute and executive order to carry out two significant missions: protection and criminal investigations.

The FTC provides a national identity theft victim complaint database containing more than 815,000 complaints, for searches of identity theft victim and suspect information across the country. But it does not have any criminal investigation authority with respect to identity theft. The FTC stresses that education is the best weapon to combat identity thieves.

The FBI is also involved in identity theft investigations. The U.S. Postal Service investigates identity theft cases that involve theft of U.S. mail, but that constitutes only about six percent of the total identity theft cases.

FTC

As noted earlier, the FTC does not have any criminal investigation authority in identity theft cases, but it has established an identity theft case referral program. Under this program, staff members create preliminary investigative reports by examining patterns of activity in their database. They refine the data using FTC's resources and then forward their reports to the appropriate task force or other law-enforcement agencies for further investigation and potential prosecution. In addition, the FTC staff uses sophisticated analytical software to find related complaints and combine information with other data sources available from the FBI.

Secret Service

The Secret Service protects the president and vice president, their families, heads of state, and other designated individuals; it also investigates threats against these protectees and investigates crimes involving U.S. currency. Since 1984, the Secret Service's investigative responsibilities have expanded to include crimes that involve financial institution fraud, computer and telecommunications fraud, false identification documents, access device fraud, advance fee fraud, electronic funds transfers, and money laundering as it relates to the agency's core violations.

As of January 2008, the Secret Service had 29 Financial Crimes Task Forces and 24 Electronic Crimes Task Forces that focus, to varying degrees, on identity theft–related crimes. The Financial Crimes Task Forces are controlled through Secret Service offices in Atlanta, Austin, Baltimore, Charlotte, Chicago, Cleveland, Dallas, Ft. Myers, Houston, Jacksonville, Kansas City, Las Vegas, Little Rock, Memphis, Miami, New Orleans, Newark, Norfolk, Oklahoma City, Omaha, Orlando, Riverside, San Antonio, San Diego, St. Louis, Springfield, Tampa, Tulsa, and Washington, D.C. The Electronic Crimes Task Forces are located in Secret Service offices in Atlanta, Baltimore, Birmingham, Boston, Buffalo, Charlotte, Chicago, Cleveland, Columbia (South Carolina), Dallas, Houston, Las Vegas, Los Angeles, Louisville, Miami, Minneapolis, and New York City.

The Secret Service's role in identity theft investigations is especially critical because of the jurisdictional problems involved. A classic example is the case of Max Ray Butler. In 2007, a high-tech undercover investigation by the U.S. Secret Service led to the indictment of a California man on wire fraud and identity theft charges. Max Ray Butler, 35, of San Francisco, California, was indicted by a federal grand jury in Pittsburgh, Pennsylvania, following his arrest on September 5, 2007. The arrest and indictment were the result of an ongoing Internet-based investigation targeting individuals involved in numerous illegal activities that included the purchase, sale, and exploitation of various financial instruments and personal identification information and documents.

The indictment alleges that Butler, using the online alias "Iceman," was associated with Internet sites known for illegal carding activity. Specifically, the indictment alleged Butler to be the cofounder and administrator of "CardersMarket," a notorious carding website. According to the indictment, Butler sold tens of thousands of credit card numbers belonging to others through websites such as Carders-Market, a virtual safe haven for those involved in the theft, use, and sale of credits cards and other personal information.

This investigation involved the Secret Service's Criminal Investigative Division, and agents from the Pittsburgh Field Office, Vancouver Resident Office (Canada), Santa Ana Resident Office, and San Francisco Field Office investigated this case. The Federal Bureau of Investigation, the Vancouver Police Department (Canada), the Newport Beach Police Department, the Orange County Sheriff's Office in California, and the Pennsylvania Attorney General's Office provided additional assistance. The U.S. attorney's office for the Western District of Pennsylvania prosecuted the case.

"Cybercrime has evolved significantly over the last several years with criminals regularly targeting the personal and financial information of ordinary citizens, as well as the confidential and proprietary information of companies engaged in e-commerce," said U.S. Secret Service Deputy Assistant Director Michael Merritt. "The Secret Service actively continues to adapt our investigative techniques to progressively combat these emerging threats to our nation's financial infrastructure."

The two primary resources that the Secret Service provides to law enforcement are the eInformation Network and the eLibrary. The U.S. Secret Service Extranet—the eInformation Network—provides an information-sharing platform for the Secret Service and its partners in the law-enforcement and financial-services industries. The network enables the Secret Service to communicate with law-enforcement agencies through several unique online resources. Only registered members may access these websites.

The Secret Service eLibrary website is a secure site for law-enforcement and qualified financial-crime investigators. It is a unique collection of resource databases on a variety of topics. The eLibrary website is based on the premise that sharing information can make law enforcement and financial crime investigators even more effective.

The Secret Service records criminal complaints, assists victims in contacting other relevant investigative and consumer protection agencies, and works with other federal, state, and local law-enforcement and reporting agencies to identify perpetrators. Identity theft crimes investigated by the Secret Service include, but are not limited to, the following:

- Credit card/access device fraud (skimming)
- Check fraud
- Bank fraud
- False identification fraud
- Passport/visa fraud

The Secret Service makes the following recommendations to victims of credit card fraud or identity theft:

- If the complaint is essentially a noncriminal dispute with a retailer or other business, the victim must immediately dispute the charge(s) in writing with the customer-relations office of his or her credit card company.

- If an individual has been the victim of credit card fraud or identity theft, he or she should:

- Report the crime to the police immediately
- Get a copy of the police report or case number to provide to the credit card company, bank, or insurance company
- Immediately contact the credit card issuer(s)
- Get replacement cards with new account numbers and ask that the old account be processed as "account closed at consumer's request" for credit record purposes
- Follow up this telephone conversation with a letter to the credit card company that summarizes this request

- The victim should call the fraud units of the three credit-reporting bureaus, report the theft of the credit cards or numbers, ask that the accounts be flagged, and add a victim's statement to the report that requests that bureaus contact him or her to verify future credit applications.

- The victim should keep a log of all conversations with authorities and financial entities.

- As with any personal information, the victim should only provide his or her credit card number to known merchants. Also, the victim should remember to protect his or her Social Security number. The victim has to provide a Social Security number for employment and tax purposes, but it is not necessary for many businesses.

- The victim should notify the Social Security Administration's Office of Inspector General if he or she suspects that his or her Social Security number has been used fraudulently.

Federal Bureau of Investigation

In January 2008, the FBI was participating in 21 task forces and working groups dedicated to identity theft and over 80 other financial crimes task forces. In cities such as Detroit, Chicago, Los Angeles, and Salt Lake City, identity fraud task forces were realizing significant success. For example, in 2005, the Detroit Metropolitan Identity Fraud Task Force accumulated the following statistical accomplishments: 23 search warrants, 23 arrest warrants, 37 arrests, 11 indictments, 29 convictions, 69 fraud cells identified, and 23 identity fraud organizations dismantled. In addition, the FBI has dedicated analytical resources to combating the identity theft problem and is working with the FTC to develop a system that will analyze large streams of identity theft data and refer the results to law-enforcement agencies in order to proactively target organized groups of identity thieves. In addition, in 2008, the FBI's Cyber Division had more than 90 task forces and more than 80 working groups, consisting of federal, state, and local law-enforcement personnel that investigate all cybercrime violations, including identity theft and Internet fraud.

The total number of FBI identity theft–related cases decreased from 1,678 in 2005 to 1,255 in 2006, and FBI field offices have been pursuing identity theft charges in many of the investigations, ranging from traditional bank fraud cases to counterterrorism cases. To utilize their resources effectively, investigations typically focus on organized groups of identity thieves and criminal enterprises, which are the most difficult to investigate and often involve a substantial number of victims.

The FBI Cyber Division has conducted a number of investigative initiatives into various types of online crime that involve identity theft:

- **Operation Retailers & Law Enforcement Against Fraud (RELEAF):** RELEAF is an international investigative initiative directed at the related problems of "reshipping" (i.e., the use of one or more people in the receiving of merchandise that criminals have fraudulently ordered from retailers, often using others' credit cards, and the shipping of that merchandise to other participants in the fraud scheme to evade detection by retailers and law enforcement) and money laundering. This initiative involves more than 100 private-sector participants and numerous law-enforcement agencies and has produced more than 150 investigations.

- **Digital Phishnet:** Digital Phishnet is a phishing and identity theft initiative involving more than 60 organizations (banks, ISPs, and e-commerce companies) that assisted in the development of more than 100 investigations.

- **Operation Slam Spam:** Operation Slam Spam is a criminal-spam and malicious-code investigative initiative that is supported daily by more than 20 small and medium enterprises. An antispam email list provided intelligence on current cybercrimes, which involved over 95 industry members. In addition, 12 industries provided analysts who are colocated with the Internet Crime Complaint Center (IC3) and Cyber Initiative and Resource Fusion Unit (CIRFU) to support this project, which resulted in more than 100 investigations.

The FBI has established InfraGard, a national information-sharing network between the FBI, an association of businesses, academic institutions, state and local law-enforcement agencies, and other participants dedicated to increasing the security of United States infrastructures. InfraGard has more than 11,800 members in 79 chapters throughout the United States. InfraGard's goals, at both the national and local levels, include increasing the level of information and reporting between InfraGard members and the FBI on matters related to counterterrorism, cybercrime, and other major crime programs.

The FBI has also initiated consumer education programs to make consumers more aware of the perils of leaving personal information unprotected. The financial services industry is also doing its part to make its financial products less susceptible to fraud.

For identity theft crimes involving the Internet, the FBI and the National White Collar Crime Center (NW3C) have established the Internet Crime Complaint Center (IC3). IC3's mission is to serve as a vehicle to receive, develop, and refer criminal complaints regarding the rapidly expanding arena of cybercrime. IC3 gives the victims of cybercrime a convenient and easy-to-use reporting mechanism that alerts authorities of suspected criminal or civil violations. For law-enforcement and regulatory agencies at the federal, state, local, and international level, IC3 provides a central referral mechanism for complaints involving Internet-related crimes.

IC3 accepts online Internet-crime complaints from either the victim, from law enforcement, or from a third party to the complainant. When filing a complaint, the following information is needed:

- The victim's name, mailing address, and telephone number

- The name, address, telephone number, and Web address, if available, of the individual or organization alleged to have defrauded the victim

- Specific details on how, why, and when the victim believes he or she was defrauded

- Any other relevant information necessary to support the complaint

The complaint may be filed online at *www.ic3.gov/complaint.*

NCIC

The FBI's National Crime Information Center (NCIC) is a computerized database of documented criminal-justice information available to virtually every law-enforcement agency nationwide, 24 hours a day, 365 days a year. The NCIC became operational in January 1967 with the goal of assisting law enforcement in apprehending fugitives and locating stolen property. NCIC's goal has since expanded to include locating missing persons, providing data on identity theft, and further protecting law-enforcement personnel and the public. The NCIC was reorganized in 2000 to provide more effective assistance to law enforcement, and it currently maintains 18 nationwide subject files on individuals, including the identity theft–victim profiles, sex-offender lists, and criminal background checks.

U.S. Postal Inspection Service

In 2005, the U.S. Postal Inspection Service (USPIS), a subdivision of the U.S. Postal Service, created the Intelligence Sharing Initiative. This is a website that allows inspectors and fraud investigators representing retail and financial institutions and major mailers to share information relating to identity theft, financial-crimes investigations, and prevention methods. This effort came more than 15 years after the Inspection Service began a Credit Card Mail Security Initiative to work more effectively with the credit card industry to reduce fraud losses.

As of January 2008, the Postal Inspection Service actively led 14 financial crimes task forces/working groups in the following places: Atlanta, Birmingham, Boston, Hawaii, Los Angeles, Memphis, New York, Northern Kentucky, Philadelphia, Phoenix, Pittsburgh, Richmond, Springfield (MO), and St. Louis. The Postal Inspection Service was also the coleader of task forces in Chicago, Salt Lake City, St. Paul/Minneapolis, and Oklahoma City.

In 1992, the USPIS started the Credit Card Mail Security Initiative (CCMSI) in an effort to work more effectively with the credit card industry. A coordinated crime-prevention effort was needed to reduce fraud losses and allow law enforcement to concentrate investigative attention on organized criminals. Results were immediate: nonreceipt fraud losses were reduced 35 percent from 1992 to 1993. In 2003, the USPIS broadened the scope of the meetings and included other significant trends that were taking place, such as counterfeit check schemes, Internet fraud, and bank fraud schemes. Since the focus expanded, the name of the group was changed from the Credit Card Mail Security Initiative to the Financial Industry Mail Security Initiative (FIMSI). This group meets three times a year and provides a forum for agency representatives to identify and share trend data. Representatives from the retail and financial industries and federal, state, and local law-enforcement agencies participate in these meetings. Experts in their respective fields give timely presentations on current trends at these meetings.

National Criminal Intelligence Resource Center

The National Criminal Intelligence Resource Center (NCIRC) is sponsored by the Bureau of Justice Assistance (BJA) for the purpose of providing a secure website developed to serve as a "one-stop shop" for local, state, tribal, and federal law enforcement to keep up with the latest developments in the field of criminal intelligence. This site contains information regarding law-enforcement intelligence operations and practices. Criminal justice professionals now have a centralized resource information bank to access a multitude of criminal intelligence resources in a secure environment.

NCIRC can only be accessed through the secure Regional Information Sharing Systems (RISS) network (RISSNET) and the FBI's Law Enforcement Online (LEO). For access to RISSNET, go to *www.iir.com/riss/*.

United States Attorney's Offices

U.S. Attorneys lead many identity theft task forces and working groups in cities such as Eugene, Philadelphia, and St. Louis. Approximately 27 U.S. Attorney's Offices participate in identity theft task forces or working groups, one U.S. Attorney's Office participates in a task force that investigates identity theft and white-collar crime, and other U.S. Attorney's Offices are in the process of forming identity theft task forces or working groups.

U.S. Immigration and Customs Enforcement

By January 2008, U.S. Immigration and Customs Enforcement (ICE) had established Document and Benefit Fraud Task Forces (DBFTFs) in 11 cities across the country to enhance interagency communications and to improve each agency's effectiveness in fraud investigations. The DBFTFs consist of federal, state, and local agencies, and they are colocated at ICE facilities. The DBFTFs combine the resources, authorities, and expertise of each of their partners to disrupt and dismantle organizations that commit various types of fraud and to deter the perpetration of fraud. The DBFTFs aggressively pursue many types of fraud that, by their nature, encompass identity theft. Additionally,

ICE is aggressively focusing its anti-identity theft efforts in the area of worksite enforcement, and it is working with other departments and agencies to establish a comprehensive approach for employers to identify and employ authorized workers and reduce the use of counterfeit identification.

IRS Criminal Investigation Division

In January 2008, approximately one-quarter of the Internal Revenue Service Criminal Investigation (IRS CI) division's 30 field offices had representatives on identity theft task forces. Some field offices had representatives in multiple judicial districts.

IRS CI's Questionable Refund Program (QRP) and Return Preparer Program (RPP) focus on identifying and stopping fraudulent tax-refund claims schemes. These schemes often involve hundreds of returns, with refunds totaling hundreds of thousands or even millions of dollars of revenue. These schemes can create significant problems for legitimate taxpayers by denying them the refunds to which they are entitled. Investigating and prosecuting those responsible for these ambitious schemes rank among IRS CI's highest priorities. Although identity theft is not a component of all fraudulent refund schemes, the rise of identity theft has helped fuel an increase in these schemes and other tax frauds, specifically employment-tax fraud. The IRS is also developing improved screening and detection processes to more effectively identify future fraudulent refund schemes.

Department of State—Bureau of Diplomatic Security

Since 2005, the State Department's Bureau of Diplomatic Security (DS) has been working on an initiative to address the use of identities of deceased people to obtain U.S. passports. As part of this initiative, some of the DS field offices have had several arrests and successful prosecutions, including some asset forfeiture cases. Some of these investigations resulted in the arrests of fugitives who had assumed the identities of others many years earlier in order to flee justice. DS plans to expand this initiative to all of its field offices.

One example of the value of this initiative involves the prosecution of Christopher J. Clarkson. On March 15, 2006, Clarkson pleaded guilty in Florida to bank fraud and was required to forfeit $500,000 in assets. Clarkson was a member of a widely known gang of bank robbers who reportedly robbed more than 100 banks and armored cars in the 1970s and 1980s in both Canada and the United States. For nearly 30 years, Clarkson used the identity of Stephen Duffy, a boy who had lived in California and died there at age four in 1948. Using Duffy's identity, which he had apparently stolen in the late 1970s, Clarkson lived in Hollywood, Florida, and worked as a successful real-estate broker. DS investigators found irregularities in "Duffy's" California driver's license because of the year of the true Duffy's death. Further investigation, including the discovery that Clarkson had applied for a passport in Duffy's name, led DS agents and Florida law enforcement to arrest Clarkson in October 2005.

NATIONAL ORGANIZATIONS

Anti-Phishing Working Group

The Anti-Phishing Working Group (APWG) is an industry association focused on eliminating the identity theft and fraud that result from the growing problem of phishing and email spoofing. The APWG has more than 2,300 members and more than 1,500 companies and government agencies participating in its activities. It provides a forum to discuss phishing issues, to define the scope of the phishing problem in terms of hard and soft costs, and to share information and best practices for eliminating the problem. Where appropriate, the APWG also shares this information with law enforcement. Membership is open to qualified financial institutions, online retailers, ISPs, the law-enforcement community, and solutions providers. Certain members of the APWG have worked closely with federal law enforcement on other initiatives.

Liberty Alliance

Liberty Alliance was formed in September 2001. It is a global consortium of more than 150 leading merchants, service providers, technology vendors, and government organizations that work together to address the technical and business issues associated with developing an open standard for federated network identity. The alliance is engaged in the ongoing release of open technical specifications, as well as business and policy guidelines to help companies deploy federated identity services across a broad range of products, services, and devices. The alliance has held workshops on identity theft prevention in Chicago, Illinois, and Tysons Corner, Virginia. These workshops brought together law-enforcement and private-sector representatives to explore potential technological and procedural solutions to the problem of identity fraud.

International Association of Financial Crimes Investigators

The International Association of Financial Crimes Investigators (IAFCI) is a nonprofit international organization that engages in training and information sharing about financial fraud, fraud investigation, and fraud-prevention methods. Its members are drawn from law enforcement, the banking and credit card sectors, and other companies. IAFCI members have access to the IAFCI Network, a secure international electronic fraud information network that allows them to broadcast warnings to all participating members and to request investigative assistance; a complete International Membership Directory listing invaluable investigative contacts worldwide; quarterly newsletters that alert IAFCI members to the latest schemes of fraud criminals; and the IAFCI International Annual Training Seminar, where members can learn a variety of fraud-prevention techniques, as well as the latest technological advances and in-the-field instructions to stop fraud.

INTERPOL

In 2002, Interpol created a database on stolen and lost travel documents (SLTD). By January 2008, the database contained information on more than 15 million stolen or lost travel documents from 123 countries. Searches of this database led to the detection of more than 5,000 individuals attempting to use these documents. Interpol's database allows law enforcement anywhere in the world to instantly run a check against the SLTD database. For more information on Interpol's database, go to the organization's website at *www.interpol.int.*

CHAPTER 5

PROSECUTING IDENTITY THEFTS

CHAPTER OUTLINE

- Federal Prosecution
- Aggravated Identity Theft
- Prosecution Under the Credit Card Fraud Act
- State Prosecutions

Frank Abagnale, Jr., a teenage identity thief, managed to cash more than $2.5 million dollars in fraudulent checks in 26 different countries before he was caught. The movie *Catch Me if You Can*, starring Leonardo DiCaprio, was based on Abagnale's autobiography of the same name. He was finally convicted of fraud, forgery, and swindling. Abagnale served 6 months in a French prison, 6 months in a Swedish prison, and 5 years (of a 12-year sentence) at the Federal Correction Institution in Petersburg, Virginia.

In 1974, the federal government released him on the condition that he would help the federal authorities to catch fraud and scam artists—without pay. After his release, Abagnale unsuccessfully tried several jobs, including cook, grocer, and movie projectionist. According to his autobiography, he approached a bank with an offer to speak to the bank's staff and show various tricks that paperhangers use to defraud banks. (Paperhangers is a term used to describe individuals who are in the habit of writing worthless checks.) Abagnale made an offer to the bank management: if the staff did not find his speech helpful, they owed him nothing; otherwise, they owed him $50 and would spread his name to other banks. The bank staff found his speech helpful, and Abagnale began a legitimate career as a security consultant.

He later founded Abagnale & Associates, which advises businesses on fraud. He claims he has raised enough money and paid back all those he scammed over his criminal career. Abagnale is now a multimillionaire through his legal fraud-detection and avoidance-consulting business based in Tulsa, Oklahoma.

FEDERAL PROSECUTION

The primary federal criminal laws used against identity thieves include:

- The Credit Card Fraud Act, 18 U.S. Code, section 1029
- The Identity Theft and Assumption Deterrence Act (Identity Theft Act), Pub. L. No. 105-318, 112 Stat. 3007 (1998) (amended 18 U.S. Code, section 1028).

  (Note that most states have also enacted laws criminalizing identity theft.)

Credit Card Fraud Act

The Credit Card Fraud Act covers fraud that extends beyond credit card misuse. The act makes it a felony to "knowingly and with intent to defraud" use or purchase goods aggregating $1,000 or more or to possess 15 or more unauthorized "access devices." Access devices include account numbers and personal identifiers that can be used "to obtain money, goods, services, or any other thing of value or that can be used to initiate a transfer of funds. The courts have construed mere possession of counterfeit access devices to be a violation of the act.

The Credit Card Fraud Act includes penalties of up to 15 years and a fine. It also allows for restitution to the victim. However, the act considers the bank, credit issuer, or merchant to be the victim rather than the person whose identity was stolen, based on the fact that the credit issuer is financially liable for the fraudulent purchases.

In *United States v. Iredia*, 866 F.2d 114, 120 (5th Cir. 1989), the rule was established that a person can be charged with separate offenses for each unauthorized use of a credit card in excess of $1,000 (rather than aggregating the uses into one count).

One defendant was convicted under the Credit Card Fraud Act for operating a "cloning" cell phone business. He argued that carriers (wireless telephone companies) are not damaged by the use of cloned cellular phones, since carriers continue to be able to bill for calls made on them. The court held that cloning cellular phones enables users to have phones they have not paid for, and this defrauds carriers of activation fees and monthly service fees and falls squarely within the act as illuminated by legislative history. (For more information on this case, see *United States v. Yates*, (1995, ED Ky) 914 F. Supp. 152.)

The Credit Card Fraud Act also reaches the misuse of telephone access codes, since legislative history indicates that Congress intended the definition of "access device" to be "broad enough to encompass technological advances"; the terms "unauthorized" and "counterfeit" are not mutually exclusive, where codes were both counterfeit because they were fictitious and forged, and unauthorized because they were obtained with intent to defraud. Legitimate access codes were nevertheless counterfeit, since it was plausible that the defendant fabricated codes that happened to be identical to valid computer-access codes. It is not necessary for each of the code numbers to be active, since legislative history does not require this, and the definitional section of the statute contemplates misuse of revoked or canceled access codes. (*United States v. Brewer*, (1987, CA5 Tex) 835 F. 2d 550)

Identity Theft and Assumption Deterrence Act

The Identity Theft Act provides for punishment of individuals for the unauthorized transfer or use of "means of identification." The act does not explicitly govern theft of credit card or bank numbers, which are considered access devices and are protected under the Credit Card

Fraud Act. The U.S. Sentencing Commission considers that the unauthorized use of credit cards may be prosecuted under either or both of the acts. The Sentencing Commission has stated that the Identity Theft Act includes criminal activities that may also be prosecuted under approximately 180 other federal criminal statutes. "Means of identification" under the Identity Theft Act include a person's name, date of birth, Social Security number, driver's license number, passport number, electronic identification number, address or routing code, and unique biometric data, such as fingerprint, voice print, or retina or iris image. (18 U.S.C. 1028(d)(7)(A)-(C))

In one case where the defendant used real Social Security numbers on bogus identification documents with fictitious names, the court held that a sentence enhancement was applicable under the Identity Theft Act. The court stated that 18 U.S. Code § 1028 did not require that name and Social Security number be used together to qualify as a means of identification. (*United States v. Melendrez*, (2004, CA9 Or.) 389 F. 3d 829.) However, six blank cards which contained no name or Social Security number and which had on them the Liberty Bell, which had never before appeared on Social Security cards, were not identification documents under 18 U.S.C. § 1028. (*United States v. Gros*, (1987, CA6 Ohio) 824 F. 2d 1487) Blank resident-alien cards from which a defendant intended to produce counterfeit identification cards were considered identification cards, as defined by 18 USCS § 1028, since the plain language of § 1028(d) does not support the contention that the statute is applicable only to completed documents. (*United States v. Castellanos*, (1999, CA7 Ill) 165 F. 3d 1129)

An essential element of 18 USCS § 1028(a)(3) is that the government must prove that a defendant's intended use for a false identification document must have violated particular federal, state, or local law. The government should not, however, attempt to shift the burden of proof to the defendant by suggesting that there were no possible lawful uses for phony identifications. (*United States v. Rohn*, (1992, CA4 Md) 964 F. 2d 310)

Federal Jurisdiction

Under the U.S. federalist system, the federal government has only limited jurisdiction. For either the Credit Card Fraud Act or the Identity Theft Act to apply, there must be some involvement or effect on interstate commerce.

In a prosecution under the Identity Theft Act, the transfer of a false identification document to an undercover officer, who had no intention of using it to travel across state or foreign lines or in any manner that would affect interstate or foreign commerce, nevertheless satisfied the jurisdictional element of 18 U.S.C. § 1028(c)(3)(A); if the defendant had accomplished his intended goals, transfer would have been in or would have affected interstate or foreign commerce. (*United States v. Villarreal*, (2001, CA5 Tex) 253 F. 3d 831) In another case, where the defendant obtained identifying information of individuals and used this information to obtain fraudulent driver's licenses, evidence that the defendant used one of these licenses to rent a storage facility where the defendant received mail as part of an identity theft scheme was sufficient to establish significant effect on interstate commerce. (*United States v. Klopf*, (2005, CA11 Fla) 423 F. 3d 1228)

Difference between the Two Acts

A big difference between the Identity Theft Act and the Credit Card Fraud Act is that the Identity Theft Act considers the victim to be the person whose identity was stolen and allows sentencing enhancements based on factors such as the number of victims and the harm done to their reputation. However, it does not include a restitution provision for a person whose identity has been stolen, therefore the classification of the individual as the victim does not help that much. An important advantage of the Identity Theft Act over the Credit Card Fraud Act is that federal law-enforcement agents have jurisdiction to initiate an investigation earlier because the Identity Theft Act criminalizes the act of stealing the information with intent to perpetrate a fraud, rather than having to wait until the information is used for fraudulent purposes, as required under the Credit Card Fraud Act.

AGGRAVATED IDENTITY THEFT

In 2004, the U.S. Congress enacted the Identity Theft Penalty Enhancement Act (ITPEA). This act did not change the substantive identity theft laws, but it increased penalties for identity theft–related crimes. It also created a new crime of "aggravated identity theft," defined as using a stolen identity to commit other crimes. The law adds a minimum sentence of two years to any felony punishment for crimes committed using stolen personal information and a five-year sentence enhancement if the stolen identity was used during a terrorism offense. The 2004 act was a modification of the Identity Theft Investigation and Prosecution Act of 2003.

Excerpts from California Congressman Adam B. Schiff (before the Subcommittee on Crime, Terrorism, and Homeland Security, and the Committee on the Judiciary, March 23, 2004)

All forms of identity theft are problematic, but the stealing of one's identity for the purpose of committing other serious crimes, including murder and terrorism, is especially egregious and demands even stronger action. For this reason, I have joined my colleague, Mr. Carter, in introducing the Identity Theft Penalty Enhancement Act, legislation that will make it easier for prosecutors to target those identity thieves who steal an identity for the purpose of committing other serious crimes.

The bill stiffens penalties to deter such offenses and strengthens the ability of law enforcement to go after identity thieves and prove their case. The legislation also makes changes to close a number of gaps identified in current Federal law.

With advances in technology and the Internet, identity theft has been transformed from a basic street crime involving a stolen wallet or stolen [PIN] number into a sophisticated crime. Nationwide computer networks have given hackers the ability to access a large number of identities that can be quickly shared with large organized networks of criminals.

Prosecution of Aggravated Identity Theft

In *United States v. Kowal*, 486 F. Supp. 2d 923, (N.D. Iowa 2007), the defendant was charged with using the identity of a deceased person to obtain a Social Security number and various other identity documents. The defendant later changed his name when he married, but continued to use the original deceased person's birth date and surname. In a motion to dismiss the charges, the defendant contended that the government did not prove the statutory elements under 18 U.S.C. § 1028A(a)(1) (Aggravated identity theft). He argued that he did not violate the statute because the statute's reference to the stolen identity of a person referred to a living, not deceased, person and that he had stopped using the identity years ago. However, the appellate court found that, based on its language and legislative history, the statute's reference to "person" referred to both living and deceased persons. The court also found that the defendant's change of name did not sever the ties linking him to the original deceased person's identity, including his birth date. Thus, the defendant had used the means of identification of another person, as required by the statute. The following is an excerpt from the court's opinion:

> 18 U.S.C. § 1028A punishes conduct that is directly related to serious crimes of identity theft. The statute uses the same language in both subsections: It punishes whomever knowingly transfers, possesses, or uses, without lawful authority, a means of identification of another person, 18 U.S.C. § 1028A(a)(1) and (a)(2). Congress surely did not intend to exempt from punishment the terrorist who assumed the identity of a person who was no longer living. Had Congress intended to exclude deceased persons from the definition of "person" in the aggravated identity theft statute, it could have simply inserted the word "living" into the text of 18 U.S.C. § 1028A(a)(1). In other words, Congress could have defined aggravated identity theft as the use, possession, or transfer of means of identification of another living person during or in relation to an enumerated felony. The United States District Court for the Northern District of Iowa finds

Congress's omission of the word "living" from the text of §
1028A(a)(1) to be purposeful.

When an actual individual's Social Security number is paired with a
fictitious name on a subsequently obtained means of identification, it
does not necessarily sever the ties linking the victims and the Social
Security numbers.

Elements of Aggravated Identity Theft

The elements of an offense are the required items that the government
must establish beyond a reasonable doubt before a conviction may be
upheld. To determine the specific elements of each crime, it is often
helpful to look at court decisions on that issue. An excellent case on
the elements of aggravated identity theft is *United States v. Godin*, 476
F. Supp. 2d 1 (D. Me. 2007).

Cori Godin was charged with numerous counts of bank fraud and
Social Security fraud, as well as aggravated identity theft pursuant to
18 USC § 1028A(a)(1). Godin pleaded guilty to all counts except the
charge of aggravated identity theft, on which she went to trial.

According to 10 U.S. Code Section 1028A(a)(1):

> Whoever, during and in relation to any felony violation enu-
> merated in subsection (c), knowingly transfers, possesses, or
> uses, without lawful authority, a means of identification of
> another person shall, in addition to the punishment pro-
> vided for such felony, be sentenced to a term of imprison-
> ment for two years.

Godin stipulated that she committed two of the enumerated felonies,
and she stipulated that she knew that the means of identification she
used—a Social Security number—was not her own. It was undisputed
at trial that the Social Security number she used in the fraud was the
valid Social Security number of another individual who resides in the
state of Maine. The jury convicted Godin.

Godin's position throughout the litigation was that because the statute uses the word "knowingly," the government had the burden to prove that she knew that the means of identification she used belonged to another person. Based on that legal argument, Godin filed a motion to dismiss the aggravated identify theft charge for lack of evidence that Godin knew that the Social Security number belonged to another person. (Defendant's motion to dismiss count 17 of the indictment (Docket Item 19)) Because the government did not concede Godin's lack of knowledge, the judge declined to render an abstract legal interpretation of the statute before trial. At trial, the judge also denied a motion for acquittal at the close of the government's case before he decided the legal question, because he found that the jury could believe (based on circumstantial evidence) that the defendant knew that the numbers she used belonged to another person.

At the charge conference, the parties once again argued the legal question of how far the "knowingly" element extends—whether it extends only to "use . . . without lawful authority, a means of identification" or whether it also extends to "of another person." The trial judge expressed on the record his view that this was a close issue. In the end, the trial judge gave the jury the following instructions:

> To convict Cori Godin of this offense, the government must prove each of the following elements beyond a reasonable doubt:
>
> - First, Cori Godin committed bank fraud and/or Social Security fraud felony violations. The parties stipulated that she did so.
>
> - Second, during and in relation to one or both of those other felony violations, Cori Godin knowingly used a means of identification without lawful authority.
>
> - Third, that means of identification belonged to another person.
>
> "Knowingly" means that the act was done voluntarily and intentionally, not because of mistake or accident. The govern-

ment must prove that Cori Godin knew that she did not have lawful authority to use the means of identification in question. The government is not required to prove that she knew the means of identification actually belonged to another person.

The judge gave this instruction for the following reasons. First, although not strongly persuasive in either direction, the syntax permits this reading of the statute.

Second, despite one case in the Western District of Washington that says "knowingly" modifies the entire predicate, *United States v. Beachem*, 399 F. Supp. 2d 1156 (W.D. Wash. 2005), the thrust of the case law supports the conclusion that "knowingly" does not modify "of another person." See *United States v. Montejo*, 442 F.3d 213 (4th Cir. 2006); *United States v. Contreras-Macedas*, 437 F. Supp.2d 69 (D.D.C. 2006). All these cases suggest that "knowingly" modifies only the verbs and thus the conduct involved—"transfers, possesses, or uses"—and not anything that follows it. *Montejo*, 442 F.3d at 215: "Good usage requires that the limiting modifier, the adverb 'knowingly,' be as close as possible to the words which it modifies, here, 'transfers, possesses, or uses.'"

The Judge in *Montejo* explained the law regarding the issue by stating: "If, during a bank-fraud conspiracy, a person hands a defendant a sealed envelope asking her to transfer it and its contents to another and she knowingly does so, she has knowingly transferred the envelope and its contents. But if she believes the statement that the envelope contains only a birthday card, when in fact it contains a forged Social Security card, the government surely would not contend that she should receive the enhanced penalty. The word "knowingly" must modify not just the verb, but also at least the object that immediately follows the verb, namely, 'a means of identification.'"

Third, although the holdings of the *Montejo* line of cases is that "knowingly" only modifies "transfers, possesses, or uses," the language and rationale from the cases strongly suggest that the defendant must know that he or she was using a means of identification without lawful authority to be convicted under section 1028A. If a defendant believed that he was using a means of identification that legally belonged to him, when in fact he was using a means of identification that belonged to another person, he would not be subject to conviction under § 1028A(a)(1). These opinions fail to explain how 1028A(a)(1) can require so much if "knowingly" modifies only the verb and nothing else. The only way to reconcile what these cases say—that the government must prove that the defendant knew that the means of identification was fraudulent but need not prove that the defendant knew the means of identification belonged to another person—with the language of 1028A is to say that "knowingly" modifies "use . . . without lawful authority, a means of identification."

Fourth, the purpose of the statute supports this reading. It is, after all, a statute about identity theft, *Montejo*, 442 F.3d at 217. Here, Godin used the Social Security number of an innocent Maine resident in a scheme to defraud financial institutions across the state. That Maine resident was a victim of identity theft, whether Godin knew that she was stealing his identity or not. A person who unlawfully transfers, possesses, or uses a means of identification that does not belong to him or her does so at the risk that it belongs to someone else.

In *U.S. v. Hines*, the defendant was convicted of identity theft, as the government satisfied the "knowingly" requirement of 18 USCS § 1028A(a)(1) with the defendant's admission that he gave police a false name, and his use of another's name and Social Security number to defraud police satisfied the "means of identification" requirement. (*United States v. Hines*, 2007, CA8 Mo 472 F. 3d 1038.)

The elements of aggravated identity theft, 18 U.S.C. § 1028A, are:

- Knowing use, possession, or transfer, without lawful authority, of the means of identification of another person

- That such conduct occurred during and in relation to a felony enumerated in 18 U.S.C. § 1028A(c)

> ### *United States v. Aguilar-Morales,*
> ### U.S. Dist. LEXIS 73801 (N.D. Iowa Oct. 2, 2007)
> ### Excerpt from the Judge's Opinion
>
> [For] the crime of aggravated identity theft, a violation of 18 U.S.C. § 1028A(a)(1), the government had to prove beyond a reasonable doubt that defendant (1) knowingly used (2) the "means of identification" of another person (3) without lawful authority (4) during and in relation to the offense charged in count one through three of the indictment. The court concluded that defendant did not need to know that the means of identification was actually assigned to another person in order to be guilty of aggravated identify theft.

Punishment for Aggravated Identity Theft

Law 18 USCS § 1028A(a)(1) requires that a mandatory sentence of two years imprisonment be imposed on a person who knowingly transfers, possesses, or uses a means of identification that belongs to someone else while committing another enumerated felony; this mandatory two-year term must be imposed consecutively, with whatever sentence is imposed for conviction on the enumerated felony. (*U.S. v. Montejo*, (2005, ED Va) 353 F. Supp. 2d 643)

Statute of Limitations for Identity Theft

The statute of limitations provides that prosecution must commence within a certain time period after a crime is committed. Pursuant to 18 U.S.C. § 3282—which applies to all noncapital federal offenses for which a statute of limitations is not expressly provided by law—the statute of limitations for an identity theft charge, 18 U.S.C. § 1028(a)(7), is five years (18 U.S.C. § 3282) The long-established general rule is that a statute of limitations begins to run on the day following the day on which the event giving rise to the cause of action occurred. (*United States v. Lnu*, U.S. Dist. LEXIS 29485 (S.D.N.Y. Apr. 12, 2007))

Is the Government Required to Prove That the Identity Was Stolen?

Law 18 U.S.C. § 1028A(a)(1) plainly requires that the transfer, possession, or use of the means of identification of another person be "without lawful authority." Nothing in the plain language of the statute requires that the means of identification must have been stolen for a § 1028A(a)(1) violation to occur. For sure, stealing and then using another person's identification would fall within the meaning of "without lawful authority." However, there are other ways someone could possess or use another person's identification, yet not have "lawful authority" to do so.

In one ruling, the court noted that it bears repeating that the documents that the defendant, Hurtado, had in the victim's name (Colon) were (1) a birth certificate, (2) a Social Security card, (3) a driver's license with Hurtado's photograph, (4) a bank debit card, (5) a library card, and (6) vehicle registration and insurance. There is no requirement of financial harm in § 1028A(a)(1), and the fact that Hurtado did not cause the real Colon financial harm is irrelevant. What Hurtado did was knowingly use a means of identification of another person, knowing full well that he was not Colon. (*United States v. Hurtado*, U.S. App. LEXIS 26874 (11th Cir. Fla. Nov. 21, 2007))

PROSECUTION UNDER THE CREDIT CARD FRAUD ACT

The Credit Card Fraud Act is a broad act designed to cover situations where individuals use counterfeit access devices (which includes credit cards). To successfully prosecute a person under the Credit Card Fraud Act, the government must establish that the defendant knowingly and with the intent to defraud:

- Produces, uses, or traffics in one or more counterfeit access devices

- Traffics in or uses one or more unauthorized access devices during any one-year period and by such conduct, obtains anything of value aggregating $1,000 or more during that period

- Possesses 15 or more devices which are counterfeit or unauthorized access devices

- Traffics in, has control or custody of, or possesses device-making equipment

- Effects transactions, with one or more access devices issued to another person or persons, to receive payment or any other thing of value during any one-year period, the aggregate value of which is equal to or greater than $1,000

- Solicits a person, without the authorization of the issuer of the access device, for the purpose of:
    - Offering an access device
    - Selling information regarding, or an application to obtain, an access device

- Uses, produces, traffics in, has control or custody of, or possesses a telecommunications instrument that has been modified or altered to obtain unauthorized use of telecommunications services

- Uses, produces, traffics in, has control or custody of, or possesses a scanning receiver

- Uses, produces, traffics in, has control or custody of, or possesses hardware or software, knowing it has been configured to intercept or modify telecommunication-identifying information; this is information associated with or contained in a telecommunications instrument so that the instrument may be used to obtain telecommunications service without authorization

- Knowingly and with intent to defraud, without the authorization of the credit-card-system member or its agent, causes or arranges for another person to present to the member or its agent, for payment, one or more evidences or records of transactions made by an access device

- Affects interstate or foreign commerce with the offense

Knowledge or Intent

In enacting the Credit Card Fraud Act, Congress focused specifically on credit card fraud so that the act only covers fraud in which the intent was to defraud the credit card holder or credit-card company, not cases where the the credit card is used as false identification. (*United States v. Blackmon*, (1988, CA2 NY) 839 F. 2d 900) The act prohibits a third party from using a credit card to defraud the issuer with the connivance of the cardholder, even if the latter had obtained the card without intent to defraud the issuer; this is because legislative history reveals intent to protect the issuer from acts of credit card fraud. (*United States v. Jacobowitz*, (1989, CA2 NY) 877 F. 2d 162)

In *United States v. Tunning*, (1995, CA6 Ky) 69 F. 3d 107, the defendant's plea of guilty to credit card fraud in violation of 18 USCS § 1029 was not supported by sufficient factual basis, since, although government did recite numerous facts, it failed to identify specific evidence it would use to prove them. The defendant's admission that he obtained the credit card by using false information failed to establish his intent to defraud, which could not be inferred.

In *United States v. Klopf*, the defendant obtained the identifying information of individuals and used this information to obtain fraudulent driver's licenses and to open credit card accounts in the individuals' names. Klopf argued that there was no intent to defraud because the accounts remained open and he made regular payments on them, but requisite intent was sufficiently established since Klopf clearly intended to deceive the credit card issuing institutions into believing he was the individual named on the various credit cards. (*United States v. Klopf*, (2005, CA11 Fla) 423 F. 3d 1228.)

An essential element of the crime is the intent to defraud, so it follows that good faith on the part of the defendant is a complete defense to a charge of access device fraud. If a defendant actually believes that he or she was authorized to use the access devices and took reasonable steps to check out that belief, then the defendant acted in good faith. A defendant, however, has no burden to establish a defense of good faith. The burden is on the government to prove fraudulent intent and the consequent lack of good faith beyond a reasonable doubt.

Evidence of Loss

The Credit Card Fraud Act does not require that the government prove that actual loss occurred. For example, a violation of the act occurred where a store owner knowingly called authorization for bank approval on phony credit cards, but later altered them so that the banks would not honor them. (*United States v. Scartz*, (1988, CA6 Ohio) 838 F. 2d 876) In one case where a defendant was charged with fraud and not theft, the actual loss to the bank was an outstanding credit card balance prior to the discovery of the offense; it was not the total amount charged on four credit cards before making payments prior to indictment, since this figure more realistically reflected the amount of loss. (*United States v. Allison*, (1996, CA9 Hawaii) 86 F. 3d 940)

In another case, the evidence demonstrating the victims' losses was sufficient to support the defendant's convictions for credit card fraud, despite the defendant's argument that the victims suffered no loss because they were able to get paid back by their credit card companies. This did not square with the law, as "loss" is measured at the moment the credit cards were charged, and if the charge was fraudulent at the time it was made, the loss was concomitant with a criminal act; the victims' later efforts to mitigate any loss through other means was irrelevant to the case. (*United States v. Goldstein*, (2006, CA2 NY) 442 F. 3d 777)

Interstate Commerce Requirement

In prosecution under the Credit Card Fraud Act for the use of a counterfeit access device, it is sufficient to show that a bank manager made an interstate phone call to a credit card authorization center to report the defendant's use of the card. This establishes the jurisdictional requirement of an effect on interstate commerce, since Congress intended the act to provide broad jurisdictional basis. (*United States v. Lee*, (1987, CA4 Md) 818 F. 2d 302)

Under 18 USCS § 1029, illicit possession of out-of-state credit card account numbers is an offense affecting interstate commerce, and there is no requirement to show an actual or potential effect on interstate commerce. (*United States v. Rushdan*, (1989, CA9 Cal) 870 F. 2d 1509) In *United States v. Clayton*, the government was not required to prove a substantial effect on interstate commerce as an element of the charged offenses under the act, since telephones are instruments of interstate commerce and no further inquiry is necessary. (*United States v. Clayton*, (1997, CA9 Cal) 108 F. 3d 1114) However, in *United States v. Spinner*, an indictment that failed to allege an effect on interstate commerce in the first count was jurisdictionally defective, and it could not be saved by the fact that the second count did allege jurisdictional element. (*United States v. Spinner*, (1999, CA3 Pa) 180 F. 3d 514)

In the aforementioned *United States v. Klopf*, the defendant obtained individuals' identifying information and used this information to obtain fraudulent driver's licenses and to open credit card accounts in their names Klopf engaged in interstate financial transactions by making purchases and withdrawals with fraudulently obtained credit cards, and this conduct was sufficient to establish that the transactions affected interstate commerce. (*United States v. Klopf*, (2005, CA11 Fla) 423 F. 3d 1228)

Other Issues Involved in Prosecution

The Credit Card Fraud Act is not unconstitutionally vague merely because of its lack of definition of access device, even though some hypothetical applications of the term might raise constitutional problems; this is because a defendant could not plausibly claim to believe that he or she could lawfully, knowingly use a stolen credit card or use a forged credit card receipt to obtain unauthorized payment. (*United States v. Lee*, (1987, CA4 Va) 815 F. 2d 971)

The act cannot be applied to satellite television descramblers, since nothing in plain wording, the legislative history of the act, or its judicial interpretation indicates that Congress intended the statute to apply to anything other than direct accounting losses. (*United States v. McNutt*, (1990, CA10 Okla) 908 F. 2d 561) The act does not apply to tumbling cellular telephones used for the purpose of free riding on cellular telephone systems. In *United States v. Brady*, the government was unable to show that a telephone accessed an identifiable account for which a record of debits and credits was created and maintained and which resulted in direct accounting losses. (*United States v. Brady*, (1993, CA10 Utah) 13 F. 3d 334) The act applies to credit cards obtained from credit card companies through false applications. Since the defendant intended to defraud the person whose credit was relied on and the companies issuing cards, the unauthorized user was not required to obtain the credit card directly from the victim. (*United States v. Akinkoye*, (1999, CA4 Md) 185 F. 3d 192)

Credit card account numbers printed on the backs of checks and possessed with the intent to engage in fraudulent credit card schemes are unquestionably covered by the definition of access device found in 18 USCS § 1029; an exception to § 1029 for access devices used to initiate a transfer of funds originated solely by paper instrument does not apply, despite the fact that the account numbers were present on the paper checks; the exception in § 1029 is limited to situations involving the passing of bad or forged checks, as legislative history explains. (*United States v. Caputo*, (1987, CA2 NY) 808 F. 2d 963, 22 Fed Rules Evid Serv 447)

According to *United States v. Brewer*, (1987, CA5 Tex) 835 F. 2d 550, the act applies to the misuse of fictitious, forged, and unauthorized (because they were obtained with an intent to defraud) telephone access codes; legitimate access codes could have been counterfeit, since it was plausible that a defendant could fabricate codes which happen to be identical to valid computer access codes; it is not necessary for each of the required 15 code numbers to be active, since legislative history does not require this, and the definitional section of the statute contemplates the misuse of revoked or canceled access codes.

(*United States v. Brewer*, (1987, CA5 Tex) 835 F. 2d 550) The unauthorized use of a credit card account number covering a valid, but unassigned, account constitutes an access device by which fraud was perpetrated under 18 USCS § 1029, even though no actual account existed. (*United States v. Taylor*, (1991, CA8 Minn) 945 F. 2d 1050)

STATE PROSECUTIONS

In state prosecutions, interstate commerce or jurisdiction is not as important because to establish state jurisdiction, the state only needs to establish a connection with that state. This is normally accomplished by establishing that at least one act required by the state statute was committed within that state.

Elements of the Crime

In states, the elements of identity theft vary according to the statute. A representative statute is New York Penal Code § 190.78. Under that statute, the elements of the offense of identity theft in the third degree are as follows:

- A person is guilty of identity theft in the third degree when he or she knowingly and with intent to defraud assumes the identity of another person by presenting himself or herself as that other person, or by acting as that other person, or by using personal identifying information of that other person, and thereby:
  - Obtains goods, money, property or services or uses credit in the name of such other person or causes financial loss to such person or to another person or persons
  - Commits a Class A misdemeanor or higher level crime

Felony or Misdemeanor

State statutes vary as to whether the crime of identity theft is a felony or a misdemeanor. For example, in California, up through 1998, identity theft was a misdemeanor. After January 1999, it could be charged as either a misdemeanor or a felony. In general, a misdemeanor may be punished by confinement of up to one year in jail and a felony maybe punished by confinement in a state prison for more than one year.

Pennsylvania (18 Pa. C.S.A., section 4120) uses an approach that is employed in many states. The statute provides the following information about the value of property and services:

- If the value obtained is less than $2,000 the offense is a misdemeanor of the first degree.

- If the total value involved was $ 2,000 or more, the offense is a felony of the third degree.

- Regardless of the total value involved, if the offense is committed in furtherance of a criminal conspiracy, the offense is a felony of the third degree.

- Regardless of the total value involved, if the offense is a third or subsequent offense under this section, the offense is a felony of the second degree.

- If the person who commits the offense is a caregiver and the victim of the offense is 60 years of age or older or a care-dependent person, the grading of the offense shall be one grade higher than specified in the above sections.

The New York Penal Code classifies identity theft as:

- Class A misdemeanor under section 190.78 & 190.81

- Class E felony under section 190.79 & 190.82

- Class D felony under section 190.80 & 190.83

In New York, the classification depends on the value of property and/or services received and the manner in which the crime was committed.

Forfeiture of Property Involved

In most states, if the thief uses a computer to commit a crime, the computer and other related equipment are subject to forfeiture. For example, in *People v. Warren*, Cal. App. LEXIS 10445 (2005), the California Attorney General stated that in light of the pervasive use of computers to accomplish identity theft offenses, it is contrary to public policy to return to a defendant convicted of identity theft the very equipment that made it possible for him or her to commit the crime, whether or not the equipment actually contains contraband. However, for forfeiture to occur under the California statute, the state must file a petition for forfeiture, and the defendant has a right to a hearing to determine whether any property or property interest is subject to forfeiture under the statute. At the hearing, the prosecution bears the burden of proof by a preponderance of the evidence that the computers that are the subject of its forfeiture petition are the same ones the defendant used to accomplish his or her identity theft offense.

Defenses to State Identity Theft Statutes

State statutes frequently include affirmative defenses in their identity theft statutes. An affirmative defense is one in which the burden of establishing the defense rests with the defendant. A representative statute on this issue is the New York Penal Code § 190.84. That code section provides that in any prosecution for identity theft or unlawful possession of personal identification information pursuant to this article, it shall be an affirmative defense that the person charged with the offense:

- Was under 21 years of age at the time of committing the offense, and the person used or possessed the personal identification information of another solely for the purpose of purchasing alcohol

- Was under 18 years of age at the time of committing the offense, and the person used or possessed the personal identification information of another solely for the purpose of purchasing tobacco products

- Used or possessed the personal identification information of another person solely for the purpose of misrepresenting their own age to gain access to a place to which access is restricted based on age

Double Jeopardy

Can a state convict a person of identity theft and another offense in which the false identity was used to commit a crime without violating the constitutional protection against double jeopardy? That issue was present in a Florida case, where the defendant, Sibley, was charged with seven counts: Count 1: organized fraud; Count 2: fraudulent use of personal identification information; Count 3: grand theft; and Counts 4–7: uttering a forged instrument. Sibley appealed his convictions and sentences on double jeopardy grounds. He argued that Counts 2–7 are subsumed in Count 1. The court affirmed Sibley's convictions and sentences on all counts except Count 3 for grand theft.

The court stated that convictions arising out of the same criminal episode for organized fraud and grand theft violated double jeopardy. However, convictions for organized fraud, fraudulent use of personal identification information, and uttering forged instruments do not violate double jeopardy. The court stated that the test was to compare the elements of the crimes; if it is apparent that each contains elements the other does not then double jeopardy does not apply. For example, organized fraud requires proof of an ongoing course of conduct and deprivation of property. Fraudulent use of personal identification information does not require proof of these elements, but does require proof of using or possessing someone's personal identification information. Organized fraud does not. Accordingly, convictions and sentences for both arising out of the same criminal episode do not violate double jeopardy. (*Sibley v. State*, 955 So. 2d 1222 (Fla. Dist. Ct. App. 5th Dist. 2007))

The *Sibley* case states the general rule for both the federal and state courts. Since identity theft occurs because the thief wants to use the information to commit another crime, the issue of double jeopardy will be present in most prosecutions. Identity theft is stealing the information, and the other offense, generally theft or fraud, is the use of that information to commit another crime. In these cases, the courts will rarely hold that the prohibition against double jeopardy prevents the state or federal government from trying the criminal for both offenses.

Venue

"Venue" refers to the geographical location of the trial. Under the U.S. Constitution, Amendment VI, the accused has a right to be tried in the judicial district in which the crime occurred. Accordingly, the venue of an identity theft case is in the judicial district in which the crime occurred. We need to look at the court decisions to determine where proper venue lies in a case involving identity theft.

In *Ex parte Egbuonu*, 911 So. 2d 748, (Ala. Crim. App. 2004), this issue is discussed. In March 2003, the defendant was arrested in California and charged with first-degree identity theft of an Alabama resident, under Alabama Code § 13A-8-192. The charges stemmed from items sent to a post office box in California addressed to one James Roberson, a captain in the Jefferson County Sheriff's Department. The post office box was traced to the defendant, Egbuonu. Egbuonu was returned to Alabama in October 2003. Bail was set at $100,000. In July 2004, Egbuonu filed a petition for a writ of habeas corpus in Jefferson County, Alabama—the county where he was incarcerated. Egbuonu alleged that he was being illegally detained in the Jefferson County jail because, he argued, the statute that determined the venue for the crime of identity theft, § 13A-8-196, Ala. Code 1975, was unconstitutional. Specifically, he argued that he had a right to be tried in the judicial district in which the crime occurred, and that was in California.

In denying his writ, the Alabama appellate court stated that identity theft, by its definition, was a continuing offense that in most instances will occur in more than one county or even more than one state. However, where there is no legislation on the matter of venue, courts look to the purpose of the statute defining the offense. Venue in a criminal case, though a constitutional matter, requires an inquiry into what conduct the statute proscribes. The test is best described as a substantial contact rule that takes into account a number of factors: the site of the defendant's acts, the elements and nature of the crime, the locus of the effect of the criminal conduct, and the suitability of each district for accurate fact-finding. Places that suffer the effects of a crime are entitled to consideration for venue purposes. Such districts have an obvious contact with the litigation in their interest in preventing such effects from occurring. To some extent, this factor overlaps with the definition and nature of the crime. The court held that the Alabama legislature specifically designated that venue was proper either in the county where the crime took place or where the victim resided. The court held that the statute complied with the constitutional requirements because the victim resided in Alabama.

In a case with similar facts, a Georgia appellate court agreed with the Alabama court and held that the Georgia Constitution Article VI, § II, ¶ VI does not limit venue in a criminal case to one county. It provides for trial in whatever county the offense was committed. A crime may be ongoing or continuing, in which case venue would be appropriate in any county in which the offense occurred. The Georgia court stated that the crime was committed in any county in which one of the elements was committed or in the county in which the victim lived. (*State v. Mayze*, 622 S.E.2d 836, 2005 Fulton County D. Rep. 3521 (2005))

Jurisdiction

Jurisdiction refers to the power of a court to try the subject matter of the case. There are two types of jurisdiction. Subject matter jurisdiction refers to the power of the court to exercise its authority over the subject matter. Personal jurisdiction refers to the power of the court to exercise its authority over the defendant. Having the defendant present in court generally satisfies personal jurisdiction.

Under subject matter jurisdiction, an Alabama court would not have jurisdiction to prosecute a defendant for the violation of a California statute. In the Egbuonu case discussed above, the defendant was tried for violating an Alabama statute while in California. The defendant's actions in stealing the identity of an Alabama citizen probably violated the identity theft statutes of both California and Alabama. Accordingly, he could be tried in both states. He could be tried in California for violating a California statute and in Alabama for violating an Alabama statute. In determining whether Egbuonu violated the California statute, we would need to look at the elements of the offense as set forth in the California Penal Code, not the Alabama Code.

There is no requirement that all elements of the offense be committed in California. If any one of the elements occurred in that state then that is sufficient to give California jurisdiction. If the effects of his criminal conduct affected a person in Alabama and he has committed all the required elements of the Alabama statute, then the offender is also guilty of a crime in Alabama. A similar result would occur where an individual mails a box of poisoned candy from California to a person in Alabama and the receiver dies from the poison. In this example, the sender would be guilty of murder in California where he or she committed the act and in Alabama where he or she killed the victim. The defendant could be tried in both states for murder, and it would not be double jeopardy because each case would be tried under different state statutes. Egbuonu was probably also guilty of the federal crime of identity theft since he used the U.S. Mail.

CHAPTER 6

REBUILDING AFTER IDENTITY THEFT

The average victim of identity theft loses more than $6,000 and spends more than 600 hours trying to rebuild his or her life.

CHAPTER OUTLINE

- Introduction
- Duty to Cooperate with Victims
- Documenting the Theft
- Dealing with Credit Reporting Companies
- Dealing with Creditors, Debt Collectors, and Merchants
- Limiting Your Loss from Identity Theft
- Other Federal Rights
- Other State Rights
- Restitution
- Wrongful Arrest
- Lawsuits Based on Negligence
- Violation of Fair Credit Reporting Act
- Need to Establish Monetary Damages
- Recovery of Attorney Fees

INTRODUCTION

This chapter focuses on helping victims to recover from identity theft crimes. The next section deals with the duty imposed by federal legislation to cooperate with the victim. In addition, most states have imposed similar duties on entities and public agencies. In some states, the legal duty to cooperate and assist the victim may be broader than those required by federal law. As noted earlier, identity theft can have serious psychological effects on the victim. Accordingly, the victim should be treated with compassion, and cooperation should be volunteered. Another consistent problem suffered by victims of this crime is wrongful arrest. Unfortunately, there is little protection or financial help provided in the statutes regarding this problem. As noted later in the chapter, it is difficult to establish a recoverable claim of wrongful arrest in a civil case. This is an area or concern that probably will increase and cause more problems for innocent individuals. Accordingly, it is an area that victims' rights organizations and other public agencies need to address.

DUTY TO COOPERATE WITH VICTIMS

In addition to the federal requirements, states have also imposed a duty on certain entities to cooperate with victims of identity theft. Most states have requirements similar to California Penal Code § 530.8, which requires that if a person discovers that he or she is a victim of identity theft:

- The victim should present the entity with which the false application was filed or the account was opened.

- The victim should obtain a copy of a police report and identifying information that the unauthorized person used to complete the application or to open the account.

- The victim or a law enforcement officer specified by the person shall be entitled to receive information related to the application or account, including a copy of the unauthorized person's application or application information and a record of transactions or charges associated with the application or account.

Upon request by the victim, the entity with which the application was filed shall inform him or her of the categories of identifying information that the unauthorized person used to complete the application or to open the account. The person or entity with which the application was filed or the account was opened shall provide copies of all paper records, records of telephone applications or authorizations, or records of electronic applications or authorizations, without charge, within ten business days of receipt of the victim's request and submission of the required copy of the police report and identifying information.

The request must be in writing and signed before a notary or other person authorized to take an acknowledgement. If the victim authorizes a law-enforcement officer to obtain the information, the written statement must:

- Authorize disclosure for a stated period

- Specify the name of the agency or department to which the disclosure is authorized

- Identify the types of records that the requesting person authorizes to be disclosed

- Include in the statement a notice that the requesting person has the right at any time to revoke the authorization

If any entity fails to produce a court order, the court in the jurisdiction in which the victim resides or in which the request for information was issued may issue an order to the entity. At the victim's request, the attorney general, the district attorney, or the prosecuting city attorney may file a petition to compel the attendance of the person or entity in possession of the records and order the production of the requested records to the court. The petition shall contain a declaration from the victim stating when the request for information was made, that the information requested was not provided, and what response, if any, the person or entity made. The petition shall also contain copies of the police report and the request for information made upon the person or entity in possession of the records. The court shall keep these two documents confidential. The petition and copies of the police report and the application shall be served upon the person or entity in possession of the records. The court shall hold a hearing on the petition no later than ten court days after the petition is served and filed. The court shall order the release of records to the victim as required.

In addition to any other civil remedy available, the victim may bring a civil action against the entity for damages, injunctive relief or other equitable relief, and a penalty of 100 dollars per day for noncompliance, plus reasonable attorneys' fees.

Identity Theft Victims' Statement of Rights
(Proposed Handout for Victims)

Federal and state laws protect victims of identity theft. These laws have to do with documenting the theft; dealing with credit reporting companies; dealing with creditors, debt collectors, and merchants; and limiting your financial losses caused by the theft of your identity.

DOCUMENTING THE THEFT

You have the right to:

- File a report with a law-enforcement agency and ask for a copy of it to show how your identity has been misused.

This report is often called a police report. An identity theft report is a second kind of report. It is a police report with more detail. To be an identity theft report, it should have enough information about the crime that the credit reporting companies and the businesses involved can verify that you're a victim and can know which accounts or information have been affected. It's the report that will give you access to many of the rights described here.

The FTC's Identity Theft Complaint form is a good place to start documenting the theft of your identity. This form asks you for the kind of detail that the identity theft report requires. Once you fill this form out online and print it, you can use it with the police report to create your identity theft report.

DEALING WITH CREDIT REPORTING COMPANIES

You have the right to:

- Place a 90-day initial fraud alert on your credit files. You would do this if you think you are—or may become—the victim of identity theft.

A fraud alert tells users of your credit report that they must take reasonable steps to verify who is applying for credit in your name. To place a 90-day fraud alert, contact just one of the three nationwide credit reporting companies. The one you contact is required to notify the other two.

- Place a seven-year extended fraud alert on your credit files.

You would do this if you know you are a victim of identity theft. You would need to give an identity theft report to each of the credit reporting companies. Each credit reporting company would ask you to give them some way for potential creditors to reach you, like a phone number. They would place this contact information on the extended fraud alert as a signal to those who use your credit report that they must contact you before they can issue credit in your name.

- Get one free copy of your credit report and a summary of your rights from each credit reporting company.

You can get these when you place a 90-day initial fraud alert on your credit reports. When you place an extended fraud alert with any credit reporting company, you have the right to two copies of that credit report during a 12-month period. These credit reports are in addition to the free credit report that all consumers are entitled to each year.

- Ask the credit reporting companies to block fraudulent information from appearing on your credit report.

To do this, you must submit a copy of a valid identity theft report. The credit reporting companies then must tell any creditors who gave them fraudulent information that it resulted from identity theft. The creditors may not then turn the fraudulent debts over to debt collectors.

- Dispute fraudulent or inaccurate information on your credit report with a credit reporting company.

The credit reporting company must investigate your charges and fix your report if they find that the information is fraudulent.

- In many states, you have the right to restrict access to your credit report through a credit freeze.

A credit freeze makes it more difficult for an identity thief to open a new account in your name. Your state attorney general's office has information about using a credit freeze where you live.

DEALING WITH CREDITORS, DEBT COLLECTORS, AND MERCHANTS

You have the right to:

- Have a credit report free of fraudulent accounts. Once you give creditors and debt collectors a copy of a valid identity theft report, they may not report fraudulent accounts to the credit reporting companies.

- Get copies of documents related to the theft of your identity—for example, applications used to open new accounts or transaction records—if you give the company a valid police report.

- Tell the company to give the documents to a specific law-enforcement agency; that agency doesn't have to get a subpoena for the records.

- Stop the collection of fraudulent debts. You may ask debt collectors to stop contacting you to collect on fraudulent debts. You may also ask them to give you information related to the debt, like the names of the creditors and the amounts of the debts.

In many states, you have the right to be notified by a business or organization that has lost or misplaced certain types of personal information. Contact your state attorney general's office for more information.

LIMITING YOUR LOSS FROM IDENTITY THEFT

Various laws limit your liability for fraudulent debts caused by identity theft.

- Fraudulent Credit Card Charges

You cannot be held liable for more than $50 for fraudulent purchases made with your credit card, as long as you let the credit card company know within 60 days of when the credit card statement with the fraudulent charges was sent to you. Some credit card issuers say cardholders who are victims of fraudulent transactions on their accounts have no liability for them at all.

- Lost or Stolen ATM/Debit Card

If your ATM or debit card is lost or stolen, you may not be held liable for more than $50 for the misuse of your card, as long as you notify the bank or credit union within two business days after you realize the card is missing. If you do not report the loss of your card promptly, your liability may increase.

- Fraudulent Electronic Withdrawals

If fraudulent electronic withdrawals are made from your bank or credit union account, and your ATM or debit card has not been lost or stolen, you are not liable, as long as you notify the bank or credit union in writing of the error within 60 days of the date the bank or credit union account statement with the fraudulent withdrawals was sent to you.

- Fraudulent Checks

Under most state laws, you are only liable for a limited amount for fraudulent checks issued on your bank or credit union account, as long as you notify the bank or credit union promptly. Contact your state banking or consumer protection agency for more information.

- Fraudulent New Accounts

Under most state laws, you are not liable for any debt incurred on fraudulent accounts opened in your name and without your permission. Contact your state attorney general's office for more information.

OTHER FEDERAL RIGHTS

Identity theft victims have other rights when the identity thief is being prosecuted in federal court. For example, under the Justice for All Act, the U.S. Department of Justice says identity theft victims have the right:

- To be reasonably protected from the accused
- To reasonable, accurate, and timely notice of any public court proceeding, any parole proceeding involving the crime, or any release or escape of the accused

- To not be excluded from any such public court proceeding unless the court determines that the identity theft victim's testimony would be materially altered if he or she heard other testimony at that proceeding

- To be reasonably heard at any public proceeding in the district court involving release, plea, sentencing, or any parole proceeding

- To confer with the attorney for the government in the case

- To full and timely restitution as provided by law

- To proceedings free from unreasonable delay

- To be treated with fairness and with respect for his or her dignity and privacy

OTHER STATE RIGHTS

You may have additional rights under state laws. Contact your state attorney general's office to learn more.

Additional Victims' Rights under State Legislation

In addition to the federal rights discussed earlier in this book, many states have enacted legislation that provides even more rights for citizens of those states. For example, California, the number one state for identity thefts, has enacted extensive legislation. A copy of their additional rights is set forth below.

California Civil Code § 1785.15.3.
Statement of Rights of Victims of Identity Theft

a) In addition to any other rights the consumer may have under this title, every consumer credit reporting agency, after being contacted by telephone, mail, or in person by any consumer who has reason to believe he or she may be a victim of identity theft, shall promptly provide to that consumer a statement, written in a clear and conspicuous manner, describing the statutory rights of victims of identity theft under this title.

b) Every consumer credit reporting agency shall, upon the receipt from a victim of identity theft of a police report prepared pursuant to Section 530.6 of the Penal Code or a valid investigative report made by a Department of Motor Vehicles investigator with peace officer status regarding the public offenses described in Section 530.5 of the Penal Code, provide the victim, free of charge and upon request, with up to 12 copies of his or her file during a consecutive 12-month period, not to exceed one copy per month, following the date of the police report. Notwithstanding any other provision of this title, the maximum number of free reports a victim of identity theft is entitled to obtain under this title is 12 per year, as provided by this subdivision.

c) Subdivision (a) does not apply to a consumer reporting agency that acts only as a reseller of credit information by assembling and merging information contained in the database of another consumer reporting agency or agencies and that does not maintain a permanent database of credit information from which new credit reports are produced.

d) The provisions of this section shall become effective July 1, 2003.

RESTITUTION

In *United States v. Garcia*, 478 F. Supp. 2d 1333, 2007 U.S. Dist. LEXIS 19874 (D. Utah 2007), the court discussed the limitations of federal restitution for identity theft victims. In February 2006, Garcia pleaded guilty to two counts of aggravated identity fraud. Under a law (Identity Theft Penalty Enhancement Act, Pub. L. No. 108-275, § 2(a), 118 Stat. 831, 831 (2004) (codified at 18 USSC § 1028A)), this offense carries a mandatory minimum sentence of two years in prison. The court sentenced her to the required two-year prison term.

The court opined that, as a result of the limits of restitution, the federal statutes unfairly tied the hands of judges in crafting restitution orders. The court recommended that the federal restitution statutes be amended to give courts the appropriate power to award restitution to victims of federal offenses for all their losses.

At the sentencing hearing, the court was also required to consider what restitution was appropriate. Of course, the banks that suffered financial losses received restitution, so the court ordered Garcia to pay restitution of $539.51 to Capital One and $ 6,299.01 to GE Consumer Finance.

The next issue considered was what restitution the victim should receive. Because the banks had absorbed the loss from the phony credit cards, the victim's direct out-of-pocket loss from the identity fraud was zero. But she also suffered other losses. While she was at a gym early one morning, her car was vandalized and her purse was stolen. In her letter to the court, she detailed the items taken, including her charge cards, driver's license, Social Security card, various membership cards, gift certificates, and work keys. She estimated the replacement cost of the stolen possessions to be $1,000 and the damage to her vehicle from the break-in to be $1,500. In addition to attempting to replace her stolen cards, the victim also had to deal with fraudulent charges incurred on her VISA card, and she had to close a checking account as a result of the theft. And she lost her confidence and peace of mind:

> For several months after my purse was stolen, I worried that whoever may have ended up with my personal information and possessions would want to know more about me or victimize me further by coming to my home and breaking in to take things, or worse, to harm me or my family. For a while, I pleaded with my husband to have the locks changed and wanted to rent a mailbox at the post office rather than have

mail sent to our home. My desire to take these actions was instigated by fear. . . . I worry I will never feel secure, as I will always wonder if my personal information was distributed, and if so, to whom, and what they plan to do with it. I have several reminders on my calendar at work to request credit reports and to follow up with utility and phone companies quarterly to ensure my identification is not being used to establish new service that will most likely never be paid, and will ultimately affect me adversely. I worry that one day I will be notified that a large amount of debt, of which I know nothing, has been attributed to me. It is unsettling to feel that someone may be out in the world pretending to be me, using my good name and my credit in a criminal way and that their actions, which are not in my control, will be blamed on me.

The court also noted that most importantly, the victim suffered a loss of what she called her "most precious thing"—her free time. She had to devote considerable efforts to clearing her credit, spending time that was hard to come by because she was a wife and a "working mother" with two children. She wrote of the "significant" amount of precious time she spent "correcting the wrong done to me by Ruby Garcia."

The court stated that the kinds of losses the victim suffered were appreciated by Congress in enacting the new identify fraud penalties. Congress realized the tremendous harm that identity theft can inflict on a victim. The court quoted one of the legislation's cosponsors, Representative Lamar Smith:

> Once an identity [thief] has the personal information of another, the possibilities for abuse are endless. Identity thieves often open up credit cards or bank accounts in another person's name, go on spending sprees, and leave the victim with damaged credit. Identity theft is a serious crime and should be punished accordingly.

The court stated that identity theft necessarily harms victims severely: "A victim of identity theft usually spends a year and a half working to restore his or her identity and good name." The problem the court encountered in the *Garcia* case is hardly unique, as current law severely restricts the ability of federal trial judges to award proper restitution. The Supreme Court has held that a district court's power to order restitution must be conferred by statute. The main federal restitution statutes—18 USSC § 3663 and § 3663A—permit courts to award restitution only for several particular kinds of loss. The statutes, however, fail to give judges more general authorization to award restitution to crime victims.

The court opined that as a result of these limits, the federal statutes unfairly tie the hands of judges in crafting restitution orders. In this case, for example, there was no authority for the court to award the victim restitution for her time lost in clearing her credit record and no authority to award restitution for the cost of repairing her car or replacing her stolen property. Not only is the statute clear on this point, but case law has explicated that courts lack authority to give victims restitution for consequential losses or other losses deemed to be too remote from the offense of conviction. For example, the Seventh Circuit recently rejected the position of a victim of identity theft that she was "entitled to reimbursement for all the time she spent in the endeavor" of clearing her credit because it would take the restitution statutes "too far."

Currently, there is no authorization under federal law for general restitution to crime victims. A judge may order restitution only if the loss suffered by the victim falls within certain categories specified by statute. On recommendation of the Criminal Law Committee, the Judicial Conference agreed to support legislation that would authorize general restitution in any criminal case at the discretion of the judge when the circumstances of the case warrant it.

The court stated that in this case, and in too many others like it, the court is unable to fully "restore the victims to their prior state of wellbeing." Congress has recently acted to punish aggravated identity theft severely by creating mandatory minimum sentences for the crime. But while these changes strongly deter such crimes, they unfortunately do nothing to fully compensate the victims who suffer from such crimes. The court recommended that Congress should give federal district court judges the tools needed to fully compensate victims of aggravated identity theft—and victims of all federal crimes.

As of January 2008, the federal restitution statutes for identity theft victims—18 U.S.C. §§ 3663 and 3663A—permitted courts to award restitution only for particular kinds of loss:

- Loss of property

- Medical expenses

- Physical therapy

- Lost income

- Funeral expenses

- Expenses for participating in all proceedings related to the offense

WRONGFUL ARREST

In *Willingham v. City of Orlando*, 929 So. 2d 43, (Fla. Dist. Ct. App. 5th Dist. 2006), Willingham filed a civil complaint against the police officer, the city, and the county in the Circuit Court for Orange County (Florida). He claimed that the city was liable for false arrest and false imprisonment, that the officer was liable for false arrest, and that the county was liable for false imprisonment. The circuit court granted summary judgment to the officer, the city, and the county, and Willingham appealed. (A summary judgment dismissed the action without a trial.)

In 2000, Willingham had been issued a ticket that was dismissed because of mistaken identity, as another person had stolen his identity. For some reason, the warrant that had been issued in the case was never cancelled.

In 2005, a police officer, who was an employee of the city, arrested Willingham based on the outstanding warrant. Willingham protested that the officer had the wrong man because of the theft of his identity. The officer chose not to investigate his claim of mistaken identity. Willingham was taken to a correctional facility in the county, and he was released five days later after the staff at the facility investigated and confirmed his claims. On appeal, the court found that the officer acted reasonably under the circumstances in fulfilling the nondiscretionary requirements of his position to arrest the person named in the warrant, even if it was mistakenly issued. Therefore, the trial court acted properly in granting summary judgment in favor of the officer pursuant to the immunity issued to the officer under Fla. Stat. § 768.28(9)(a) (2003). Further, there was no special duty owed to Willingham by either the city or the county. Therefore, they were not liable for his arrest or detention. The judgment was affirmed.

The court noted that this case required the court to examine the potential liability of law-enforcement officers and their governmental employers in connection with the execution of an arrest warrant and the taking into custody of the person named in the warrant. The court concluded that no cause of action for false arrest or false imprisonment against the officer or the involved agencies could be alleged under the facts of the case.

LAWSUITS BASED ON NEGLIGENCE

What if the company you are doing business with fails to protect your personal information? That issue was involved in *King Motor Co. v. Jones*, 901 So. 2d 1017, Fla. App. LEXIS 7214, 30 Fla. L. Weekly D 1262 (Fla. Dist. Ct. App. 4th Dist. 2005).

Judith Jones became a victim of identity theft when she purchased a car at a dealership. She sued King Motor Company of Fort Lauderdale, Inc. (King Motor), alleging that a King Motor salesman used the information contained on her credit application to steal her identity and make fraudulent purchases and bank account withdrawals. Her complaint included claims for negligence, gross negligence, unfair and deceptive trade practices, and a violation of the Credit Services Organization Act.

King Motor claimed that Jones only had the rights set forth in the contract to purchase the vehicle, which required any dispute under the contract to be resolved by arbitration. The court noted that if a duty alleged to be breached is one imposed by law in recognition of public policy and is generally owed to others besides the contracting parties, then a dispute regarding such a breach is not one arising from the contract, but sounds in tort. A tort is a private wrong for which a person may bring a lawsuit. The trial court concluded that a contractually imposed arbitration requirement would not apply to such a claim.

The trial court held that this case involved tort claims based on King Motor's alleged breach of duty to keep customers' confidential and financial information safe. These claims do not implicate contractual duties created or governed by the contract but concern duties generally owed to the public, in other words, to others besides Jones. None of the allegations in the complaint require reference to or construction of any portion of the purchase and sale or financing agreement between the parties. Because this action is predicated upon a theory of negligence unrelated to the rights and obligations of the contract, it does not have a sufficient relationship to the agreement as to fall within the arbitration provision.

The Fourth District Court of Appeals, in reviewing the case, reasoned that the tort claims were based on the dealer's alleged breach of duty to keep the customer's confidential and financial information safe—duties owed generally to the public—and did not implicate the contractual duties created or governed by the parties' purchase and sales contract. Moreover, none of the allegations in the complaint required reference to, or construction of, any portion of the parties' contract. Jones was allowed to maintain her suit to recover her losses from the dealership.

VIOLATION OF FAIR CREDIT REPORTING ACT

What if a victim reports to a bank that a credit it issued was not issued to that victim and the bank still reports the failure to pay to a credit reporting agency? That issue was discussed in *Defer v. World Fin. Network Nat'l Bank*, U.S. Dist. LEXIS 76188 (E.D. Mich. Oct. 15, 2007), in which the plaintiff, Daniel P. Defer (the identity-theft victim), sued Defendant World Financial Network National Bank. Defer claimed that the bank violated the federal Fair Credit Reporting Act (FCRA), 15 U.S.C. § 1681 et seq., by failing to indicate on Defer's credit report that a credit card debt purportedly owed by him remained in dispute.

The debt arose from the use of a credit card issued by the bank on behalf of the Victoria's Secret chain of stores. This credit card account evidently was held in the name of Daniel P. Defer. The bank states that this account was opened in October of 2004 and that it was regularly used and payments were made for about a year, but that the payments then ceased and it is now past due.

According to Defer, his estranged wife has used his personal information, including his Social Security number, to open credit card accounts and run up debts in his name, all without his knowledge or consent. Upon learning of this, he sent letters to the bank and to certain credit reporting agencies denying that he owed various debts, including the outstanding debt on the credit card issued by the bank. Defer also filed a report with the local police department, claiming that he was the victim of identity theft committed by his estranged wife. According to Defer, this investigation is still ongoing, with the police still purportedly considering whether to file charges against his now ex-wife.

Upon receiving Defer's letter disputing his debt, the bank opened an investigation in early April of 2006 and purportedly advised the credit bureaus of the account's disputed status. The bank then wrote to Defer on May 18, 2006, requesting that he provide a copy of the police report he had filed regarding his ex-wife's alleged identity theft. When Defer failed to do so by June 1, 2006, the bank closed its investigation and removed the "disputed" status from its account as reflected on Defer's credit report. The suit followed, with Defer alleging that the bank violated the FCRA by failing to conduct an appropriate investigation and prematurely removing the disputed designation from the debt it claims Defer owes.

The bank made a motion to dismiss the lawsuit, stating that it properly terminated its investigation of Defer's claim of identity theft upon his failure to cooperate in the investigation by providing a copy of the police report he had filed with the police. In response, Defer asserted that he had "done everything he could do" to dispute the debt that the bank claimed he owed and that he could not provide the "finalized" police report purportedly sought by the bank until the ongoing police investigation was concluded.

As the court observed, the FCRA places distinct obligations on three types of entities: (1) consumer reporting agencies, (2) users of consumer reports, and (3) furnishers of information to consumer reporting agencies. The court noted that in this case, it is clear that the bank is in the last of these three categories. Accordingly, the FCRA establishes various prohibitions and duties with regard to the information the bank provided to consumer credit-reporting agencies, including:

- A prohibition against furnishing consumer-related information that it "knows or has reasonable cause to believe" is inaccurate (15 U.S.C. § 1681s-2(a)(1)(A))

- A prohibition against furnishing information after being notified by the consumer, and then confirming, that this information is inaccurate (15 U.S.C. § 1681s-2(a)(1)(B))

- A duty to correct any inaccuracies in information previously provided to a credit reporting agency (15 U.S.C. § 1681s-2(a)(2))

- A duty, when presented with a consumer's dispute as to the completeness or accuracy of information, not to furnish this information to a credit reporting agency without "notice that such information is disputed by the consumer," (15 U.S.C. § 1681s-2(a)(3))

- A duty, upon receiving an identity theft report from a consumer, not to furnish any information based upon this alleged identity theft to any credit reporting agency unless it "knows or is informed by the consumer that the information is correct" (15 U.S.C. § 1681s-2(a)(6)(B))

In addition, the bank had a duty, upon receiving notice from a credit reporting agency that a consumer has disputed the accuracy or completeness of information it has provided, to "conduct an investigation with respect to the disputed information" and report the results of its investigation to the credit reporting agency. (15 U.S.C. § 1681s-2(b)(1))

In this case, the bank contended that it properly reported Defer's debt as disputed and commenced the requisite investigation upon receiving a letter from him in early April of 2006 claiming that he had been the victim of identity theft, and it therefore did not owe the debt that the bank sought to collect from him. In the course of this investigation, the bank purportedly requested that Defer provide a copy of the report he had filed with the police, but he failed to comply with this request. In light of this failure, the bank maintained that it was entitled to abandon its investigation, in accordance with an FCRA provision that authorizes a consumer reporting agency to terminate its investigation of a consumer-generated dispute if the consumer fails "to provide sufficient information to investigate the disputed information." (15 U.S.C. § 1681i(a)(3)(A))

The court noted that there were at least two separate obstacles, however, to the court's acceptance of the bank's proposition as a matter of law. First, the above-quoted FCRA provision applies only to consumer reporting agencies, and not to entities, such as the bank, that furnish information to these agencies.

Nothing in the pertinent statutory provision, therefore, suggests that a furnisher of information such as the bank may abandon its investigation if it is unable to satisfy its desire for additional information through direct interaction with the consumer. Rather, the bank's apparent recourse would be to seek additional information from the credit reporting agency that gave notice of the dispute.

Apart from its reliance on an inapplicable FCRA provision, the bank also failed to establish as a matter of law that it fully discharged its investigative duty under the provision that does apply, § 1681s-2(b)(1)(A). This provision itself merely requires that furnishers of information such as the bank "conduct an investigation," without specifying what this investigation must entail or what standards might govern judicial review of this investigation. The courts, however, have construed the statute as demanding a "reasonable" investigation.

NEED TO ESTABLISH MONETARY DAMAGES

In *Randolph v. Ing Life Ins. & Annuity Co.*, 486 F. Supp. 2d 1, U.S. Dist. LEXIS 11523 (D.D.C. 2007), the plaintiffs, seven current or retired District of Columbia employees, filed a purported class action on behalf of individuals whose private personal information, including Social Security numbers, was contained on the laptop computer of a representative of the defendant, ING Life Insurance and Annuity Company ("ING"). This laptop was stolen during a burglary of the representative's home. The plaintiffs' complaint alleges two counts of invasion of privacy, one count of gross negligence, and one count of negligence. The defendant moved to dismiss the plaintiffs' complaint on the grounds that the plaintiffs failed to allege any injury in fact and thus lack standing.

The plaintiffs asserted that the "unauthorized and unconsented disclosure of an individual's name, address, date of birth, and Social Security number creates a substantial risk of identity theft" and that "nationwide studies confirm that, on average, victims of identity theft spend hundreds of hours in personal time and hundreds of dollars in personal funds to resolve their credit issues." Significantly, however, none of the plaintiffs asserted that they were actually victims of identity theft. Instead, the plaintiffs alleged that the disclosure of their information raises concerns about the plaintiffs' safety because, for example, their information could be used to find out where police personnel live. Specifically, the plaintiffs alleged that as a "direct and proximate result of [ING's] acts and omissions, they have been exposed to a risk of substantial harm and inconvenience and have incurred or will incur actual damages in purchasing comprehensive credit reports and/or monitoring of their identity and credit for the indefinite future."

The court concluded that the plaintiffs' case should be dismissed because they failed to allege a cognizable injury. To recover, a plaintiff must establish that he or she has (1) suffered an injury in fact, "an invasion of a legally protected interest which is (a) concrete and particularized and (b) actual or imminent, not conjectural or hypothetical," (2) which is fairly traceable to the crime.

RECOVERY OF ATTORNEY FEES

In *Smith v. Citifinancial Retail Servs.*, U.S. Dist. LEXIS 58723 (N.D. Cal. Aug. 2, 2007), the plaintiff, Smith, a victim of identity theft, sued the defendants, Citi, for continuing to provide false information about his financial status after he had reported the problem to them. For reasons not completely understood, what should have been a simple matter to resolve resulted in a bitterly contested year-long litigation. It was resolved when the plaintiff accepted the defendants' offer of judgment of $75,000, with costs and attorneys' fees to be determined by the court. The plaintiff then moved for an award of $200,156.25 in attorneys' fees and $5,954.16 in costs.

The underlying dispute arose out of an incident of identity theft, in which an unauthorized person opened several credit accounts in the plaintiff's name. After attempting for several years to have the defendants remove the fraudulent account from his credit report, Smith brought suit against the defendants, alleging violations of the FCRA, (15 U.S.C. § 1681 et seq.) and California's Identity Theft Statute, Cal. Civ. Code § 1798.92 et seq.

The court noted that because his FCRA action against the defendants was successful, the plaintiff is entitled to recover "the costs of the action together with reasonable attorneys' fees as determined by the court." (15 U.S.C. §§ 1681n(a)(3), 1681o(a)(2)) Similarly, California's Identity Theft Statute provides that a successful plaintiff is entitled to recover "actual damages, attorneys' fees, and costs." (Cal. Civ. Code § 1798.93(c)(5))

CHAPTER 7

VOICES OF EXPERIENCE

In this chapter, a veteran Los Angeles police officer, Sergeant Ed Dadisho, and a Los Angeles County deputy district attorney, Jonathan Fairtlough, a member of the Los Angeles County High Tech Crime Division, share their experiences and provide guidance in the investigation and filing of charges in identity theft incidents. The chapter is concluded with the reprint of an article by Assistant U.S. Attorney Sean Hoar. His article provides an excellent concluding summary of identity theft and the issues involved.

IDENTITY THEFT AND THE POLICE RESPONSE: THE INVESTIGATION

By Ed Dadisho, Sergeant, Los Angeles Police Department, Los Angeles, California

A properly structured preliminary investigation saves investigative time, involves the victim in resolution of the theft, and lays the foundation for prosecution.

The Preliminary Investigation

Generally, identity theft crimes will not be contained in one jurisdiction. Every investigation requires investigators to determine the point of compromise of the victim's identity—that is, where the offender may have obtained the victim's identification information. This will help lead to possible suspects and will often lead to additional victims.

The investigation starts with the victim's report of the theft. Victims should be informed of the steps they need to take to prepare for investigation. This enables victims to start doing something constructive immediately and helps fulfill their emotional needs. By providing a worksheet or explaining exactly what victims need to do, investigators help victims organize their thoughts and information. In preparing for the investigation, victims should gather the following information and materials and turn them over to the police investigators, being sure to keep any original documents related to the case:

- Date of birth, driver's license number, Social Security number, telephone numbers (work, home, and cellular), and email addresses of every victim in the household

- Account numbers involved in the theft and the names of primary and secondary account holders

- When and how the fraud or theft was discovered and under what circumstances the victim became aware of the identity theft

- Exact locations (addresses, businesses, persons involved) where fraudulent use of the identity occurred

- Names, addresses (home and work), phone numbers, and dates of birth of every person involved in the incident

- Names of financial institutions the victim has notified of the theft, along with the names, addresses, and phone numbers of customer service representatives or investigators who accepted the report; also, the dates and times of the reports, a brief summary of the conversation, and copies of any email messages or faxes sent to or received from the financial institutions

- Photocopies of any letters, account statements, and other documents associated with the case

- A chronological log of the theft and the victim's actions since discovering the theft, to include information about the discovery of theft or fraud, possible locations of the theft, and names or descriptions of persons around when the theft might have occurred

During the early stages of the investigation, it is important to determine the motive. The motive will help direct the investigation. The motive for financial crimes is usually greed, drugs, or revenge. Determining the motive requires investigators to conduct a detailed interview with the victim. The U.S. Secret Service, along with the IACP, has developed an outstanding 11-page document that investigators can give to the victim to fill out. This document is in effect a questionnaire filled with a variety of useful information to the investigator. This document can be obtained from the U.S. Secret Service/IACP "Identity Crime" CD-ROM; call the Secret Service or the IACP for details.

The Continued Investigation

The next steps taken by the investigator should be to examine all financial and credit bureau documents. These documents are useful and vital pieces of evidence to tie suspects to the crime and lead to their eventual prosecution. For help with this step, the investigator can contact appropriate state and local agencies, as well as the following federal agencies:

- Postal Inspection Service

- Federal Bureau of Investigation

- Bureau of Immigration and Customs Enforcement

- Social Security Administration

- Secret Service

The Secret Service has a program called the eInformation Network, an intranet site that is available, for free, to law enforcement agencies and investigators. It is an important tool for investigators in accessing bank and credit card information. For more information, go to (*www.einformation.usss.gov*). The resources available on the Secret Service eInformation Network include the following:

- Bank identification number search

- Credit card and skimming information

- Counterfeit check database

- Genuine and counterfeit identification document database

- Cybercrime resources

- Fraudulent document database

FinCEN (Financial Crimes Enforcement Network) is another excellent network for investigating identity theft and other financial crimes. FinCEN links databases maintained by the law enforcement, financial, and regulatory communities. Its purpose is to collect, analyze, and share information with law-enforcement agencies. FinCEN accesses approximately 37 different and independent databases in three main categories: law enforcement, financial, and commercial. The databases include AutoTrack, LexisNexis, the Social Security Administration Death Master File, Drug Enforcement Administration, Federal Bureau of Investigation, and Internal Revenue Service databases, to name a few.

Another excellent tool for investigators is the use of informants. Investigators should develop informants from potential suspects during the investigation. Investigators should identify possible informants by using intelligence from other law enforcement agencies or the private sector. Another good technique for developing informants is using other people who participated in some capacity in the identity theft, such as a store employee who sold goods knowing the suspect was using someone else's identity.

Investigators should consider using other means to gain access to privileged information, such as obtaining federal cooperation and funds, seeking state and federal RICO statute investigations, or using forfeiture statutes to gain access to financial records. Above all, investigators should always follow the money; this is an appropriate investigative technique in any financial crime.

In January 2002, the IACP published a model law-enforcement policy on identity theft. The purpose of the IACP policy is to enable police agencies to develop protocols for accepting, recording, and investigating the crime of identity theft. The IACP model policy suggests the following:

- An identity theft report should not normally be taken when a related crime report has already been filed with any law-enforcement agency. If a resident of your agency's jurisdiction is not satisfied that another forgery-related report is sufficient, complete an identity theft report. Note in the narrative, "Victim insisted on report," and reference related reports.

- An identity theft report should not be taken in lieu of a worthless-document report. Specific forgery-related crimes shall continue to be reported on a worthless-document report.

- The location of occurrence for an identity theft is the victim's residence. Therefore, nonresidents of your agency's jurisdiction should be referred to the law enforcement agency having jurisdiction over their residence.

- Identity theft reports shall not normally be taken telephonically. Residents of your agency's jurisdiction making telephonic inquiries should be directed to appear in person at the nearest police station with copies of supporting documentation and identification to file a report.

- Officers conducting a preliminary investigation of an identity theft shall include with the report the following:
  - Include all copies of documents supporting the allegation (credit reports, invoices, demand letters, affidavits of forgery, and so on) as pages of the report. If these documents are not available, explain in the narrative.

- Attach a copy of the victim's identification as a report page. If the victim is not in possession of identification at the time of the report, explain in the narrative.

- Include all notifications made by the victim to any financial institutions or credit reporting agencies in the narrative portion of the report.

- Have the reporting person sign the report and submit the report to a supervisor for approval.

- When the taking of the report is beyond the ability of the desk officer or requires expert knowledge, the desk officer shall refer the reporting person to a detective or agency unit specializing in theft crimes. When the concerned detective or unit is not available, referral shall be made to the watch commander. In all cases, the final interviewing officer shall take the report.

- Review the crime report and conduct any follow-up inquiries of victims or others as appropriate for clarification or expansion of information.

- Contact the FTC Consumer Sentinel law-enforcement network and search the database for investigative leads.

- Contact other involved or potentially involved law-enforcement agencies for collaboration and avoidance of duplication. These agencies include but are not limited to the following:

  - Federal law-enforcement agencies such as the U.S. Secret Service, the Federal Bureau of Investigation, and the U.S. Postal Inspection Service, as appropriate, whether or not the victim has filed a crime report with them.

  - Any state or local enforcement agency with which the victim has filed a crime report.

Obtaining Financial Information

Getting financial information for any fraud case can be a daunting task for the investigator, especially when cooperation is lacking. It is imperative that the investigator gain cooperation from both the victim and the financial organization. There are three ways of getting the financial information needed for an identity theft case: (1) search warrant, (2) subpoena power, or (3) consent. Consent is the simplest and most cost-effective. This article will assume that investigators are quite familiar with obtaining search warrants and subpoenas for their cases; therefore, we will concentrate more on obtaining consent through the victim and financial institutions.

As in other cases dealing with victims, identity theft cases require officers and investigators to develop a rapport with victims and witnesses to gain their cooperation. This is more important when dealing with victims who are experiencing an emotional crime such as identity theft, much like an assault victim. Comforting the victim and assuring them that the crime was not their fault will go a long way toward gaining their confidence and cooperation. Nevertheless, investigators should explain the potential consequences of being a victim of identity theft (the effect on the victims' credit, the financial loss, the amount of time the investigation may take, and the long-term issues relating to this crime).

Victims have an overwhelming need to be actively involved in the case because ultimately it is their reputation, their credit, and their family's livelihood on the line. Although this is the investigator's case and the officer must maintain control, giving the victim some sense of control will help develop information and evidence for a successful conviction.

Ask the victim to begin gathering and providing documentation, to include the following:

- Bank and credit card statements
- Letters from creditors

- Merchant account statements

- Any other financial documentation related to the crime

Ask the victim to obtain and voluntarily provide you the credit reports from the three major credit bureaus (Equifax, Experian, and TransUnion). A subpoena is needed from the courts if the victim does not voluntarily provide you with the credit reports. Remember, if the victim provides authorization, the investigator can get the victim's identity theft–related transaction records from creditors without first obtaining a subpoena under the 2003 amendments to the Fair Credit Reporting Act.

Advise the victim to keep a log or a diary of everything they do or everyone they talk with regarding the crime. This can be used as part of the victim impact statement during any subsequent court proceeding. The FTC or ID Theft Resources Center provides valuable information on how victims can organize their identity crime cases.

The investigator should contact the financial institution or merchant security departments and ask for (or subpoena) documentation on all fraudulent or suspect accounts.

Identifying Additional Victims

There are many reasons why an investigator should locate and identify additional victims, but among the most important is to ascertain if there is a larger, organized ring victimizing the community. One way of doing this is by quarrying the FTC Clearinghouse for other reported complaints that may be related to the case. Investigators can also contact other agencies in the area to determine if there have been similar crimes reported and possibly connected. If that is the case, these agencies can combine resources and personnel into a task force to combat the crime.

Case Preparation

Filing the case criminally can be another daunting adventure for the investigator. However, if the case is well prepared, the criminal prosecutor will be better equipped to file the case. As noted earlier, the best way of preparing the case is to have the victim play a role in the case by taking and keeping notes or a diary, requesting and collecting financial information regarding the identity theft, and taking an overall interest and partnership in the case.

The Los Angeles County District Attorney's Office has an active prosecuting unit involved with high-tech crimes. Deputy District Attorney Jeffrey McGrath indicated that the unit handles an average of 60 high-tech cases per year. Of the 60 cases, approximately 50 percent involve identity theft. Many more are brought for filing but they are declined because of the office's lack of resources. The prosecutors in the L.A. County District Attorney's Office must therefore be selective in the cases they accept for filing, and they focus on the large identity theft cases that involve organized rings with multiple victims, losses, and suspects. Because of the cases they do file and the investigations they receive from area law-enforcement agencies, the unit has a 100 percent conviction rate.

According to McGrath, the key to getting an identity theft case filed and getting a successful conviction is organization. The investigator has to organize the case logically. McGrath recommended that investigators use binders containing a contents page and dividers with tabs on each major section. In McGrath's words, "avoid the brick." A brick is a giant stack of papers the district attorney has to shuffle through. Those cases will never get filed.

The binders need to include supporting documents such as search warrants, all financial account numbers for each victim, names and addresses of the financial institutions, and documentation for subpoena duces tecum that would be admissible in court. McGrath said it is fine to get all of the financial information from the victim, but eventually the court will require these in an admissible format. The binder also needs to include an outline of expected testimony from victims and witnesses.

McGrath recommended that the investigator have an outline of the particular law that is sought for filing when dealing with district attorneys who are unfamiliar with the law. List the requested charges and enhancements on the charging sheet, along with any additional charges.

The Future

The new FACTA will invariably increase the number of victims reporting identity theft cases to local police agencies. But more reports taking is not the only problem facing local police agencies. This influx of reports will require at least a preliminary investigation if not a full investigation and filing with the local prosecutor. This reporting influx will require police agencies to look at the problem as any other crime affecting the community and to begin comprehensive problem resolution strategies.

To provide the level of service required by the community, police departments must prepare for the increase of identity theft victims reporting identity theft crimes. Police agencies can prepare by teaching the public how to prevent and report identity theft and by training officers in the prevention and investigation of identity theft crimes and other financial crimes. Having a robust community education program, such as providing pamphlets on identity theft prevention and organizing community and business meetings, will help a police department reduce the likelihood of community members being victimized.

Police officers must be knowledgeable about state and federal laws relating to identity theft and other fraud crimes so that they can identify violations involving identity theft and peripheral criminal activity that are related, such as burglary or robbery, that specifically target financial information. These peripheral crimes could lead to bigger cases involving criminal rings. Investigators should receive training in conducting complex financial crime investigations involving multiple suspects, victims, and witnesses. The investigator must be knowledgeable in interviewing techniques, evidence collection, and presentation of evidence to ensure cases are filed with the local prosecutor's office.

All of this can be done at little or no cost to local police agencies by merely asking for assistance from government or private organizations. Government agencies such as the FTC, the FBI, and the Secret Service have excellent resources and training tools; resources such as FinCEN and Consumer Sentinel are available to all law-enforcement agencies; one needs only to apply. Private nonprofit organizations such as the IACP and NW3C provide training for police officers and investigators in all facets of high-tech crimes, including identity theft. The training provided by the NW3C is available at no cost to any law-enforcement agency, along with any resource material they publish.

(Reprinted from *The Police Chief*, Vol. 72, No. 3, pp. 46–52, March 2005. Copyright held by the International Association of Chiefs of Police, 515 North Washington Street, Alexandria, VA 22314 USA. Further reproduction without express written permission from IACP is strictly prohibited.)

THINKING DIFFERENTLY ABOUT FILING IDENTITY THEFT INCIDENTS

By Jonathan Fairtlough, Deputy District Attorney, Los Angeles County High Tech Crime Division, Los Angeles, California

The following scenario should be all too familiar to investigators of identity theft. An investigative officer works up a case against an identity thief; search warrants are served, records gathered, and witnesses interviewed; and the thief is identified through hours of painstaking investigation. The officer brings a large and detailed filing package over to the office of the district attorney (DA), identifying several victims and repeated incidents. After the officer waits for hours to see a filing DA, the officer is told the case is filed with only two counts: identity theft and grand theft. Two weeks later, the officer finds out that the thief has been sentenced to probation or, even worse, was convicted of only a misdemeanor. What can the investigator do to get a better result? By following the 11 steps of case organization outlined here, officers can help to ensure a case resolution satisfactory to them.

Step One: Understand the Filing Process

All cases begin with the filing deputy DAs. Their initial review determines how many counts a given case will carry as well as if a defendant will be extradited, a felony filed, or the case sent back for further investigation. Usually, filing DAs are senior deputy district attorneys with experience in criminal prosecution who have two main responsibilities: to review and file cases in such a manner that they will result in successful prosecution and to review custody cases in sufficient time to have the matter ready for court within the statutory time period. Filing DAs must have a broad range of knowledge in criminal law and must be able to quickly identify the elements of a crime and apply the facts in the case reports to determine the appropriate charges. It is not uncommon for a filing DA to review cases of burglary, rape, murder, and driving under the influence of alcohol or drugs all in the same morning.

A large identity theft case cannot be effectively reviewed in the time available during the morning file rush unless the investigator organizes the case for filing. By organizing their identity theft cases in an appropriate manner, investigators will get a fairer and more thorough review—and therefore a better filing.

Step Two: Make an Appointment

If the case is being brought in for a warrant, then it is necessary to call the filing DA and make an appointment. Los Angeles County is probably like many other jurisdictions, so officers should not seek to file a large case on a Tuesday. In Los Angeles, Tuesday is the day when all the in-custody filings from the weekend are due. As a result, the filing DA has twice the normal workload on a Tuesday. Unless the defendant is in custody and the 48-hour rule applies, large identity theft cases should not be brought to the filing DA on a Tuesday.

If possible, officers should drop off the case file before the appointment date to give the filing DA the opportunity to review the file before the meeting. A face-to-face meeting benefits both parties, allowing the filing DA to ask questions while reviewing the material and allowing officers to justify the type of filing they feel is appropriate.

Although filed cases are the DA's responsibility, any successful prosecution results from a partnership between the investigating officer and the prosecutor, and almost all prosecutors welcome officers' active input. Investigators should always indicate their filing preferences.

Step Three: Avoid the Paper Brick File

Most identity theft packets are organized chronologically. This typically means that the first report available to the filing DA for review is the one with the least amount of information: the initial victim report, taken when the theft is discovered. This report lists the victim's name as well as the time and method of discovery of the theft—and, in most cases, nothing else. Multiple supplemental reports contained in the packet provide the information needed to make a filing decision. These supplemental reports usually have attachments five to ten times the length of the report. When complete, the entire package of reports and attachments resembles a large paper brick. When filing DAs see such a "brick" and have at best 30 minutes to review a file, they select the two counts easiest to prove for filing. They miss all the other potential charges because filing DAs do not have time to find and thoughtfully review all the evidence in a brick-shaped file.

To avoid submitting a brick, investigative officers must sort reports and separate them with tabs. Small investments of money in tabs and of time in organizing the file will enable the filing DA to review the relevant evidence with greater ease.

Step Four: Prepare the Case in Layers

In most criminal investigations, there is one crime: a single murder, rape, or arson. Identity theft, however, is never a single, stand-alone crime. It is a crime of layers, a crime committed in such a manner that criminals can commit or facilitate other crimes and still hide their identity. When an identity thief uses the name and personal information of another person to obtain a credit card, the theft enables the thief to steal money and goods from the credit card company and the merchants that accept the card. A thief who uses someone's Social Security number to get electric service activated is stealing a utility service.

Identity theft always has at least two and usually three victims every time it is committed. The first victim is the individual whose information has been used without permission (the ID victim). The second victim is the credit grantor, bank, or credit card company that accepted the information and used it to issue credit. The third victim is the merchant or provider of a service that accepted the credit card, loan, or surety and provided goods or services in exchange. For example, when an identity thief uses another's credit card to purchase a basketball, the ID victim, the credit card company, and the sporting goods store are all victims.

There are three common ways to organize a case: by victim, by location, or by crime. The type of identity theft and the type of victim will help determine the best approach. A case in which a thief uses one ID victim's credit card to shop at ten different stores is best organized by merchant victim—that is, by each store. In the filing packet, each store should have its own tab, allowing the filing DA to easily verify the facts surrounding and the witnesses to each commercial burglary and theft. When the credit cards of 200 different people have been processed through a merchant terminal, the file is best organized by ID victim, with tabs reserved for each victim's interview and credit information.

Step Five: Prepare a Short Prosecution Summary

Once the case has been organized using tabs, officers should prepare a brief summary of the case. The summary should be one page and should include a description of the victims and the method of the crime, a reference to each victim or crime location by tab, and a list of the charges sought by the investigator of the case. An effective summary reads as follows:

> This case involves the use of the personal information of three victims (see tabs 1–3) to obtain credit cards without authorization from American Express (tab 4), Discover (tab 5), Citibank (tab 6), and Sears (tab 7). These four cards were sent to a mailbox at 1234 Main Street (tab 8). Defendant 1 opened this mailbox. The four cards were used at 15 different stores in the city (tabs 9–24). Defendants 1 and 2 have been identified by store clerks at four of the locations as using each of the cards (tabs 9–12). Driver's licenses in the name of two of the victims but bearing a picture of defendant 1 were found in the possession of defendant 1 (tabs 25 and 26). An identity card in the name of the third victim but bearing a picture of defendant 2 was found in the possession of defendant 2 (tab 27). Based on this evidence, I am requesting the filing of 3 counts of identity theft, 4 counts of credit card fraud, 15 counts of commercial burglary, and 3 counts of fraudulent document possession.

A filing DA reviewing a well-organized summary can easily check each tab to see if there is enough information for the requested filing. In addition, a listing of the requested charges and statutes allows officers to remind generalist filing DAs of potential charges without having to tell them directly. The summary report is also a great way for officers to justify any enhancement of charges based on amount of loss, number or vulnerability of victims, or defendants' prior arrests and convictions.

Step Six: Make a Witness List

Getting a good filing does not necessarily ensure a successful prosecution. The next step is helping the DA get the right witnesses to court. To do so, officers need to provide a good witness list. In the sample case used in this article, there are 26 witnesses on the list. Some will be very important, such as the four clerks who identified the defendants, and others will be needed only for trial, such as the four custodians of record for the credit card companies. Unfortunately, most investigators do not prepare witness lists that allow DAs to easily determine the facts of the witness testimony. In most jurisdictions, officers fill out a form with the witness's name, address, and contact telephone number. However, this limited information does not tell the DA if the witness is a custodian of record or a key identification witness without a detailed reading of the report. To make a better witness list, simply add a one-line description of the testimony each witness is expected to give. A witness entry can look as simple as this:

John Smith, 789 Main Street, Anywhere, CA; 213-974-1234

> Custodian of record for American Express—can testify about Amex loss

Jane Johnson, 71234 Apple Street, Yourtown, CA; 213-974-1324

> Macy's employee who identified defendant 1 as the person who used the credit card of victim 2

Such a list will allow the person issuing the subpoenas to make sure that the right witnesses will be available to testify and that no unnecessary witnesses will waste their time with a needless trip to court.

Step Seven: Make a Restitution List

Identity theft and fraud cases deal with issues of restitution and loss. As mentioned earlier, an identity thief using a fraudulent credit card in the name of an ID victim to purchase a basketball can cause the cardholder, card issuer, and merchant all to suffer losses. By asking the right questions, officers can determine who suffered the financial loss. Did the sporting goods store get paid for the basketball, or was the card refused or the charge later charged back from the merchant's account? Did the credit card company have any expenses in trying to investigate who committed the theft? Was the ID victim civilly sued for the charge, and did the suit require a defense in court? What documentation do the victims have to support their loss claims?

Once these questions have been answered, investigators should prepare a restitution report. The report should list what each victim is owed and on what information victims base their loss claims. This report should be kept separate from the main file so that it can be given to courts, clerks, and probation officers without turning over the entire police report.

All states view victim restitution as a primary right, but identity theft cases can take considerable time to wind their way through the court system. Investigators are often asked to provide a restitution list months after their cases have been filed. One hour spent organizing this information at the time of filing can save many hours later.

Step Eight: Ask for SDTs at the Time of Filing

At the time of the filing, officers should ask the filing DA to issue a subpoena duces tecum (SDT) for the records that the officer has obtained via search warrant. Although it seems like a waste of resources, it actually saves the prosecution and the victim time and money. Records obtained via search warrant must be authenticated by a witness, the custodian of record. However, in many jurisdictions, records obtained by subpoena are considered authentic and admissible once received by the court. Since many of the records used in an identity theft case fall under the business records exception, if the records are obtained by an SDT, the prosecutor can introduce the records without calling a witness. This conserves resources and allows for the easy presentation of evidence.

Step Nine: Prepare for Bail Hearings

Because identity thieves exploit the information and credit of others, officers should review with the prosecutor any bail defendants offer to ensure that it has not been obtained through another identity theft or other felonious means. In most jurisdictions, prosecutors can file a motion with an affidavit from the investigating officer explaining why the bail should be checked to make sure it has not been feloniously obtained. Investigators are used to considering this in narcotics cases, but identity theft cases with multiple victims should merit the same consideration. Draft an affidavit that outlines how the defendant has access to other people's information and how that access can be used to obtain funds to post bail. A copy of the filing report should be attached to the affidavit; this ensures that all the facts can be considered by the court in reviewing bail.

Step Ten: Call the Prelim DA

The tabbed, organized case file is forwarded by the filing DA to the preliminary hearing court. This court is where the first offer is made and where the case is scheduled on the same calendar as multiple other cases, all handled by the same DA. Preliminary hearing DAs (prelim DAs) are often among the most junior members of the office, yet they handle the busiest calendar in the courthouse. They have to read and prepare every case on their calendar. Investigators should make a point of confirming the receipt of the tabbed file with the prelim DA.

The prosecution summary will allow the prelim DA to understand the case and make an appropriate offer. The tabbed filing packet will assist in the presentation of the case at the preliminary hearing and the trial. The appearance of the organized, tabbed file makes defendants fully aware of the extent and detail of the case against them and can encourage an early disposition.

Step Eleven: Form a Task Force with the DA

Finally, investigating officers should consider the benefits of a collaborative task force model, where multiple agencies and the prosecutor's office work together to fight identity theft. Identity thieves rarely respect jurisdictional boundaries, and identity theft legislation and the methods available for filing charges are constantly being updated. A prosecutor assigned to the vertical prosecution of identity theft cases produces the best results for investigations. Vertical prosecution enables all aspects of the prosecution of a given case, from filing to trial, to be handled by one DA intimately familiar with the case.

A jurisdiction's size does not limit a department's ability to set up a collaborative task force. When a vertically assigned prosecutor regularly schedules a time period to be a part of the task force, case results will significantly improve. Investigators who are flexible and creative in respecting the limits to which DAs can cover their entire workload will find that everyone can work better to improve results in the fight against identity theft.

(Reprinted from *The Police Chief*, Vol. 74, No. 5, pp. 46–52, May 2007. Copyright held by the International Association of Chiefs of Police, 515 North Washington Street, Alexandria, VA 22314 USA. Further reproduction without express written permission from IACP is strictly prohibited.)

IDENTITY THEFT: THE CRIME OF THE NEW MILLENNIUM

The following material was reprinted from the U.S. Attorney's Bulletin, March 2001, pp. 7–23. In the article, Sean B. Hoar, Assistant United States Attorney, District of Oregon provides an overview of identity theft crime and a detailed summary of the law.

The Nature of the Problem

Identity theft has been referred to by some as the crime of the new millennium. It can be accomplished anonymously, easily and with a variety of means, and the impact upon the victim can be devastating. Identity theft is simply the theft of identity information such as a name, date of birth, Social Security number (SSN), or a credit card number. The mundane activities of a typical consumer during the course of a regular day may provide tremendous opportunities for an identity thief: purchasing gasoline, meals, clothes, tickets to an athletic event, or home-improvement tools; renting a car or a video; purchasing gifts or trading stock online; receiving mail or taking out the garbage or recycling. Any activity in which identity information is shared or made available to others creates an opportunity for identity theft.

It is estimated that identity theft has become the fastest growing financial crime in America and perhaps the fastest growing crime of any kind in our society. (*Identity Theft: Is There Another You? Joint Hearing before the House Subcomms. on Telecommunications, Trade, and Consumer Protection, and on Finance and Hazardous Materials, of the Comm. on Commerce*, 106th Cong. 16 (1999) (testimony of Rep. John B. Shadegg)) The illegal use of identity information has increased exponentially in recent years. In fiscal year 1999 alone, the Social Security Administration (SSA) Office of Inspector General (OIG) Fraud Hotline received approximately 62,000 allegations involving SSN misuse. The widespread use of SSNs as identifiers has reduced their security and increased the likelihood that they will be the object of identity theft. The expansion and popularity of the Internet to effect commercial transactions has increased the opportunities to commit crimes involving identity theft. The use of the Internet to post official information for the benefit of citizens and customers has also increased opportunities to obtain SSNs for illegal purposes.

On May 31, 1998, in support of the Identity Theft and Assumption Deterrence Act, the General Accounting Office (GAO) released a briefing report on issues relating to identity fraud entitled "Identity

Fraud: Information on Prevalence, Cost, and Internet Impact Is Limited." The report found that methods used to obtain identity information ranged from basic street theft to sophisticated, organized crime schemes involving the use of computerized databases or the bribing of employees with access to personal information on customer or personnel records. The report also found the following: In 1995, 93 percent of arrests made by the U.S. Secret Service Financial Crimes Division involved identity theft. In 1996 and 1997, 94 percent of financial crimes arrests involved identity theft. The Secret Service stated that actual losses to individuals and financial institutions which the Secret Service had tracked involving identity fraud totaled $442 million in fiscal year 1995, $450 million in fiscal year 1996, and $745 million in fiscal year 1997. The SSA OIG stated that SSN misuse in connection with program fraud increased from 305 in fiscal year 1996 to 1,153 in fiscal year 1997. Postal Inspection investigations showed that identity fraud was perpetrated by organized crime syndicates, especially to support drug trafficking and had a nationwide scope. TransUnion Corporation, one of the three major national credit bureaus, stated that two-thirds of its consumer inquiries to its fraud victim department involved identity fraud. Such inquiries had increased from an average of less than 3,000 a month in 1992 to over 43,000 a month in 1997. VISA USA, Inc., and MasterCard International, Inc., both stated that overall fraud losses from their member banks were in the hundreds of millions of dollars annually. MasterCard stated that dollar losses relating to identity fraud represented about 96 percent of its member banks' overall fraud losses of $407 million in 1997.

Victims of identity theft often do not realize they have become victims until they attempt to obtain financing on a home or a vehicle. Only then, when the lender tells them that their credit history makes them ineligible for a loan, do they realize something is terribly wrong. When they review their credit report, they first become aware of credit cards for which they have never applied, bills long overdue, unfamiliar billing addresses, and inquiries from unfamiliar creditors. Even if they are able to identify the culprit, it may take months or years, tremendous emotional anguish, many lost financial opportunities, and large legal fees to clear up their credit history.

How Does Identity Theft Occur?

Identity theft occurs in many ways, ranging from careless sharing of personal information to intentional theft of purses, wallets, mail, or digital information. In public places, for example, thieves engage in "shoulder surfing," watching you from a nearby location as you punch in your telephone calling card number or credit card number, or they listen in on your conversation if you give your credit card number over the telephone. Thieves may obtain information from your personal computer while you are online at home and they are anonymously sitting in the comfort of their own home. Outside your home, thieves steal your mail, garbage, or recycling. Outside medical facilities or businesses, thieves engage in "dumpster diving," going through garbage cans, large dumpsters, or recycling bins to obtain identity information which includes credit or debit card receipts, bank statements, medical records like prescription labels, or other records that bear your name, address, or telephone number.

In a recent case in the District of Oregon, a ring of thieves obtained identity information by stealing mail, garbage, and recycling material, and by breaking into cars and hacking into websites and personal computers. The thieves traded the stolen information for methamphetamine, cellular telephones, or other favors. Before they were arrested, they had gained access to an estimated 400 credit card accounts and had made an estimated $400,000 in purchases on those fraudulently obtained accounts. One aspect of the case involved the theft of preapproved credit card solicitations; they activated the cards and had them sent to drop boxes or third-party addresses. Another scam involved taking names, dates of birth, and SSNs from discarded medical, insurance, or tax information and obtaining credit cards at various sites on the Internet. The thieves found most credit card companies to be unwitting allies. One of the thieves boasted about successfully persuading a bank to grant a higher credit limit on a fraudulently obtained credit card account. Another aspect of the case involved the use of a software application to hack into commercial websites or personal computers and to mirror keystrokes to capture credit card account information. Two of the offenders were prosecuted federally for conspiracy to commit computer fraud and mail theft under 18 U.S.C. §1030(a)(4), 371 and 1708, and they consented to the forfeiture of computer equipment obtained as a result of the fraud-related activity pursuant to 18 U.S.C. § 982(a)(2)(B). One defendant was sentenced to serve a 41 month term of imprisonment and pay $70,025.98 in restitution. (*United States v. Steven Collis Massey*, CR 99-60116-01-AA (D.Or. 1999)) The other defendant was sentenced to serve a 15-month term of imprisonment and to pay $52,379.03 in restitution. (*United States v. Kari Bahati Melton*, CR 99-60118-01-AA (D. Or. 1999))

How Can Identity Theft Be Investigated and Prosecuted?

The investigation of identity theft is labor intensive, and individual cases are usually considered to be too small for federal prosecution. Perpetrators usually victimize multiple victims in multiple jurisdictions. Victims often do not realize they have been victimized until weeks or months after the crime has been committed and can provide little assistance to law enforcement. In short, identity theft has become the fastest-growing financial crime in America and perhaps the fastest-growing crime of any kind in our society, because offenders are seldom held accountable. Consequently, it has become a priority for the Departments of Justice and Treasury and the Federal Trade Commission (FTC) to pursue effective means of prevention, investigation, and prosecution of identity theft offenses. Toward that end, workshops were recently held for the purpose of identifying the best practices to combat identity theft, including remediation, prevention, and law-enforcement strategies. Workshop participants included prevention specialists, federal agency representatives, state and federal investigators, and state and federal prosecutors.

The opinion of workshop participants is that law-enforcement agencies at all levels, federal and nonfederal, must work together to investigate identity theft. Multiagency task forces have proven successful in investigating and prosecuting identity theft. By utilizing task forces, member agencies pool scarce resources to investigate and prosecute identity theft offenses, and provide prevention training. Workshop participants also indicated that outreach to private industry is necessary as a prevention strategy, and it facilitates the identification of offenders.

Identity theft cases involving large numbers of victims present unique challenges. One challenge is communication with victims. Communication is necessary to obtain fundamental investigative information, including loss and restitution information. In complex cases, it is imperative to devise a system for communication with the victims at the outset of the case. The assistant U. S. attonrney (AUSA) should work with victim/witness units to identify the best communication system for the case. The AUSA should also work with the system administrator to develop a link from the district's website for online communication with victims. The link can provide access to a database into which victims can enter case-related information. The link can also be used to provide updates on the status of the case. Notification to the victims regarding their use of the website can be provided through a form letter accompanying an investigative survey which must be completed, in any event, to obtain loss and restitution information.

Federal Criminal Laws

There are a number of federal laws applicable to identity theft, some of which may be used for prosecution of identity theft offenses, and some of which exist to assist victims in repairing their credit history. The primary identity theft statute is 18 U.S.C. § 1028(a)(7) and was enacted on October 30, 1998, as part of the Identity Theft and Assumption Deterrence Act (Identity Theft Act). The Identity Theft Act was needed because 18 U.S.C. § 1028 previously addressed only the fraudulent creation, use, or transfer of identification *documents*, and not the theft or criminal use of the underlying personal *information*. The Identity Theft Act added § 1028(a)(7) which criminalizes fraud in connection with the unlawful theft and misuse of personal identifying information, regardless of whether the information appears or is used in documents. Section 1028(a)(7) provides that it is unlawful for anyone to knowingly transfer or use, without lawful authority, a means of identification of another person with the intent to commit, or to aid or abet, any unlawful activity that constitutes a violation of federal law or that constitutes a felony under any applicable state or local law.

The Identity Theft Act amended the penalty provisions of § 1028(b) by extending its coverage to offenses under the new § 1028(a)(7) and applying more stringent penalties for identity thefts involving property of value. Section 1028(b)(1)(D) provides for a term of imprisonment of not more than 15 years when an individual commits an offense that involves the transfer or use of one or more means of identification if, as a result of the offense, anything of value aggregating $1,000 or more during any one year period is obtained. Otherwise, § 1028(b)(2)(B) provides for imprisonment of not more than three years. The Identity Theft Act added § 1028(f) which provides that attempts or conspiracies to violate § 1028 are subject to the same penalties as those prescribed for substantive offenses under § 1028.

The Identity Theft Act amended § 1028(b)(3) to provide that if the offense is committed to facilitate a drug trafficking crime, or in connection with a crime of violence, or is committed by a person previously convicted of identity theft, the individual is subject to a term of imprisonment of not more than 20 years. The Identity Theft Act also added § 1028(b)(5) which provides for the forfeiture of any personal property used or intended to be used to commit the offense.

Section 1028(d)(3) defines "means of identification," as used in § 1028(a)(7), to include "any name or number that may be used, alone or in conjunction with any other information, to identify a specific individual." It covers several specific examples, such as name, Social Security number, date of birth, and government-issued driver's license and other numbers; unique biometric data, such as fingerprints, voice print, retina or iris image, or other physical representation; unique electronic identification number; and telecommunication identifying information or access device.

Section 1028(d)(1) modifies the definition of "document-making implement" to include computers and software specifically configured or primarily used for making identity documents. The Identity Theft Act is intended to cover a variety of individual identification information that may be developed in the future and utilized to commit identity theft crimes.

The Identity Theft Act also directed the United States Sentencing Commission to review and amend the Sentencing Guidelines to provide appropriate penalties for each offense under Section 1028. The Sentencing Commission responded to this directive by adding U.S.S.G. § 2F.1.1(b)(5) which provides the following:

(5) If the offense involved:

(A) the possession or use of any device-making equipment;

- the production or trafficking of any unauthorized access device or counterfeit access device; or

- (i) the unauthorized transfer or use of any means of identification unlawfully to produce or obtain any other means of identification; or (ii) the possession of [five] or more means of identification that unlawfully were produced from another means of identification or obtained by the use of another means of identification, increase by two levels. If the resulting offense level is less than level 12, increase to level 12.

These new guidelines take into consideration the fact that identity theft is a serious offense, whether or not certain monetary thresholds are met. For most fraud offenses, the loss would have to be more than $70,000 for the resulting offense level to be level 12. (U.S.S.G. § 2F.1.1(b)(1)(G)) In providing for a base offense level of 12 for identity theft, the Sentencing Commission acknowledged that the economic harm from identity theft is difficult to quantify, and that whatever the identifiable loss, offenders should be held accountable. Identity theft offenses will usually merit a two-level increase because they often involve more than minimal planning or a scheme to defraud more than one victim. (U.S.S.G. § 2F.1.1(b)(2)) Identity theft offenses may also provide for two- to four-level upward organizational role adjustments when multiple defendants are involved. (U.S.S.G. § 3B1.1)

The Identity Theft Act also directed the FTC to establish a procedure to log in and acknowledge receipt of complaints from victims of identity theft, to provide educational materials to these victims, and to refer the complaints to appropriate entities. The FTC has responded to this directive by developing a website, great educational materials, a hotline for complaints, and a central database for information. The website can be found at *www.consumer.gov/idtheft*. The hotline is 877-ID THEFT. Identity theft complaints are entered into Consumer Sentinel, a secure, online database available to law enforcement. The FTC has become a primary referral point for victims of identity theft and a tremendous resource for these victims and law enforcement.

Other Federal Offenses

Identity theft is often committed to facilitate other crimes, although it is frequently the primary goal of the offender. Schemes to commit identity theft may involve a number of other statutes, including identification fraud (18 U.S.C. § 1028(a)(1)-(6)), credit card fraud (18 U.S.C. § 1029), computer fraud (18 U.S.C. § 1030), mail fraud (18 U.S.C. § 1341), wire fraud (18 U.S.C. § 1343), financial institution fraud (18 U.S.C. § 1344), mail theft (18 U.S.C. § 1708), and immigration document fraud (18 U.S.C. § 1546). For example, computer fraud may be facilitated by the theft of identity information when stolen identity is used to fraudulently obtain credit on the Internet. Computer fraud may also be the primary vehicle to obtain identity information when the offender obtains unauthorized access to another computer or website to obtain such information. These acts might result in the offender being charged with both identity theft under 18 U.S.C. § 1028(a)(7) and computer fraud under 18 U.S.C. § 1030(a)(4). Regarding computer fraud, note that U.S.S.G. § 2F.1.1(c)(1) provides a minimum guideline sentence, notwithstanding any other adjustment, of a six month term of imprisonment if a defendant is convicted of computer fraud under 18 U.S.C. § 1030(a)(4).

Several examples of how identity theft schemes may involve other statutes may be helpful. These include the case of an offender who fraudulently obtains identity information by posing as an employer in correspondence with a credit bureau. This offender might appropriately be charged with both identity theft under 18 U.S.C. § 1028(a)(7) and mail fraud under 18 U.S.C. § 1341. An offender who steals mail thereby obtaining identity information might appropriately be charged with identity theft under 18 U.S.C. § 1028(a)(7) and mail theft under 18 U.S.C. § 1708. The offender who fraudulently poses as a telemarketer thereby obtaining identity information might appropriately be charged with both identity theft under 18 U.S.C. § 1028(a)(7) and wire fraud under 18 U.S.C. § 1343.

Recent Federal Cases

A number of cases have recently been prosecuted under 18 U.S.C. § 1028(a)(7), including the following:

In the Central District of California, a man was sentenced to a 27 month term of imprisonment for obtaining private bank account information about an insurance company's policyholders, while serving as a temporary employee of the company. Thereafter, he used that information to deposit over $764,000 in counterfeit bank drafts and withdraw funds from accounts of policyholders. *United States v. Anthony Jerome Johnson*, CR 99-926 (C.D. Ca. Jan. 31, 2000).

In the District of Delaware, one defendant was sentenced to a 33-month term of imprisonment and $160,910.87 in restitution, and another defendant to a 41-month term of imprisonment and $126,298.79 in restitution for obtaining names and SSNs of high-ranking military officers from an Internet website and using them to apply online for credit cards and bank and corporate credit in the officers' names. (*United States v. Lamar Christian*, CR 00-3-1 (D. Del. Aug. 9, 2000); *United States v. Ronald Nevison Stevens*, CR 00-3-2 (D. Del. Aug. 9, 2000))

In the District of Oregon, seven defendants have been sentenced to imprisonment for their roles in a heroin/methamphetamine trafficking organization, which included entering the United States illegally from Mexico and obtaining SSNs of other persons. The SSNs were then used to obtain temporary employment and identification documents in order to facilitate the distribution of heroin and methamphetamine. In obtaining employment, the defendants used false alien registration receipt cards, in addition to the fraudulently obtained SSNs, which provided employers enough documentation to complete employment verification forms. Some of the defendants also used the fraudulently obtained SSNs to obtain earned income credits on tax returns fraudulently filed with the Internal Revenue Service. Some relatives of narcotics traffickers were arrested in possession of false documents and were charged with possessing false alien registration receipt cards and with using the fraudulently obtained SSNs to obtain employment.

Federal Credit Laws

It is important for training purposes and to assist victims in repairing damage to their credit history that prosecutors have at least a cursory understanding of credit laws that impact identity theft. The Fair Credit Reporting Act establishes procedures and time frames for correcting mistakes on credit records and requires that your record only be provided for legitimate business, credit, or employment needs. (15 U.S.C. § 1681 ets eq.) The Truth in Lending Act limits liability for unauthorized credit card charges in most cases to $50. (15 U.S.C. § 1601 et seq.) The Fair Credit Billing Act establishes procedures for resolving billing errors on credit card accounts *if* the unauthorized charge is reported within certain time frames. (15 U.S.C. § 1666) The Fair Debt Collection Practices Act prohibits debt collectors from using unfair or deceptive practices to collect overdue bills that your creditor has forwarded for collection. (15 U.S.C. § 1692) The Electronic Fund Transfer Act provides consumer protections for transactions using a debit card or electronic means to debit or credit an account. It also limits a consumer's liability for unauthorized electronic fund transfers if the unauthorized transfer is reported within certain time frames. (15 U.S.C. § 1693) If an ATM or debit card is reported lost or stolen within two business days of the loss or theft, the losses are limited to $50. If reported after two business days but within 60 days of the first statement showing an unauthorized transfer, the losses are limited to $500. Otherwise, losses may only be limited by the amount obtained. (15 U.S.C. § 1693(g)(a))

State Criminal Laws

Most states have laws prohibiting the theft of identity information. Where specific identity theft laws do not exist, the practices may be prohibited under other state laws, or the states may be considering such legislation. The following is a list of current state laws which prohibit the theft of identity information: Ariz. Rev. Stat. § 13-2008; Ark. Code Ann. § 5-37-227; Cal. Penal Code § 530.5; 2000 Colo. Legis. Serv. ch. 159 (May 19, 2000); 1999 Conn. Acts 99-99; Del. Code Ann. tit. 11, § 854; Fla. Stat. Ann. § 817.568; Ga. Code Ann. § 16-9-121 to 16-9-127; Idaho Code § 18-3126; 720 Ill Comp.Stat. 5/16G; Ind. Code § 35-43-5-4 (2000); Iowa Code § 715A.8; Kan. Stat. Ann. § 21-4018; Ky. Rev. Stat. Ann. § 514.160; La. Rev. Stat. Ann. § 67.16; Me. Rev. Stat. Ann. tit. 17-A, § 354-2A; Md. Ann. Code art. 27, § 231; Mass. Gen. Laws ch. 266, § 37E; Minn. Stat. Ann. § 609.527; Miss. Code Ann. § 97-19-85; Mo. Rev. Stat. § 570.223; Neb. Rev. State. § 28-101; Nev. Rev. Stat. § 205.465; N.H. Rev. Stat. Ann. § 638:26; N.J. Stat. Ann. § 2C:21-17; N.C. Gen. Stat. § 14-113.20; N.D. Cent. Code § 12.1-23-11; Ohio Rev. Code Ann. 2913.49; Okla. Stat. tit. 21, § 1533.1; Or. Rev. Stat. § 165.800; Pa. Cons. Stat. Ann. § 420; R.I. Gen. Laws § 11-49.1-1; S.C. Code Ann. § 16-13-500; S.D. Codified Laws 20; Tenn. Code Ann. § 39-14-150; Tex. Penal Code Ann. § 35.51; Utah Code Ann. § 76-6-1101-1104; Va. Code Ann. § 18.2-186.3; Wash. Rev. Code § 9.35; W. Va. Code Ann. § 61-3-54; Wis. Stat. § 943.201; Wyo. Stat. Ann. § 6-3-901.

How Can Identity Theft Be Prevented?

While it is extremely difficult to prevent identity theft, the best approach is to be proactive and take steps to avoid becoming a victim. As prosecutors, it is important to learn how to prevent identity theft in order to provide training to law enforcement and private industry. We can also complement the assistance to victims provided by our victim/witness units. A thorough guide to preventing and responding to identity theft can be found in *Privacy Piracy! A Guide to Protecting Yourself from Identity Theft*, by Mari Frank and Beth Givens, Office Depot, 1999. Related information can be found at *www.identitytheft.org*. The FTC has also published a helpful guide entitled *ID Theft: When Bad Things Happen to Your Good Name*, FTC, August 2000. This and related information can be found at *www.consumer.gov/idtheft*. Also, the United States Postal Inspection Service has produced an excellent video about identity theft entitled *IDENTITY THEFT: The Game of the Name*.

Only Share Identity Information When Necessary.

Be cautious about sharing personal information with anyone who does not have a legitimate need for the information. For instance, credit card numbers should never be provided to anyone over the telephone unless the consumer has initiated the call and is familiar with the entity with whom they are doing business. Likewise, SSNs should not be provided to anyone other than employers or financial institutions who need the SSN for wage, interest, and tax reporting purposes. Businesses may legitimately inquire about a SSN if doing a credit check for purposes of financing a purchase. Some entities, however, may simply want the SSN for record-keeping purposes. Businesses may choose to not provide a service or benefit without obtaining a person's SSN, but the choice as to whom a SSN is provided should be exercised with caution. In the event an entity, such as a hospital or a Department of Motor Vehicles (DMV), assigns a SSN as a patient or client identification number, the customer should request that an alternative number be assigned.

When in Public, Exercise Caution When Providing Identity Information.

"Shoulder surfers" regularly glean such information for their fraudulent use. Be especially cautious when entering account information at an Automated Teller Machine (ATM), or when entering long-distance calling card information on a public telephone. Likewise, be cautious when orally providing this type of information on a public telephone. Also, do not put identity information, such as an address or license plate number, on a key ring or anything similar that can easily be observed or lost. Identity information on such objects simply provides thieves easier means of finding and accessing homes and cars.

Do Not Carry Unnecessary Identity Information in a Purse or Wallet.

According to the FTC Identity Theft Clearinghouse, the primary means for thieves to obtain identity information is through the loss or theft of purses and wallets. To reduce the risk that identification information might be misappropriated, only carry the identity information necessary for use during the course of daily activities, such as a driver's license, one credit or debit card, an insurance card, and membership cards that are regularly required for use. There should be no need to carry a Social Security card or anything containing a SSN. Likewise, there should be no need to carry a birth certificate or a passport. These items should be kept under lock and key in a safe or a safety deposit box. Credit or debit cards that are not regularly used should also be removed from a purse or wallet. The fewer pieces of identification carried in a purse or wallet, the easier it is to identify an individual piece that may have been lost or stolen, and the easier the task of notifying creditors and replacing such information should a purse or wallet be lost or stolen.

Secure Your Mailbox.

According to the FTC, the second most successful means for thieves to obtain identity information is through stolen mail. Many thieves follow letter carriers at a discreet distance and steal mail immediately after it has been delivered to a residential mailbox. Do not place outgoing mail in residential mailboxes. Doing so, especially raising a red flag on a mailbox to notify the postal carrier of outgoing mail, is simply an invitation to steal. Deposit outgoing mail in locked post office collection boxes or at a local post office. If you prefer to have mail delivered to your residential address, install a mailbox which is secured by lock and key. Promptly remove mail after it has been delivered to your mailbox.

Secure Information on Your Personal Computer.

Similar to telephonic inquiries, credit card numbers should not be provided to anyone on the Internet unless the consumer has initiated the contact and is familiar with the entity with whom they are doing business. In addition to cautiously choosing with whom identity information is shared, computer users should install a firewall on their personal computers to prevent unauthorized access to stored information. A personal firewall is designed to run on an individual personal computer and isolate it from the rest of the Internet, thereby preventing unauthorized access to the computer. The user sets the level of desired security and the firewall inspects each packet of data to determine if it should be allowed to get to or from the individual machine, consistent with the level of security. A firewall is especially necessary for Digital Subscriber Line (DSL), cable modem, or other "always-on" connections. There are a number of quality firewall software applications that can be downloaded as freeware from sites on the Internet.

Keep Financial and Medical Records in a Secure Location.

Thieves may be more interested in identity information from which they can access credit than in physical property. It is important, therefore, to keep all financial and medical records, and any other information containing identity information, in a secure location under lock and key.

Shred Nonessential Material Containing Identity Information.

All nonessential documentary material containing any type of identity information should be shredded prior to being placed in garbage or recycling. The term "nonessential" should be interpreted as anything that an individual or business is not required by law or policy to retain. For individuals this includes credit or debit card receipts, canceled bank checks and statements, outdated insurance or financial information, and junk mail, especially preapproved credit applications and subscription solicitations. For businesses or medical facilities, this includes receipts of completed credit or debit card transactions, outdated client files, or prescription labels. The best shredding is done through a crosscut shredder which cuts paper into small pieces, making it extremely difficult to reconstruct documents. Expired credit or debit cards should also be cut into several pieces before being discarded.

"Sanitize" the Contents of Garbage and Recycling.

All nonessential documentary material containing any type of identity information should be shredded before being placed in garbage or recycling. While junk mail or old financial documents may appear to be innocuous, they can be a gold mine when obtained by an identity thief.

Ensure That Organizations Shred Identity Information.

Many businesses, firms, and medical facilities are not sensitive to privacy issues arising from discarded material. Many of these entities regularly dispose of material containing customer identity information, e.g., customer orders, receipts, prescription labels, etc., into garbage cans, dumpsters, or recycling bins without shredding the material. Tremendous damage can be done by these practices. Customers of businesses, clients of firms, and patients of medical facilities should insist that all data be shredded before being discarded and that all retained data be kept in secure storage.

Remove Your Name from Mailing Lists.

Removing a name from a mailing list reduces the number of commercial entities having access to the identity information. It also reduces the amount of junk mail, including preapproved credit applications and subscription solicitations, thereby reducing the risk that the theft of such mail will compromise privacy. Many financial institutions, such as banks and credit card companies, and even state agencies, market identity information of customers unless a request is received, in writing, that such information is not to be shared. Customers of such businesses and agencies should submit such requests, notifying the entity in writing of their desire to opt out of any mailing lists and to not have identity information shared.

To opt out of the mailing lists of the three major credit bureaus (Equifax, Experian, and TransUnion), call 888-5OPT-OUT. To opt out of many national direct mail lists, write the Direct Marketing Association, DMA Preference Service, P.O. Box 9008, Farmingdale, NY 11735-9008. To opt out of many national direct email lists, visit *www. e-mps.org.* To opt out of many national telemarketer lists, send your name, address, and telephone number to the Direct Marketing Association, DMA Telephone Preference Service, P.O. Box 9014, Farmingdale, NY 11735-9014.

Carefully Review Financial Statements.

Promptly review all bank and credit card statements for accuracy. Pay attention to billing cycles. A missing bill may mean a thief has taken over an account and changed the billing address to avoid detection. Report any irregularities to the bank or credit card company immediately.

Periodically Request Copies of Credit Reports.

Credit reports are available for $8 from the three major credit bureaus (Equifax, Experian, and TransUnion). Credit bureaus must provide a free copy of the report if it is inaccurate due to fraud and it is requested in writing. The reports should be reviewed carefully to make sure no unauthorized accounts have been opened or unauthorized changes made to existing accounts.

To order a report from Equifax, visit *www.equifax.com*, call 800-685-1111, or write P.O. Box 740241, Atlanta, GA 30374-0241. To order a report from Experian, visit *www.experian.com*, call 888-EXPERIAN (397-3742), or write P.O. Box 949, Allen, TX 75013-0949. To order a report from Trans Union, visit *www.tuc.com*, call 800-916-8800, or write P.O. Box 1000, Chester, PA 19022.

What Steps Should Be Taken by a Victim of Identity Theft?

When someone realizes they have become a victim of identity theft, they should take the following steps while keeping a log of all conversations, including dates, names, and telephone numbers. The log should indicate any time spent and expenses incurred in the event restitution can be obtained in a civil or criminal judgment against the thief. All conversations should be confirmed in writing with the correspondence sent by certified mail, return receipt requested. All correspondence should be kept in a secure location, under lock and key.

First, the victim should contact the fraud departments of each of the three major credit bureaus (Equifax, Experian, and TransUnion), inform the representative of the identity theft, and request that a "fraud alert" be placed on their file, as well as a statement asking that creditors call the victim before opening any new accounts. This can help prevent an identity thief from opening additional accounts in the victim's name. The victim should inquire about how long the fraud alert will remain on the file, and what, if anything, must be done to extend the alert if necessary. Copies of credit reports from the credit bureaus should also be ordered. The reports should be reviewed carefully to identify unauthorized accounts or unauthorized changes to existing accounts. Also, if the reports indicate that any "inquiries" were made from companies that opened fraudulent accounts, a request should be made to remove the "inquiries" from the report. A request should also be made for the credit bureaus to notify those who have received a credit report in the last six months and alert them to the disputed and erroneous information. The victim should request a new copy of the reports after a few months to verify that the requested changes have been made and to ensure no new fraudulent activity has occurred.

To report fraud to Equifax, visit *www.equifax.com*, call 800-525-6285, and write P.O. Box 740241, Atlanta, GA 30374-0241. To report fraud to Experian, visit *www.experian.com*, call 888-EXPERIAN, and write P.O. Box 949, Allen TX 75013-0949. To report fraud to Trans Union, visit *www.tuc.com*, call 800-680-7289, and write Fraud Victim Assistance Division, P.O. Box 6790, Fullerton, CA 92634.

Second, the victim should contact the security or fraud departments for any creditors of accounts in which fraudulent activity occurred. The telephone numbers for these creditors can be obtained from the credit bureaus. Creditors can include businesses, credit card companies, telephone companies and other utilities, and banks and other lenders. All conversations should be confirmed with written correspondence. It is particularly important to notify credit card companies in writing because it is required by the consumer protection laws set forth above. The victim should immediately close accounts that have been tampered with and open new ones with new Personal Identification Numbers (PINs) and passwords.

Third, the victim should file a report with a local police department or the police department where the identity theft occurred, if that can be determined. The victim should obtain a copy of the police report in the event creditors need proof of the crime. Even if the thief is not apprehended, a copy of the police report may assist the victim when dealing with creditors. The victim should also file a complaint with the FTC. The FTC should be contacted on its Identity Theft Hotline toll-free at 877-ID THEFT (438-4338), TDD at 202-326-2502, by mail at FTC Identity Theft Clearinghouse, 600 Pennsylvania Avenue, N.W., Washington, DC 20580, or at *www.consumer.gov/idtheft*.

Fourth, certain situations may require additional action by the victim. For instance, if an identity thief has stolen mail, it should be reported to a local postal inspector. A phone number for the nearest postal inspection service office can be obtained from a local post office or the U.S. Postal Service website at *www.usps.com/postalinspectors*. If financial information has been obtained, the financial entity (the bank, brokerage firm, credit union, credit card company, etc.) should be contacted, the fraudulently affected accounts closed, and new accounts opened with new PINs and passwords, including affected ATM cards. Payment should be stopped on any stolen checks, and banks or credit unions should be asked to request the appropriate check verification service to notify retailers not to accept the checks. Three check verification companies that accept reports of check fraud directly from consumers are: Telecheck: 800-710-9898; International Check Services: 800-631-9656; and Equifax: 800-437-5120. If investments or securities may have been affected, brokers should be notified and the victim should file a complaint with the Securities and Exchange Commission (SEC). A complaint can be filed with the SEC at the SEC Enforcement Complaint Center, 450 Fifth Street, N.W., Washington, DC 20549-0202; its website *www.sec.gov*, email *enforcement@sec.gov*, or fax 202-942-9570.

If new phone service has fraudulently been established in a victim's name or billing for unauthorized service is made to an existing account, the victim should contact the service provider immediately to cancel the account and/or calling card and open new accounts with new PINs and passwords. If a victim has difficulty removing fraudulent charges from an account, a complaint should be filed with the Federal Communications Commission (FCC). A complaint can be filed with the FCC at the FCC Consumer Information Bureau, 445 12th Street, S.W., Room 5A863, Washington, DC 20554; the FCC Enforcement Bureau website *www.fcc.gov/eb*, email *fccinfo@fcc.gov*, telephone 888-CALL FCC, or TTY 888-TELL FCC.

If someone is using a victim's SSN to apply for a job or to work, it should be reported to the Social Security Administration (SSA). The victim should first visit the SSA's website at *www.ssa.gov*, read the Guidelines for Reporting Fraud, Waste, Abuse, and Mismanagement, and then call the SSA Fraud Hotline at 800-269-0271, and file a report at SSA Fraud Hotline, P.O. Box 17768, Baltimore MD 21235, fax 410-597-0118 or email *oig.hotline@ssa.gov*. The victim should also call the SSA at 800-772-1213 to verify the accuracy of earnings reported under the SSN and to request a copy of the victim's Social Security Personal Earnings and Benefit Estimate Statement. The statement should reveal earnings posted to the victim's SSN by the identity thief. If an SSN has been fraudulently used, the Internal Revenue Service (IRS) Taxpayer Advocates Office should be contacted. The fraudulent use of an SSN might result in what appears to be an underreporting of a victim's taxable income and an attempt by the IRS to collect taxes on the underreported income. The IRS Taxpayer Advocates Office can be contacted at 877-777-4778 or *www.treas.gov/irs/ci*.

If someone has fraudulently obtained a driver's license or photographic identification card in a victim's name through an office of a DMV, the local DMV should be contacted and a fraud alert should be placed on the license. Likewise, if someone has stolen any other identification document, the entity responsible for creating the document should be contacted and informed of the theft. If a passport has been lost or stolen, the United States State Department should be contacted at Passport Services, Correspondence Branch, 1111 19th Street, N.W., Suite 510 Washington, DC 20036, or *www.travel.state.gov/passport_services.html*. If someone has stolen a health insurance card, the theft should be reported to the insurer. Subsequent insurance statements should be reviewed for fraudulent billing.

If someone has fraudulently filed for bankruptcy in a victim's name, the U.S. Trustee should be contacted in the region where the bankruptcy was filed. A listing of the U.S. Trustees can be found at *www.usdoj.gov/ust*. A written complaint must be filed describing the situation and providing proof of the victim's identity. The U.S. Trustee, if appropriate, will make a referral to criminal law-enforcement authorities. The victim should also file a complaint with the FBI in the city where the bankruptcy was filed.

In rare instances, an identity thief may create a criminal record under a victim's name by providing the identity when arrested. Victims of this type of problem should contact the FBI and initiate a request that the victim's name be cleared, and retain an attorney to resolve the problem as procedures for clearing one's name may vary by jurisdiction.

Conclusion

Identity theft was clearly identified as a serious crime two years ago when the Identity Theft Act was passed. Since that time great strides have been made to combat the problem, but much work remains to be done. Law-enforcement agencies at all levels, federal and nonfederal, must work together to develop strategies for the investigation and prosecution of offenders. At the same time, the law enforcement community must work closely with private industry to develop effective education and prevention programs. The crime of the new millennium will not fade away soon, nor will passive efforts soften the devastating impact upon its victims. Yet with hard work, cooperation, and effective communication between law enforcement and the public, identity thieves will be held accountable in this new millennium.

(Sean B. Hoar has been an AUSA since 1991 and is the Computer and Telecommunications Coordinator (CTC) for the southern half of the District of Oregon. As such, he prosecuted the first case in the United States under the No Electronic Theft Act (NET Act), involving criminal copyright infringement on the Internet. He is primarily concerned with developing partnerships with local, state, and federal law-enforcement agencies to prevent, investigate, and prosecute cybercrime.)

SUMMARY OF FEDERAL LEGISLATION ON IDENTITY THEFT

FEDERAL LEGISLATION DISCUSSED

- Identity Theft Act, 18 U.S.C. § 1028(a)(7)

- Aggravated Identity Theft Act, 18 U.S.C. § 1028A

- Computer Fraud and Abuse Act (CFAA), 18 U.S.C. § 1030(a)(4)

- Fair Credit Reporting Act (FCRA), 15 U.S.C. § 1681-1681X, amended by the Fair and Accurate Credit Transactions Act of 2003 (FACTA), Pub. L. No. 108-159, 117 Stat. 1952

- Credit Card Fraud Act, 18 U.S.C. 1029

- Gramm-Leach-Bliley Act (GLB Act), 15 U.S.C. § 6801-09

- Federal Trade Commission Act (FTC Act), 15 U.S.C. § 45(a)

- Electronic Fund Transfer Act (15 U.S.C. § 1693-1693r)

- USA Patriot Act, 31 U.S.C. § 5318(l)

- Health Insurance Portability and Accountability Act Of 1996 (HIPAA), 42 U.S.C. § 1320d

- Drivers Privacy Protection Act of 1994 (DPPA), 18 U.S.C. § 2721-2725

- Family Educational Rights and Privacy Act (FERPA), 20 U.S.C. § 1232g

- Department of Veterans Affairs Information Security Act of 2006, 38 U.S.C. § 5721-28

- Intelligence Reform and Terrorism Prevention Act (IRTPA) of 2004 (Pub. L. 108-458)

- Real ID Act of 2005 (Pub. L. 109-13)

IDENTITY THEFT ACT

The Identity Theft Act (18 U.S.C. § 1028(a)(7)) generally prohibits knowingly transferring, possessing, or using a means of identification of another person in connection with any unlawful activity that constitutes a violation of federal law or that constitutes a felony under any applicable state or local law. The act is discussed in chapters 1 and 5.

AGGRAVATED IDENTITY THEFT ACT

The Aggravated Identity Theft Act, 18 U.S.C. § 1028A(a), prohibits knowingly transferring, possessing, or using a means of identification of another person, during and in relation to any of numerous specified federal felonies listed in that section. This act is discussed in chapter 5.

The act requires that a mandatory sentence of two years imprisonment be imposed on a person who knowingly transfers, possesses, or uses a means of identification that belongs to someone else while committing another enumerated felony; this mandatory two-year term must be imposed consecutively, with whatever sentence is imposed for conviction on the enumerated felony. The term "person" includes all human beings, regardless of whether they are living at the time their identity is stolen and used. For a person to be convicted of aggravated identity theft, the prosecutor must prove that an accused individual: "(1) during and in relation to any felony violation that is enumerated in § 1028A(c), (2) knowingly transfers, knowingly possesses, or knowingly uses, (3) means of identification of another person, (4) without lawful authority." (*U.S. v. Montejo*, (2005, ED Va) 353 F. Supp. 2d 643)

In *United States v. Hines*, (2007, CA8 Mo) 472 F. 3d 1038, the defendant was convicted of aggravated identity theft when the government satisfied the "knowingly" requirement of 18 U.S.C.S § 1028A(a)(1) by showing that the defendant admitted that he gave the police a false name, and his use of another's name and Social Security number to defraud police satisfied the "means of identification" requirement.

COMPUTER FRAUD AND ABUSE ACT

The Computer Fraud and Abuse Act (CFAA), 18 U.S.C. § 1030(a)(4), generally prohibits the unauthorized accessing of a computer with an intent to defraud and thus furthering the fraud and obtaining anything of value. This statute has been used effectively to charge defendants engaging in identity theft by unlawful accessing of computers where the evidence shows that the data was taken as part of a fraud scheme. Second, 18 U.S.C. § 1030(a)(2) generally prohibits the theft of information from a computer, but limits a federal court's jurisdiction to instances in which the thief uses an interstate communication to access that computer (unless the computer belongs to the federal government or a financial institution). Third, 18 U.S.C. § 1030(a)(5) prohibits actions that cause "damage" to computers—that is, actions that impair the "integrity or availability" of data or computer systems. Absent special circumstances, however, the loss caused by the conduct must exceed $5,000 in order for it to constitute a federal crime.

"Without authorization," as used in the Computer Fraud and Abuse Act, means no access authorization, and "exceeds authorized access" means to go beyond access permitted. *Lockheed Martin Corp. v. Speed*, (2006, MD Fla) 81 USPQ2d 1669, 19 FLW Fed D 939. The term "fraud," as used in 18 U.S.C.S § 1030(a)(4), which penalizes defendants who gain access to a computer with an intent to defraud, means wronging of a person of property rights by dishonest methods or schemes, rather than fraud in its common-law sense. (*Shurgard Storage Ctrs. v. Safeguard Self Storage, Inc.*, (2000, WD Wash)

119 F. Supp. 2d 1121) 18 USCS § 1030(a)(5) criminalizes computer crime that damages individuals and corporations alike. (*United States v. Middleton*, (2000, CA9 Cal) 231 F. 3d 1207, 2000 CDOS 9194, 2000 Daily Journal DAR 12198)

Law 18 U.S.C. § 1030(e)(2)(B) provides that the term "protected computer" means a computer which is used in interstate or foreign commerce or communication, including a computer located outside the United States that is used in a manner that affects interstate or foreign commerce or communication in the United States.

Indictment need not be dismissed in business settings due to lack of allegation of damage done to an "individual," since the obvious purpose of 18 USCS § 1030 is to protect the use of computers and most computer usage, particularly that which could result in monetary damage. It does not make sense that Congress would seek to protect the integrity of computers and their information but limit that protection to natural persons and not include business entities more likely to use computers. (*United States v. Middleton*, (1999, ND Cal) 35 F. Supp. 2d 1189, affd (2000, CA9 Cal) 231 F. 3d 1207, 2000 CDOS 9194, 2000 Daily Journal DAR 12198)

FAIR CREDIT REPORTING ACT

The Fair Credit Reporting Act (FCRA), 15 U.S.C. § 1681–1681X, amended by the Fair and Accurate Credit Transactions Act of 2003 (FACTA), Pub. L. No. 108-159, 117 Stat. 1952, contains requirements designed to protect the privacy of consumer report information, which includes accounts, credit history, and employment information. Under the FCRA, consumer-reporting agencies are prohibited from distributing consumer reports except for specified "permissible purposes." These entities must maintain reasonable procedures to ensure that they provide consumer reports only for these purposes, such as by verifying the identities of persons obtaining consumer reports and their intended use of the information. The FACTA amendments to the FCRA added a number of new requirements, many of which have been or are being implemented through rule-making. Several of these new requirements are intended to prevent identity theft or assist victims in the recovery process. The rules most relevant to data security are discussed below.

FACTA was enacted to prevent identity theft, improve resolution of consumer disputes, improve the accuracy of consumer records, and make improvements in the use of, and consumer access to, credit information. It provides that consumers have the right to request a free consumer report annually from the major credit reporting agencies (CRAs). It also allows consumers to put a fraud alert on their credit file. The act also requires that CRAs block or cease reporting fraudulent or allegedly fraudulent information on a consumer's record when the consumer submits a police report and appropriate identifying information.

FACTA also includes restrictions on the circumstances under which consumer reporting agencies may furnish consumer reports that contain medical information about consumers. In particular, a consumer reporting agency may not furnish a consumer report that contains medical information about a consumer except under certain delineated circumstances involving consumer consent to the furnishing of the report, or if the information is limited to account status and is reported in a manner that does not reveal the nature of the medical treatment.

Disposal Rule

The FACTA amended the FCRA to include a number of provisions designed to increase the protection of sensitive consumer information. One such provision required the financial regulatory agencies and the FTC to promulgate a coordinated rule designed to prevent unauthorized access to consumer-report information by requiring all users of such information to have reasonable procedures to dispose of it properly.

The rule applies to any entity that maintains consumer reports or information derived from consumer reports. The rule does not address when entities must dispose of such information, but rather how they must dispose of it: by using disposal practices that are reasonable and appropriate to prevent the unauthorized access to or use of information in a consumer report. The standard is flexible and allows the organizations and individuals covered by the rule to determine what measures are reasonable based on the sensitivity of the information, the costs and benefits of different disposal methods, and changes in technology. For the federal bank regulatory agencies, these requirements are included in their Interagency Security Guidelines. The SEC's disposal rule requirements are included in the SEC's Regulation S-P (17 C.F.R. § 248.30(b)).

Identity Theft Red Flags

The Identity Theft Red Flags and Address Discrepancies Rule was established pursuant to the FACTA ("Red Flags Rule"), Pub. L. No. 108-159, 117 Stat. 1952, Sections 114 and 315; all provisions of the rule will not become effective until November 8, 2008. The regulations require every financial institution and creditor to develop and implement a written identity theft prevention program that includes policies and procedures for detecting, preventing, and mitigating identity theft in connection with account openings and existing accounts. The program must be risk-based and tailored to the size and complexity of each financial institution or creditor and the nature and scope of its activities. Credit card and debit card issuers must develop policies and procedures to assess the validity of a request for a change of address that is followed closely by a request for an additional or replacement card. In addition, as required by the statute, the proposed regulations require users of consumer reports to develop reasonable policies and procedures regarding notices of address discrepancies that they receive from a consumer reporting agency (CRA). If a user of a consumer report receives notice from a CRA that the address a consumer has provided to obtain the report "substantially differs" from the consumer's address in the CRA's file, the user must reasonably confirm an accurate address for the consumer and provide it to the CRA.

CREDIT CARD FRAUD ACT

The Credit Card Fraud Act, 18 U.S.C. 1029, makes it a felony to "knowingly and with intent to defraud," use, purchase goods aggregating $1,000 or more with, or possess 15 or more unauthorized "access devices." Access devices include account numbers and personal identifiers that can be used to "to obtain money, goods, services, or any other thing of value or that can be used to initiate a transfer of funds." The Credit Card Fraud Act includes penalties of up to 15 years and a fine. It also allows for restitution to the "victim," although the act considers the bank, credit issuer, or merchant to be the victim rather than the person whose identity was stolen, because the credit issuer is financially liable for the fraudulent purchases.

The act defines an unauthorized access device as any access device that is lost, stolen, expired, revoked, canceled, or obtained with an intent to defraud. It is a violation of the act for a person to knowingly, and with intent to defraud, traffic in or use one or more unauthorized access devices during any one-year period and obtain anything of value aggregating $1,000 or more during that period.

In one case where the defendant stole credit cards from letters, intending to send the cards to another criminal in exchange for money, the defendant's offense involving trafficking of credit cards was upheld because trafficking was sufficient to satisfy the requirement under the act. (*United States v. Alli*, (2006, CA1 RI) 444 F. 3d 34)

In *United States v. Yates*, the defendant was convicted under the act for cloning cellular phones, even though he argued that carriers were not damaged by use of cloned cellular phones since the carriers continued to be able to bill for calls made on them; but he was convicted because cloning cellular phones to enable users to have extension phones defrauds carriers of activation fees, and monthly service fees, and falls squarely within ambit of § 1029(a) as illuminated by legislative history. (*United States v. Yates*, (1995, ED Ky) 914 F. Supp. 152)

GRAMM-LEACH-BLILEY ACT

The Gramm-Leach-Bliley Act (GLB Act), 15 U.S.C. § 6801-09, addresses privacy and security obligations of financial institutions. Financial institutions are defined broadly as those entities engaged in "financial activities," such as banking, lending, insurance, loan brokering, and credit reporting. (12 C.F.R. § 225.28, 225.86)

The GLB Act addresses two distinct types of protection for personal information: protection of security and protection of privacy. Various federal agencies, including the federal bank regulatory agencies, the Federal Trade Commission (FTC), and the Securities and Exchange Commission (SEC), have issued regulations or guidelines addressing both the security and privacy provisions of the GLB Act.

The security provisions require that the agencies write standards for financial institutions regarding appropriate physical, technical, and procedural safeguards to ensure the security and confidentiality of customer records and information, and to protect against anticipated threats and unauthorized access to such information. The privacy provisions require financial institutions to give notice to their customers of their information-sharing practices and to provide customers with an opportunity to opt out of information sharing with certain unaffiliated third parties in certain circumstances.

Interagency Security Guidelines

The Interagency Security Guidelines, jointly issued by the federal bank regulatory agencies in 2001, require each financial institution under their jurisdiction to have a written information security program designed to meet the statutory objectives of Title V of the GLB Act and section 216 of the Fair and Accurate Credit Transactions Act of 2003 (FACTA) regarding disposal of consumer information derived from consumer reports. See 12 C.F.R. Part 30, App. B (national banks); 12 C.F.R. Part 208, App. D-2 and Part 225, App. F (state member banks and holding companies); 12 C.F.R. Part 364, App. B (state nonmember banks); 12 C.F.R. Part 570, App. B (savings associations); 12 C.F.R. Part 748, App. A (credit unions). Under the guidelines, the institution's board of directors must approve the program and assess the risks to its customer information, identify reasonably foreseeable internal and external threats that could result in unauthorized disclosure or misuse of its customer information. The board must assess the likelihood and potential damage of these threats, taking into account the institution's size and complexity, the nature and scope of its activities, and the sensitivity of the customer information it handles. Each of the requirements in the guidelines regarding proper disposal of customer information also applies to the disposal of consumer information. The institution must then design its information security program to control the identified risks.

Information Security Program

The guidelines stipulate certain minimum specific security measures that should be considered and adopted if appropriate to the institution's risk profile. These measures include access controls on customer information systems, encryption of electronic customer information, monitoring systems to detect actual and attempted attacks on customer information systems, and response programs that specify actions to be taken when an institution suspects or detects unauthorized access to customer information.

Each institution must also train its staff to implement the program and oversee its arrangements with service providers that have access to its customer information. This includes using due diligence in selecting service providers, requiring by contract that service providers implement appropriate safeguard measures that satisfy the guidelines, and monitoring the activities of service providers, where necessary, to control the risks the institution has identified that may be posed by the service provider's access to the institution's customer information.

An institution's information security program must be dynamic. Institutions must routinely test their systems and address any weaknesses they discover. Institutions must adjust their programs to address new threats to customer information, changes in technology, and new business arrangements.

Safeguard Rules

FTC Standards for Safeguarding Customer Information (Safeguards Rule), 16 C.F.R. Part 314, were drafted in compliance with the GLB Act. The FTC's Safeguards Rule applies to a wide variety of financial institutions that are not subject to the jurisdiction of other federal or state authorities under the GLB Act. Among the institutions that fall under the Safeguards Rule are nonbank mortgage lenders, loan brokers, some state-regulated financial or investment advisers, tax preparers, providers of real estate settlement services, and debt collectors. The FTC's regulation applies only to companies that are "significantly engaged" in such financial activities.

Like the Interagency Security Guidelines, the Safeguards Rule requires financial institutions to develop a written information security plan that describes their procedures to protect customer information. Further, the rule requires covered entities to take certain procedural steps, including: (1) assigning employees to oversee the program, (2) conducting a risk assessment, (3) designing and implementing an information safeguards program, (4) contractually requiring service providers to protect customers' information, and (5) evaluating and adjusting the program in light of relevant circumstances. However, given the wide variety of entities (large and small) that are covered, the rule mandates a data security plan that accounts for each entity's particular circumstances, including its size and complexity, the nature and scope of its activities, and the sensitivity of the customer information it handles.

Privacy Rule

The Privacy Rule, issued by the federal bank regulatory agencies and the FTC, implements the privacy provisions of the GLB Act with respect to financial institutions under their respective jurisdictions. (16 C.F.R. Part 313 (FTC); 12 C.F.R. Parts 40 (OCC), 216 (FRB), 332 (FDIC), 573 (OTS), and 716 (NCUA)) Subject to certain exceptions, it prohibits financial institutions from disclosing nonpublic personal information to nonaffiliated third parties without first providing consumers with notice and the opportunity to opt out of the disclosure. The notice and opt-out must be provided no later than when a customer relationship arises, and then annually for the duration of that relationship, or at a reasonable time before the disclosure in the case of noncustomers. The notice must be "a clear and conspicuous notice that accurately reflects [the financial institution's] privacy policies and practices," including policies and practices related to security.

FEDERAL TRADE COMMISSION ACT

The Federal Trade Commission Act (FTC Act), 15 U.S.C. § 45(a), prohibits "unfair or deceptive acts or practices in or affecting commerce" and gives the FTC broad jurisdiction over a wide variety of entities and individuals operating in commerce. Prohibited deceptive practices include making false or misleading claims about the privacy and security provided for consumer information. The FTC Act also prohibits unfair practices, including unfair practices affecting consumer data. Practices are unfair if they cause or are likely to cause consumers substantial injury that is neither reasonably avoidable by consumers nor offset by countervailing benefits to consumers or competition. The FTC has used this authority to challenge a variety of injurious practices, including companies' failure to provide reasonable and appropriate security for sensitive consumer data such as Social Security numbers and financial account information. (See the discussion of enforcement actions below.) The federal bank regulatory agencies have also enforced Section 5 of the FTC Act against financial institutions under their jurisdiction.

ELECTRONIC FUND TRANSFER ACT

The Electronic Fund Transfer Act (15 U.S.C. § 1693-1693r) establishes the rights, liabilities, and responsibilities of participants in electronic fund transfer systems. The act requires financial institutions to adopt certain practices respecting such matters as transaction accounting, preauthorized transfers, and error resolution, and it sets liability limits for losses caused by unauthorized transfers.

USA PATRIOT ACT

Under the USA Patriot Act, 31 U.S.C.. § 5318(l), Customer Identification Program Rules were established. Banks, savings associations, credit unions, broker-dealers, mutual funds, and futures commission merchants are required to follow verification procedures under rules issued by the federal bank regulatory agencies, the Department of Treasury, the CFTC, and the SEC under section 326 of the USA Patriot Act. The implementing rules require every covered entity to design and implement a customer identification program (CIP) that includes policies and procedures for verifying the identity of a person opening a new account. While the primary purpose of the regulations implementing the USA Patriot Act was to deter terrorist financing and money laundering, the CIP regulations also play a role in preventing identity theft.

HEALTH INSURANCE PORTABILITY AND ACCOUNTABILITY ACT

The Health Insurance Portability and Accountability Act of 1996, (HIPAA), 42 U.S.C. § 1320d et seq., prohibits certain entities (including health plans, health-care clearinghouses, and certain healthcare providers) from disclosing to third parties an individual's protected health information without prior authorization, subject to some exceptions, such as the disclosure of patient records by covered entities for purposes of routine treatment, insurance, payment, or, in limited circumstances, credit reporting relating to account information.

Like the GLB Act Safeguards Rule, the HIPAA Privacy Rule requires covered entities under its jurisdiction to have in place "appropriate administrative, technical, and physical safeguards to protect the privacy of protected health information." (45 C.F.R. § 164.530(c)) The HIPAA Security Rule similarly seeks to protect the confidentiality, integrity, and availability of electronic protected health information by specifying a series of administrative, technical, and physical security procedures for covered entities to use to assure the security and confidentiality of electronic protected health information.

DRIVERS PRIVACY PROTECTION ACT

The Drivers Privacy Protection Act of 1994 (DPPA), 18 U.S.C. § 2721-2725, prohibits the disclosure of a driver's personal information (i.e., individual photograph, Social Security number, and driver identification number) obtained in connection with a motor vehicle record. The DPPA contains exceptions that allow for certain disclosures of such information, such as for use by an insurer or to provide notice to the owners of towed or impounded vehicles. The DPPA also prohibits an individual from knowingly obtaining a driver's personal information for a use not permitted under the act and from making a false representation to obtain any such information.

FAMILY EDUCATIONAL RIGHTS AND PRIVACY ACT

The Family Educational Rights and Privacy Act (FERPA), 20 U.S.C. § 1232g, 34 C.F.R. Part 99, protects the privacy of student education records. The law applies to all schools that receive funds under an applicable program of the U.S. Department of Education. FERPA gives parents certain rights with respect to their children's education records; these rights transfer to the student when he or she reaches the age of 18 or attends a school beyond the high-school level. Under FERPA, a parent or an eligible student has the right to inspect and review the student's education records maintained by the school and to request that a school correct records that the parent or eligible student believes to be inaccurate or misleading. Furthermore, schools generally must have written permission from the parent or eligible student to release any information from a student's education record, subject to certain exceptions, such as disclosures to appropriate parties in connection with financial aid to a student. Schools may disclose "directory" release information—including a student's name, address, telephone number, and date and place of birth—but must provide advance notice to parents and eligible students and allow them a reasonable amount of time to opt out of the disclosure.

DEPARTMENT OF VETERANS AFFAIRS INFORMATION SECURITY ACT

Department of Veterans Affairs Information Security Act of 2006, 38 U.S.C. § 5721-5728, establishes a comprehensive information security program for the Department of Veterans Affairs (VA) and outlines requirements for the VA's response to data breaches. The act provides that if it appears that VA-sensitive information may have been compromised, and an independent data breach analysis determines that a reasonable risk of potential misuse exists, then the VA must offer credit protection services to the record subjects. The following credit protection services must be prescribed in VA regulations: notification of the record subjects, data mining, fraud alerts, data-breach analyses, credit monitoring, identity theft insurance, and credit protection services. In addition, the VA must comply with Congressional notification requirements regarding data breaches. The act requires all VA contracts in which the contractor will have access to VA-sensitive information to contain provisions prohibiting the contractor from sharing the information with other entities, except to perform the contract. This requires the contractor to report any data breaches to the agency and to pay liquidated damages to the VA for any data breach involving sensitive VA information.

INTELLIGENCE REFORM AND TERRORISM PREVENTION ACT

The Intelligence Reform and Terrorism Prevention Act (IRTPA) of 2004 (Pub. L. 108-458) improves identification information security and requires a national strategy for combating international terrorist travel. As part of this plan, the law contains provisions for robust travel document screening and authentication and for improved training for a variety of federal officials who come into contact with fraudulent identification documents. The law also requires that part of the strategic plan will be to disrupt terrorists' production and use of false travel documents. It also requires that the president lead international efforts to provide for the detection of counterfeit or stolen foreign travel documents and to criminally punish those involved in such crimes.

One section of the law focuses on biometrics. The law requires that biometric identifier technology be studied, be included in airport access controls, and be incorporated into a new, uniform law-enforcment officer credential. The law also requires that a plan be developed to accelerate the full implementation of an automated biometric entry and exit system.

The law also focuses on improving identification documents, from requiring that improved pilots' licenses be developed to providing for the creation of federal standards for birth certificates, driver's licenses, and personal identification cards. The law included security enhancements for Social Security cards, such as restricting the issuance of multiple replacement cards and establishing minimum standards for verification of documents. Additionally, the law prohibits the use of Social Security numbers on driver's licenses.

REAL ID ACT

The Real ID Act of 2005 (Pub. L. 109-13) supplements the requirements of state driver's licenses and identification cards for use by federal agencies. The law requires a number of verification measures before such identification is issued, including that the state verify the validity of supporting documents. The law also mandates that identification cards used for federal purposes expire every eight years and be produced in secure environments by personnel with appropriate clearances. It further requires that state identification cards that do not meet the federal security requirements state so on their face and that all states provide electronic access to other states of their motor vehicle databases.

RELATED FEDERAL STATUTES

Often, identity theft cases are tried under other related federal criminal statutes. The most frequently used statutes are listed below:

- Mail fraud (18 U.S.C. § 1341)

- Wire fraud (18 U.S.C. § 1343)

- Financial institution fraud (18 U.S.C. § 1344)

- Access device fraud (18 U.S.C. § 1029)

- Social Security number fraud [42 U.S.C. § 408(a)(7)(B))

In cases involving false documents, such as visas, passports, or other documents relating to identification, federal prosecutors can also charge a variety of identification document offenses. These include:

- Identification document fraud (18 U.S.C. § 1028(a)(1)–(6))

- False statement in application and use of a passport (18 U.S.C. § 1542)

- Forgery or false use of a passport (18 U.S.C. § 1543)

- Misuse of a passport (18 U.S.C. § 1544)

- Fraud and misuse of visas, permits, and other documents (18 U.S.C. § 1546)

STATE IDENTITY THEFT LEGISLATION

STATE LAWS ON CREDIT INFORMATION AND PERSONAL INFORMATION

All states and the District of Columbia have some form of legislation that prohibits identity theft, and in all of those jurisdictions, except for Maine, identity theft can be a felony. In general, 11 states appear to use a narrower approach to criminalizing identity theft by focusing on the use of personal identifying information with intent to defraud. Other states use a broader approach to criminalization that often includes unauthorized use, as well as the possession, creation, recording, obtaining, selling, giving, or transmitting of personally identifiable information. State laws concerning identity theft change frequently. One of the trends has been to make criminal law more specific, for example, making it a separate crime to traffic in stolen identities or to engage in phishing.

ALABAMA

Alabama Code Sect. 13A-8-190 through 201 13A-8-190

13A-8-191	13A-8-197
13A-8-192	13A-8-198
13A-8-193	13A-8-199
13A-8-194	13A-8-200
13A-8-195	13A-8-201
13A-8-196	

Section 11 requires the credit reporting agencies (CRAs) to block false information from consumer victims' credit reports within 30 days of a consumer submitting a court order for the identity thief's conviction to the CRA.

CALIFORNIA

California Office of Privacy Protection
www.privacyprotection.ca.gov

COLORADO

Colorado Revised Statutes 12-14.3-106.5 through 108 and CRS
12-14.3-106.5
12-14.3-107
12-14.3-108
16-18.5-103

IDAHO

Idaho Code Section 28-51-102
(This code requires credit-reporting agencies to block inaccurate information resulting from an identity theft upon receipt of a police report.)

RHODE ISLAND

Rhode Island Gen. Laws Section 6-13-17
(This law states that unless required by federal law, no person shall require that a consumer of goods or services disclose a Social Security number incident to the sale of consumer goods or services. Exceptions, however, include insurance companies, health care, or pharmaceutical companies that may require the consumer to furnish a Social Security number. Also, a consumer may be required to furnish his or her Social Security number when applying for a credit card.)

WASHINGTON

Rev. Code Washington Section 19.182.160
(This code requires credit reporting agencies to block inaccurate information resulting from an identity theft upon receipt of a police report.)

STATE LAWS ON IDENTITY THEFT

U.S. States and the District of Columbia

Alabama	Ala. Code § 13A-8-190 through 201
Alaska	Alaska Stat. § 11.46.565
Arizona	Ariz. Rev. Stat. § 13-2008
Arkansas	Ark. Code Ann. § 5-37-227
California	Cal. Penal Code § 530.5-8
Colorado	Colorado Art 5 § 18-5-901
Connecticut	Conn. Stat. § 53a-129a (criminal)
	Conn. Stat. § 52-571h (civil)
Delaware	Del. Code Ann. tit. II, § 854
District of Columbia	District of Columbia Title 22, Section 3227
Florida	Fla. Stat. Ann. § 817.568
Georgia	Ga. Code Ann. § 16-9-120 through 128
Hawaii	HI Rev. Stat. § 708-839.6
	HI Rev. Stat. § 708-839.7
	HI Rev. Stat. § 708-839.8
Idaho	Idaho Code § 18-3126
Illinois	720 Ill. Comp. Stat. 5/16 G

Indiana	Ind. Code § 35-43-5-3.5
Iowa	Iowa Code § 715A.8 (criminal)
	Iowa Code § 714.16.B (civil)
Kansas	Kan. Stat. Ann. § 21-4018
Kentucky	Ky. Rev. Stat. Ann. § 514.160
Louisiana	La. Rev. Stat. Ann. § 14:67.16
Maine	ME Rev. Stat. Ann. tit. 17-A § 905-A
Maryland	Md. Code Ann. art. 27 § 231
Massachusetts	Mass. Gen. Laws ch. 266 § 37E
Michigan	Mich. Comp. Laws § 750.285
Minnesota	Minn. Stat. Ann. § 609.527
Mississippi	Miss. Code Ann. § 97-19-85
Missouri	Mo. Rev. Stat. § 570.223
Montana	Mon. Code Ann. § 45-6-332
Nebraska	NE Rev. Stat. § 28-608 & 620
Nevada	Nev. Rev. Stat. § 205.463-465
New Hampshire	NH Rev. Stat. Ann. § 638:26
New Jersey	NJ Stat. Ann. § 2C:21-17
New Mexico	NM Stat. Ann. § 30-16-24.1
New York	NY CLS Penal § 190.77 through 190.84

North Carolina	NC Gen. Stat. § 14-113.20-23
North Dakota	N.D.C.C. § 12.1-23-11
Ohio	Ohio Rev. Code Ann. § 2913.49
Oklahoma	Okla. Stat. tit. 21 § 1533.1
Oregon	Or. Rev. Stat. § 165.800
Pennsylvania	18 Pa. Cons. State § 4120
Rhode Island	RI Gen. Laws § 11-49.1-1
South Carolina	SC Code Ann. § 16-13-500, 501
South Dakota	SD Codified Laws § 22-30A-3.1
Tennessee	TCA § 39-14-150 (criminal)
	TCA § 47-18-2101 (civil)
Texas	Tex. Penal Code § 32.51
Utah	Utah Code Ann. § 76-6-1101-1104
Vermont	V.S.A. 13 § 2030
Virginia	Va. Code Ann. § 18.2-186.3
Washington	Wash. Rev. Code § 9.35.020
West Virginia	W. Va. Code § 61-3-54
Wisconsin	Wis. Stat. § 943.201
Wyoming	Wyo. Stat. Ann. § 6-3-901

U.S. Territories

Guam   9 Guam Code Ann. § 46.80

U.S. Virgin Islands (Does not have a specific
                            identity theft law.)

STATE CONSUMER AGENCIES

Many states have consumer protection agencies, and the states' attorneys general have information and guidance for businesses to help them protect consumers' sensitive information. Examples of states providing this type of guidance include:

California

California has created an Office of Privacy Protection to promote and protect consumers' rights. This office makes numerous publications available to assist businesses in complying with federal and state safeguard requirements, as well as improving their general information security practices. In its publication, *A California Business Privacy Handbook* (available at *www.privacyprotection.ca.gov/recommenda tions/ca_business_privacy_hb.pdf*), the state's Office of Privacy Protection describes basic techniques that companies can use to protect personal information and prevent identity theft, such as controlling access to personal information and securely disposing of materials containing sensitive consumer information. Likewise, in its *Recommended Practices for Protecting the Confidentiality of Social Security Numbers* (available at *www.privacyprotection.ca.gov/recommenda tions/ssnrecommendations.pdf*), the state provides businesses with information on federal and state laws regarding the collection, use, and confidentiality of Social Security numbers, as well as recommended practices like reducing the unnecessary collection of Social Security numbers and eliminating the public display of Social Security numbers.

New York

The New York State Office of Cyber Security and Critical Infrastructure Coordination has published *Best Practices and Assessment Tools to Promote Cyber Security Awareness*. This guide includes advice specifically directed at corporations and small businesses.

Wisconsin

Wisconsin has an agency to address consumers' privacy rights, the Office of Privacy Protection within the Wisconsin Department of Agriculture, Trade and Consumer Protection division. This office provides guidance for small businesses through its website, *www.privacy.wi.gov/business/business.jsp*, which recommends actions like limiting the collection of sensitive information and screening and training employees.

RESOURCES TO FIGHT IDENTITY THEFT

FBI Internet Fraud Complaint Center

www.ifccfbi.gov

Federal Deposit Insurance Corporation (FDIC)

www.fdic.gov

Federal Trade Commission (FTC)

The FTC offers help to victims. File your case with the FTC Consumer Response Center. Include your police report number. Use the FTC uniform affidavit form.

Telephone: 877-ID-THEFT

www.consumer.gov/idtheft

Federal Reserve System

www.federalreserve.gov

Internal Revenue Service

www.irs.gov

Office of the Comptroller of the Currency (OCC)

www.occ.treas.gov

Office of Justice Programs (OJP)

www.ojp.gov

Office for Victims of Crime (OVC)

www.ojp.usdoj.gov/ovc

Securities and Exchange Commission (SEC)

www.sec.gov

U.S. Department of Justice (DOJ)

www.usdoj.gov/criminal/fraud/idtheft.html

U.S. Postal Inspection Service (USPIS)

https://postalinspectors.uspis.gov

U.S. Secret Service (USSS)

www.secretservice.gov

U.S. Social Security Administration (SSA)

www.socialsecurity.gov

U.S. Treasury Department, Financial Crimes Division

www.treas.gov/usss/financial_crimes

STATES

California Office of Privacy Protection

ww.privacy.ca.gov

Colorado Attorney General's Office

www.ago.state.co.us/idtheft/clients.cfm

New Jersey Department of Banking and Insurance

www.state.nj.us/dobi/division_consumers/finance/identitytheft.htm

Wisconsin Department of Agriculture, Trade and Consumer Protection, Office of Privacy Protection

www.privacy.wi.gov

NATIONAL ORGANIZATIONS

Anti-Phishing Working Group

www.antiphishing.org

Centers for Medicare and Medicaid Services

www.cms.gov

Earthlink Identity Protection Center

www.earthlink.net/mysecurity/identity

Identity Theft Resource Center (ITRC)

www.idtheftcenter.org

National Conference of State Legislatures (NCSL)

www.ncsl.org/programs/lis/privacy/idt-01legis.htm

National Consumer Law Center

www.consumerlaw.org

National Credit Union Administration (NCUA)

www.ncua.gov

Privacy Rights Clearinghouse (PRC)

Telephone: 619-298-3396

www.privacyrights.org

Small Business Administration (SBA)

www.sba.gov/beawareandprepare/cyber.html

U.S. Chamber of Commerce

www.U.S.C.hamber.com/sb/security

UNIVERSITIES

Harvard University

www.hupd.harvard.edu/id_theft.php

Northwestern University

www.it.northwestern.edu/security/protectingprivacy/index.html

Pennsylvania State University

http://consumerissues.cas.psu.edu/pdfs/creditprivacyidentity.pdf

Tulane University

www.tuhscpd.tulane.edu/safety/idtheft.htm

University of California—Los Angeles

www.ucpd.ucla.edu/ucpd/programs_persafe.html

University of Kansas

www.privacy.ku.edu/idtheft

University of Michigan

www.identityweb.umich.edu

University of Minnesota

www.safecomputing.umn.edu/safepractices/idtheft.html

University of Missouri—Kansas City

www.umkc.edu/adminfinance/police/tips/identity.asp

University of Oklahoma

www.ou.edu/oupd/idtheft.htm

University of Utah

www.it.utah.edu/leadership/security/identity.html

Yale University

www.yale.edu/security/goodmeasures/protectingyouridentity.html

IDENTITY THEFT PUBLICATIONS AVAILABLE ONLINE

Anti-Phishing Working Group

www.antiphishing.org/phishing_archive.html

AOL—Money & Finance, Identity Theft

www.money.aol.com/creditdebt/identity

Bank of America, Identity Theft and Your Rights

www.bankofamerica.com/privacy/control.do?body=privacy

Better Business Bureau (January 26, 2005), "New Research Shows That Identity Theft Is More Prevalent Offline with Paper Than Online."

www.bbbonline.org/idtheft/safetyQuiz.asp

Center for Problem-Oriented Policing

www.popcenter.org

Business Software Alliance/Cybersafety Phishing, Do You Know if Someone Is Trying to Steal Your Identity?

www.bsacybersafety.com/index.cfm

Chase, Identity Theft

www.chase.com/ccp/index.jsp?pg_name=ccpmapp/shared/assets/page/identity_theft

California Office of Privacy Protection's Publication, Recommended Practices on Notification of Security Breach Involving Personal Information

www.privacy.ca.gov/recommendations/secbreach.pdf

Capital One, Find Out How to Protect Yourself from Fraud and Identity Theft

www.capitalone.com/fraud

Citibank, Protect Yourself

www.citibank.com/us/cards/cm/theft01.htm

Centers for Medicare and Medicaid Services,
Holding Ourselves to a Higher Standard

www.cms.hhs.gov/informationsecurity

Columbia Credit Union, Security and Identity Theft

www.columbiacu.org/identity/identity_tips.html

Commerce Bank, Identity Theft and Fraud

www.commercebank.com/about/privacy/identity.asp

Consumer Advice: What to Do If You've Given
Out Your Personal Financial Information

www.antiphishing.org/consumer_recs2.html

Department of Justice, Fraud/Identity Theft

www.usdoj.gov/ust/r16/fraud.htm

Dixon, Pam. "Medical Identity Theft: The
Information Crime That Can Kill You,"
World Privacy Forum, Spring 2006

www.worldprivacyforum.org/pdf/wpf_medicalidtheft2006.pdf

eBay, Tutorial: Spoof (Fake) Emails

www.pages.ebay.com/education/spooftutorial

ECRI Institute, Operating Room Risk
Management, Health-Care Identity Theft:
Prevention and Response March 2006

www.ecri.org/marketingdocs/0306news.pdf

Federal Reserve Bank of Boston, Identity Theft

www.bos.frb.org/consumer/identity/idtheft.htm

FDIC, Classic Cons . . . and How to Counter Them

www.fdic.gov/consumers/consumer/news/cnsprg98/cons.html

**FDIC, A Crook Has Drained Your
Account. Who Pays?**

www.fdic.gov/consumers/consumer/news/cnsprg98/crook.html

FDIC, Identity Theft

www.fdic.gov/consumers/consumer/alerts/theft.html

FDIC, When a Criminal's Cover Is Your Identity

www.fdic.gov/consumers/privacy/criminalscover/index.html

FDIC, Your Wallet: A Loser's Manual

www.fdic.gov/consumers/consumer/news/cnfall97/wallet.html

**Foley, L. "Enhancing Law Enforcement–Identity Theft
Communication" Identity Theft Resource Center**

www.idtheftcenter.org

**FTC, "Active Duty" Alerts Help Protect
Military Personnel from Identity Theft**

www.ftc.gov/bcp/conline/pubs/alerts/dutyalrt.htm

FTC, Fighting Back against Identity Theft

www.ftc.gov/bcp/edu/pubs/consumer/idtheft/idt01.htm

FTC, How Not to Get Hooked by a Phishing Scam

www.ftc.gov/bcp/edu/pubs/consumer/alerts/alt127.htm

In Spanish: *www.ftc.gov/bcp/conline/spanish/alerts/s-phishingalrt.htm*

FTC, ID Theft Audio File—Audio 1, Audio 2

www.consumer.gov/idtheft/con_pubs.htm

FTC, ID Theft Video News Release (Dial Up Version—56k)—Video 1, Video 2

www.consumer.gov/idtheft/con_pubs.htm

FTC, ID Theft: What It's All About

www.ftc.gov/bcp/conline/pubs/credit/idtheftmini.htm

FTC, Information Compromise and the Risk of Identity Theft: Guidance for Your Business

www.ftc.gov/bcp/edu/pubs/business/idtheft/bus59.htm

FTC, Medicare Part D Solicitations: Words to the Wise about Fraud

www.ftc.gov/bcp/conline/pubs/alerts/meddalrt.htm

FTC, Privacy Choices for Your Personal Financial Information

www.ftc.gov/bcp/conline/pubs/credit/privchoices.htm

FTC, Remedying the Effects of Identity Theft

www.ftc.gov/bcp/conline/pubs/credit/idtsummary.pdf

In Spanish: *www.ftc.gov/bcp/conline/spanish/credit/s-idtsummary.pdf*

FTC, Take Charge: Fighting Back against Identity Theft

www.ftc.gov/bcp/conline/pubs/credit/idtheft.htm

In Spanish: *www.ftc.gov/bcp/conline/spanish/credit/s-idtheft.htm*

FTC, What to Do if Your Personal Information Has Been Compromised

www.ftc.gov/bcp/conline/pubs/alerts/infocompalrt.htm

FTC, Your Access to Free Credit Reports

www.ftc.gov/bcp/conline/pubs/credit/freereports.htm

In Spanish: *www.ftc.gov/bcp/conline/spanish/credit/s-freereports.htm*

GetNetWise

www.getnetwise.org

International Association of Chiefs of Police, "Curbing Identity Theft" Resolutions

www.theiacp.org/Resolutions/index.cfm?fuseaction

IRS, Identity Theft and Your Tax Records

www.irs.gov/individuals/article/0,,id=136324,00.html

ITRC, Identity Theft Recovery

www.idtheftcenter.org/index.html

MasterCard, Identity Theft

www.mastercard.com/us/personal/en/securityandbasics/identitytheft/index.html

Microsoft, Security at Home: Protect Yourself

www.microsoft.com/athome/security/privacy/default.mspx

National Consumer Law Center, Protecting Older Americans from Telemarketing Scams: A Quick Guide for Advocates

www.consumerlaw.org/initiatives/seniors_initiative/concerns_tele-market.shtml

National Consumer Law Center, Protect Yourself from Identity Theft

www.consumerlaw.org/action_agenda/seniors_initiative/identity_theft.shtml

National Consumer Law Center, What to Do if You've Become the Victim of Telemarketing Fraud

www.consumerlaw.org/initiatives/seniors_initiative/telemarketing_fraud.shtml

National Consumer Law Center, What You Should Know about Your Credit Report

www.consumerlaw.org/action_agenda/seniors_initiative/content/cfactscreditreport .pdf

National Credit Union Administration, You Can Fight Identity Theft

www.ncua.gov/publications/brochures/identitytheft/phishbrochure-web.pdf

National Cyber Security Alliance, Don't Take
the Bait! Avoid Getting Hooked by "Phishers"
Trying to Steal Your Personal Information

www.staysafeonline.org/basics/pharming_tips.html

National Women's Health Information Center,
Protecting Yourself from Cybercrime

www.girlshealth.gov/safety/internet.cybercrime.htm

Neremberg, L. (June 2003), "Daily Money Management
Programs: A Protection against Elder Abuse"

*www.elderabusecenter.org/pdf/publication/dailymoneymanagement.
pdf*

Newman, Graeme R. and Megan M. McNally (2005),
"Identity Theft Literature Review," Presented at the
National Institute of Justice Focus Group Meeting

www.ncjrs.gov/pdffiles1/nij/grants/210459.pdf

OCC, Check Fraud: A Guide to Avoiding Losses

www.occ.treas.gov/chckfrd/chckfrd.pdf

OCC, Fight Back: What You Can
Do about Identity Theft

www.occ.gov/consumer/idtheft.htm

OCC, How to Avoid Becoming a
Victim of Identity Theft

www.occ.treas.gov/idtheft.pdf

OCC, Internet Pirates Are Trying to Steal
Your Personal Financial Information

www.occ.gov/consumer/phishing.htm

OJP, Preventing Identity Theft: A Guide for Consumers

www.ncpc.org/cms/cms-upload/prevent/files/idtheftrev.pdf

OVC, Identity Theft

www.ojp.gov/ovc/help/it.htm

President's Identity Theft Task Force
(April 2007), ID Task Force Report

www.ftc.gov

Privacy Rights Clearinghouse, Coping with Identity
Theft: What to Do When an Impostor Strikes

www.privacyrights.org

Social Security Administration, Frequently
Asked Questions on SSA's Internet Website

www.ssa.gov/pubs/10064.html

Social Security Administration, Identity
Theft and Your Social Security Number
(SSA Publication No. 05-10064)

www.socialsecurity.gov/pubs/10064.html

Social Security Administration, Identity Theft Links

www.socialsecurity.gov/oig/investigations/links.htm

Social Security Administration (Office of Inspector General), When Someone Else Uses Your Social Security Number Fact Sheet

www.socialsecurity.gov/oig/hotline/when.htm

Social Security Administration, New Rules for Getting a Social Security Number and Card (SSA Publication No. 05-10120)

www.socialsecurity.gov/pubs/10120.html

Social Security Administration, Your Social Security Number and Card (SSA Pub. No. 05-10002)

www.socialsecurity.gov/pubs/10002.html

U.S. Bank, Online Security

www.usbank.com/cgi_w/cfm/about/online_security/index.cfm

U.S. Chamber of Commerce, Security Toolkit for Small Businesses

www.U.S.C.hamber.com/sb/security/default.htm

U.S. Department of Justice, Office of Community Oriented Policing Services, Identity Theft

www.popcenter.org

U.S. General Accounting Office (2002), "Identity Fraud: Report No. GGD-98-1 00BR"

www.gpoaccess.gov/gaoreports/index.html

U.S. Postal Service, ID Theft Poster

www.usps.com/websites/depart/inspect/idposter.pdf

U.S. Postal Service, Identity Crisis (DVD)

www.usps.com/websites/depart/inspect/idthft_ncpw.htm

U.S. Postal Service, Identity Theft Is America's Fastest-Growing Crime

www.usps.com/websites/depart/inspect/idthft_ncpw.htm

U.S. Postal Service, Identity Theft: Stealing Your Name and Your Money

www.usps.com/websites/depart/inspect/IDtheft2.htm

U.S. Postal Service, LooksTooGoodToBeTrue.com

www.lookstoogoodtobetrue.com/fraud.aspx

U.S. Postal Service, Read These Tips to Protect Yourself from Identity Theft

www.usps.com/websites/depart/inspect/idtheftips.htm

U.S. Postal Service, Safeguard Your Personal Information

www.usps.com/cpim/ftp/pubs/pub280/welcome.htm

U.S. Treasury Department, Frequently Asked Questions: Protecting Yourself

www.treas.gov/usss/faq.shtml#identity

U.S. Treasury Department, Computer Security Bulletin—Phishing Scams

www.treas.gov/tigta/docs/phishing_alert_2006.pdf

Virginia Credit Union, Security and Identity Theft

www.vacu.org/education/security.asp

Visa USA, Protect Yourself

www.usa.visa.com/personal/security/protect_yourself/index.html

Wells Fargo, Identity Theft

www.wellsfargo.com/privacy_security/fraud/operate/idtheft

Wisconsin Department of Agriculture, Trade and Consumer Protection, Office of Privacy Protection, How Small Business Can Help in the Fight against ID Theft

www.privacy.wi.gov

> This is a copy of an ID Theft Affidavit that may be completed by the victim. The victim may also complete one online at *www.consumer. gov/idtheft/pdf/affidavit.pdf* and print copies to send to all companies involved.

INSTRUCTIONS FOR COMPLETING THE ID THEFT AFFIDAVIT

To make certain that you do not become responsible for any debts incurred by an identity thief, you must prove to each of the companies where accounts were opened in your name that you did not create the debt. The ID Theft Affidavit was developed by a group of credit grantors, consumer advocates, and attorneys at the Federal Trade Commission (FTC) for this purpose. Importantly, this affidavit is only for use where a new account was opened in your name. If someone made unauthorized charges to an existing account, call the company for instructions.

While many companies accept this affidavit, others require that you submit more, or different, forms. Before you send the affidavit, contact each company to find out if they accept it. If they do not accept the ID Theft Affidavit, ask them what information and/or documentation they require.

You may not need the ID Theft Affidavit to absolve you of debt resulting from identity theft if you obtain an Identity Theft Report. We suggest you consider obtaining an Identity Theft Report where a new account was opened in your name. An Identity Theft Report can be used to (1) permanently block fraudulent information from appearing on your credit report, (2) ensure that debts do not reappear on your credit reports, (3) prevent a company from continuing to collect debts or from selling the debt to others for collection, and (4) obtain an extended fraud alert.

The ID Theft Affidavit may be required by a company in order for you to obtain applications or other transaction records related to the theft of your identity. These records may help you prove that you are a victim. For example, you may be able to show that the signature on an application is not yours. These documents also may contain information about the identity thief that is valuable to law enforcement.

This affidavit has two parts:

- Part One, the ID Theft Affidavit, is where you report general information about yourself and the theft.

- Part Two, the Fraudulent Account Statement, is where you describe the fraudulent account(s) opened in your name. Use a separate Fraudulent Account Statement for each company.

When you send the affidavit to the companies, attach copies (NOT originals) of any supporting documents (for example, driver's license or police report). Before submitting your affidavit, review the disputed account(s) with family members or friends who may have information about the account(s) or access to them.

Complete this affidavit as soon as possible. Many creditors ask that you send it within two weeks. Delays on your part could slow the investigation. Be as accurate and complete as possible. You may choose not to provide some of the information requested. However, incorrect or incomplete information will slow the process of investigating your claim and absolving the debt. Print clearly.

When you have finished completing the affidavit, mail a copy to each creditor, bank, or company that provided the thief with the unauthorized credit, goods, or services you describe. Attach a copy of the Fraudulent Account Statement with information only on accounts opened at the institution to which you are sending the packet, as well as any other supporting documentation you are able to provide.

Send the appropriate documents to each company by certified mail, return receipt requested, so you can prove that it was received. The companies will review your claim and send you written responses telling you the outcome of their investigations. Keep a copy of everything you submit.

If you are unable to complete the affidavit, a legal guardian or someone with power of attorney may complete it for you. Except as noted, only the company will use the information you provide to process your affidavit, investigate the events you report, and help stop further fraud. If this affidavit is requested in a lawsuit, the company might have to provide it to the requesting party. Completing this affidavit does not guarantee that the identity thief will be prosecuted or that the debt will be cleared.

If you haven't already done so, report the fraud to the following organizations:

1. Any one of the nationwide consumer reporting companies to place a fraud alert on your credit report. Fraud alerts can help prevent an identity thief from opening any more accounts in your name. The company you call is required to contact the other two, which will place an alert on their versions of your report, too.

   - Equifax: 800-525-6285; *www.equifax.com*
   - Experian: 888-EXPERIAN (397-3742); *www.experian.com*
   - TransUnion: 800-680-7289; *www.transunion.com*

   In addition, once you have placed a fraud alert, you are entitled to order one free credit report from each of the three consumer reporting companies, and if you ask, they will display only the last four digits of your Social Security number on your credit reports.

2. The security or fraud department of each company where you know or believe accounts to have been tampered with or opened fraudulently. Close the accounts. Follow up in writing, and include copies (NOT originals) of supporting documents. It is important to notify credit card companies and banks in writing. Send your letters by certified mail, return receipt requested, so that you can document what the company received and when. Keep a file of your correspondence and enclosures.

When you open new accounts, use new personal identification numbers (PINs) and passwords. Avoid using easily available information, like your mother's maiden name, your birth date, the last four digits of your Social Security number, your phone number, or a series of consecutive numbers.

3. Your local police or the police in the community where the identity theft took place. Provide a copy of your ID Theft Complaint filed with the FTC (see page 248), to be incorporated into the police report. Get a copy of the police report or, at the very least, the number of the report. It can help you deal with creditors who need proof of the crime. If the police are reluctant to take your report, ask to file a Miscellaneous Incidents report or try another jurisdiction, like your state police. You also can check with your state attorney general's office to find out if state law requires the police to take reports for identity theft. Check the Blue Pages of your telephone directory for the phone number, or check *www.naag.org* for a list of state attorneys general.

4. The Federal Trade Commission. By sharing your identity theft complaint with the FTC, you will provide important

information that can help law-enforcement officials across the nation track down identity thieves and stop them. The FTC can also refer victims' complaints to other government agencies and companies for further action, as well as investigate companies for violations of laws that the FTC enforces.

You can file a complaint online at *www.consumer.gov/idtheft*. If you do not have Internet access, call the FTC's Identity Theft Hotline, toll-free: 877-ID-THEFT (438-4338); TTY: 866-653-4261; or write: Identity Theft Clearinghouse, Federal Trade Commission, 600 Pennsylvania Avenue, N.W., Washington, DC 20580. When you file an ID Theft Complaint with the FTC online, you will be given the option to print a copy of your ID Theft Complaint. You should bring a copy of the printed ID Theft Complaint with you to the police to be incorporated into your police report. The ID Theft Complaint, in conjunction with the police report, can create an Identity Theft Report that will help you recover more quickly. The ID Theft Complaint provides the supporting details necessary for an Identity Theft Report, which go beyond the details of a typical police report.

DO NOT SEND AFFIDAVIT TO THE FTC OR ANY OTHER GOVERNMENT AGENCY

ID THEFT AFFIDAVIT

Name _____ **Phone number** _____ **Page 1**

Victim Information

(1) My full legal name is

_____

(First) (Middle) (Last) (Jr., Sr., III)

(2) (If different from above) When the events described in this affidavit took place, I was known as

_____

(First) (Middle) (Last) (Jr., Sr., III)

(3) My date of birth is _____ (day/month/year)

(4) My Social Security number is _____

(5) My driver's license or identification card state and number are

_____

(6) My current address is _____
City _____ State _____
Zip Code _____

(7) I have lived at this address since _____ (month/year)

(8) (If different from above) When the events described in this affidavit took place, my address was _____
City _____ State _____
Zip Code _____

(9) I lived at the address in Item 8 from _____ until

_____

(10) My daytime telephone number is (____) _____
My evening telephone number is (____) _____

DO NOT SEND AFFIDAVIT TO THE FTC OR ANY OTHER GOVERNMENT AGENCY

Name _____ Phone number _____ Page 2

How the Fraud Occurred

Check all that apply for items 11–17:

(11) [ ] I did not authorize anyone to use my name or personal information to seek the money, credit, loans, goods, or services described in this report.

(12) [ ] I did not receive any benefit, money, goods, or services as a result of the events described in this report.

(13) [ ] My identification documents (for example, credit cards, birth certificate, driver's license, Social Security card, etc.) were stolen/lost on or about _____. (day/month/year)

(14) [ ] To the best of my knowledge and belief, the following person(s) used my information (for example, my name, address, date of birth, existing account numbers, Social Security number, mother's maiden name, etc.) or identification documents to get money, credit, loans, goods, or services without my knowledge or authorization:

Name (if known) _____
Address (if known) _____
Phone number(s) (if known) _____
Additional information (if known) _____
Name (if known) _____
Address (if known) _____
Phone number(s) (if known) _____
Additional information (if known) _____

(15) [ ] I do NOT know who used my information or identification documents to get money, credit, loans, goods, or services without my knowledge or authorization.

(16) [ ] Additional comments: (For example, description of the fraud, which documents or information were used, or how the identity thief gained access to your information.)

_____
_____
_____

(Attach additional pages as necessary.)

DO NOT SEND AFFIDAVIT TO THE FTC OR ANY OTHER GOVERNMENT AGENCY

Name _____ **Phone number** _____ **Page 3**

Victim's Law-Enforcement Actions

(17) I [ ] am [ ] am not willing to assist in the prosecution of the person(s) who committed this fraud.

(18) (check one) I [ ] am [ ]am not authorizing the release of this information to law enforcement for the purpose of assisting them in the investigation and prosecution of the person(s) who committed this fraud.

(19) (check all that apply) I [ ] have [ ] have not reported the events described in this affidavit to the police or another law-enforcement agency. The police [ ] did [ ] did not write a report.

In the event you have contacted the police or another law-enforcement agency, please complete the following:

_____	_____
(Agency #1)	(Officer/Agency taking report)
_____	_____
(Date of report)	(Report number, if any)
_____	_____
(Telephone number)	(Email address, if any)
_____	_____
(Agency #2)	(Officer/Agency taking report)
_____	_____
(Date of report)	(Report number, if any)
_____	_____
(Telephone number)	(Email address, if any)

**DO NOT SEND AFFIDAVIT TO THE FTC OR
ANY OTHER GOVERNMENT AGENCY**

Name _____ **Phone number** _____ **Page 4**

Documentation Checklist

Please indicate the supporting documentation you are able to provide to the companies you plan to notify. Attach copies (NOT originals) to the affidavit before sending it to the companies.

(20) [ ] A copy of a valid government-issued photo-identification card (for example, your driver's license, state-issued ID card, or your passport). If you are under 16 and do not have a photo ID, you may submit a copy of your birth certificate or a copy of your official school records showing your enrollment and place of residence.

(21) [ ] Proof of residency during the time the disputed bill occurred, the loan was made or the other event took place (for example, a rental/lease agreement in your name, a copy of a utility bill, or a copy of an insurance bill). (Officer/Agency personnel taking report)

(22) [ ] A copy of the report you filed with the police or sheriff's department. If you are unable to obtain a report or report number from the police, please indicate that in Item 19. Some companies only need the report number, not a copy of the report. You may want to check with each company.

Signature

I certify that, to the best of my knowledge and belief, all the information on and attached to this affidavit is true, correct, and complete and made in good faith. I also understand that this affidavit or the information it contains may be made available to federal, state, and/or local law-enforcement agencies for such action within their jurisdiction as they deem appropriate. I understand that knowingly making any false or fraudulent statement or representation to the government may constitute a violation of 18 U.S.C. § 1001 or other federal, state, or local criminal statutes and may result in imposition of a fine or imprisonment or both.

_____   _____
(Signature)   (Date signed)

_____   _____
(Notary)   (Date signed)

(Check with each company. Creditors sometimes require notarization. If they do not, please have one witness (nonrelative) sign below that you completed and signed this affidavit.)

Witness:

_____   _____   _____
(Signature)   (Printed name)   (Telephone number)

DO NOT SEND AFFIDAVIT TO THE FTC OR
ANY OTHER GOVERNMENT AGENCY

Name _____ Phone number _____ Page 5

Fraudulent Account Statement

Completing This Statement

Make as many copies of this page as you need. Complete a separate page for each company you're notifying and only send it to that company. Include a copy of your signed affidavit.

- List only the account(s) you're disputing with the company receiving this form.
- See the example below.
- If a collection agency sent you a statement, letter, or notice about the fraudulent account, attach a copy of that document (NOT the original).

I declare (check all that apply):

[ ] As a result of the event(s) described in the ID Theft Affidavit, the following account(s) was/were opened at your company in my name without my knowledge, permission, or authorization using my personal information or identifying documents:

Creditor Name/Address (the company that opened the account or provided the goods or services)	Account Number	Type of unauthorized credit/goods/services provided by creditor (if known)	Date issued or opened (if known)	Amount/Value provided (the amount charged or the cost of the goods/services)
National Bank 22 Main Street Columbus, Ohio 22722	012345	Auto loan	01/02/2008	$36,600

[ ] During the time of the accounts described above, I had the following account open with your company:

Billing name _____

Billing address _____

Account number _____

DO NOT SEND AFFIDAVIT TO THE FTC OR ANY OTHER GOVERNMENT AGENCY

EXECUTIVE SUMMARY OF THE PRESIDENT'S IDENTITY THEFT TASK FORCE REPORT (APRIL 2007)

From Main Street to Wall Street, from the back porch to the front office, from the kitchen table to the conference room, Americans are talking about identity theft. The reason: millions of Americans each year suffer the financial and emotional trauma it causes. This crime takes many forms, but it invariably leaves victims with the task of repairing the damage to their lives. It is a problem with no single cause and no single solution.

A. INTRODUCTION

Eight years ago, Congress enacted the Identity Theft and Assumption Deterrence Act, which created the federal crime of identity theft and charged the Federal Trade Commission (FTC) with taking complaints from identity theft victims, sharing these complaints with federal, state, and local law enforcement, and providing the victims with information to help them restore their good name. Since then, federal, state, and local agencies have taken strong action to combat identity theft. The FTC has developed the Identity Theft Data Clearinghouse into a vital resource for consumers and law enforcement agencies; the Department of Justice (DOJ) has prosecuted vigorously a wide range of identity theft schemes under the identity theft statutes and other laws; the federal financial regulatory agencies have adopted and enforced robust data security standards for entities under their jurisdiction; Congress passed, and the Department of Homeland Security issued draft regulations on, the REAL ID Act of 2005; and numerous other federal agencies, such as the Social Security Administration (SSA), have educated consumers on avoiding and recovering from identity theft. Many private sector entities, too, have taken proactive and significant steps to protect data from identity thieves, educate consumers about how to prevent identity theft, assist law enforcement in apprehending identity thieves, and assist identity theft victims who suffer losses.

Over those same eight years, however, the problem of identity theft has become more complex and challenging for the general public, the government, and the private sector. Consumers, overwhelmed with weekly media reports of data breaches, feel vulnerable and uncertain of how to protect their identities. At the same time, both the private and public sectors have had to grapple with difficult, and costly, decisions about investments in safeguards and what more to do to protect the public. And, at every level of government—from the largest cities with major police departments to the smallest towns with one fraud detective—identity theft has placed increasingly pressing demands on law enforcement.

Public comments helped the Task Force define the issues and challenges posed by identity theft and develop its strategic responses. To ensure that the Task Force heard from all stakeholders, it solicited comments from the public.

In addition to consumer advocacy groups, law enforcement, business, and industry, the Task Force also received comments from identity theft victims themselves. The victims wrote of the burdens and frustrations associated with their recovery from this crime. Their stories reaffirmed the need for the government to act quickly to address this problem.

The overwhelming majority of the comments received by the Task Force strongly affirmed the need for a fully coordinated approach to fighting the problem through prevention, awareness, enforcement, training, and victim assistance. Consumers wrote to the Task Force exhorting the public and private sectors to do a better job of protecting their Social Security numbers (SSNs), and many of those who submitted comments discussed the challenges raised by the overuse of Social Security numbers as identifiers. Others, representing certain business sectors, pointed to the beneficial uses of SSNs in fraud detection. The Task Force was mindful of both considerations, and its recommendations seek to strike the appropriate balance in addressing SSN use. Local law enforcement officers, regardless of where they work, wrote of the challenges of multi-jurisdictional investigations and called for greater coordination and resources to support the investigation and prosecution of identity thieves. Various business groups described the steps they have taken to minimize the occurrence and impact of the crime and many expressed support for risk-based, national data security and breach notification requirements.

These communications from the public went a long way toward informing the Task Force's recommendation for a fully coordinated strategy. Only an approach that encompasses effective prevention, public awareness and education, victim assistance, and law enforcement measures and which fully engages federal, state, and local authorities will be successful in protecting citizens and private entities from the crime.

B. THE STRATEGY

Although identity theft is defined in many different ways, it is, fundamentally, the misuse of another individual's personal information to commit fraud. Identity theft has at least three stages in its "life cycle," and it must be attacked at each of those stages:

First, the identity thief attempts to acquire a victim's personal information.

Criminals must first gather personal information, either through low-tech methods—such as stealing mail or workplace records or "dumpster diving" —or through complex and high-tech frauds, such as hacking and the use of malicious computer codes. The loss or theft of personal information by itself, however, does not immediately lead to identity theft. In some cases, thieves who steal personal items inadvertently steal personal information that is stored in or with the stolen personal items, yet never make use of the personal information. It has recently been reported that, during the past year, the personal records of nearly 73 million people have been lost or stolen, but that there is no evidence of a surge in identity theft or financial fraud as a result. Still, because any loss or theft of personal information is troubling and potentially devastating for the persons involved, a strategy to keep consumer data out of the hands of criminals is essential.

Second, the thief attempts to misuse the information he has acquired.

In this stage, criminals have acquired the victim's personal information and now attempt to sell the information or use it themselves. The misuse of stolen personal information can be classified in the following broad categories:

Existing account fraud: This occurs when thieves obtain account information involving credit, brokerage, banking, or utility accounts that are already open. Existing account fraud is typically a less costly, but more prevalent, form of identity theft. For example, a stolen credit card may lead to thousands of dollars in fraudulent charges, but the card generally would not provide the thief with enough information to establish a false identity. Moreover, most credit card companies, as a matter of policy, do not hold consumers liable for fraudulent charges, and federal law caps liability of victims of credit card theft at $50.

New account fraud: Thieves use personal information, such as Social Security numbers, birth dates, and home addresses, to open new accounts in the victim's name, make charges indiscriminately, and then disappear. While this type of identity theft is less likely to occur, it imposes much greater costs and hardships on victims.

In addition, identity thieves sometimes use stolen personal information to obtain government, medical, or other benefits to which the criminal is not entitled.

Third, an identity thief has completed his crime and is enjoying the benefits, while the victim is realizing the harm.

At this point in the life cycle of the theft, victims are first learning of the crime, often after being denied credit or employment or being contacted by a debt collector seeking payment for a debt the victim did not incur.

In light of the complexity of the problem at each of the stages of this life cycle, the Identity Theft Task Force is recommending a plan that marshals government resources to crack down on the criminals who traffic in stolen identities, strengthens efforts to protect the personal information of our nation's citizens, helps law enforcement officials investigate and prosecute identity thieves, helps educate consumers and businesses about protecting themselves, and increases the safeguards on personal data entrusted to federal agencies and private entities.

The plan focuses on improvements in four key areas:

1. Keeping sensitive consumer data out of the hands of identity thieves through better data security and more accessible education

2. Making it more difficult for identity thieves who obtain consumer data to use it to steal identities

3. Assisting the victims of identity theft in recovering from the crime

4. Deterring identity theft by more aggressive prosecution
   and punishment of those who commit the crime

In these four areas, the Task Force makes a number of recommendations summarized in greater detail below. Among those recommendations are the following broad policy changes:

- That federal agencies should reduce the unnecessary use of Social Security numbers (SSNs), the most valuable commodity for an identity thief

- That national standards should be established to require private sector entities to safeguard the personal data they compile and maintain and to provide notice to consumers when a breach occurs that poses a significant risk of identity theft

- That federal agencies should implement a broad, sustained awareness campaign to educate consumers, the private sector, and the public sector on deterring, detecting, and defending against identity theft

- That a National Identity Theft Law Enforcement Center should be created to allow law enforcement agencies to coordinate their efforts and information more efficiently and investigate and prosecute identity thieves more effectively

The Task Force believes that all of the recommendations in this strategic plan—from these broad policy changes to the small steps—are necessary to wage a more effective fight against identity theft and reduce its incidence and damage. Some recommendations can be implemented relatively quickly; others will take time and the sustained cooperation of government entities and the private sector. Following are the recommendations of the President's Task Force on Identity Theft:

PREVENTION: KEEPING CONSUMER DATA OUT OF THE HANDS OF CRIMINALS

Identity theft depends on access to consumer data. Reducing the opportunities for thieves to get the data is critical to fighting the crime. Government, the business community, and consumers have roles to play in protecting data.

Data compromises can expose consumers to the threat of identity theft or related fraud, damage the reputation of the entity that experienced the breach, and carry financial costs for everyone involved. While "perfect security" does not exist, all entities that collect and maintain sensitive consumer information must take reasonable and appropriate steps to protect it.

Data Security in Public Sector

Decrease the Unnecessary Use of Social Security Numbers in the Public Sector by Developing Alternative Strategies for Identity Management

- Survey current use of SSNs by federal government.

- Issue guidance on appropriate use of SSNs.

- Establish clearinghouse for "best" agency practices that minimize use of SSNs.

- Work with state and local governments to review use of SSNs.

Educate Federal Agencies on How to Protect Data; Monitor Their Compliance with Existing Guidance

- Develop concrete guidance and best practices.

- Monitor agency compliance with data security guidance.

- Protect portable storage and communications devices.

Ensure Effective, Risk-Based Responses to Data Breaches Suffered by Federal Agencies

- Issue data breach guidance to agencies.

- Publish a "routine use" allowing disclosure of information after a breach to those entities that can assist in responding to the breach.

Data Security in Private Sector

Establish National Standards for Private Sector Data Protection Requirements and Breach Notice Requirements

Develop Comprehensive Record on Private Sector Use of Social Security Numbers

Better Educate the Private Sector on Safeguarding Data

- Hold regional seminars for businesses on safeguarding information.

- Distribute improved guidance for private industry.

Initiate Investigations of Data Security Violations

Initiate a Multiyear Public Awareness Campaign

- Develop national awareness campaign.

- Enlist outreach partners.

- Increase outreach to traditionally underserved communities.

- Establish "Protect Your Identity" Days.

Develop Online Clearinghouse for Current Educational Resources

PREVENTION: MAKING IT HARDER TO MISUSE CONSUMER DATA

Because security systems are imperfect and thieves are resourceful, it is essential to reduce the opportunities for criminals to misuse the data they steal. An identity thief who wants to open new accounts in a victim's name must be able to (1) provide identifying information to allow the creditor or other grantor of benefits to access information on which to base a decision about eligibility and (2) convince the creditor that he is the person he purports to be.

Authentication includes determining a person's identity at the beginning of a relationship (sometimes called verification) and later ensuring that he is the same person who was originally authenticated. But the process can fail: Identity documents can be falsified; the accuracy of the initial information and the accuracy or quality of the verifying sources can be questionable; employee training can be insufficient; and people can fail to follow procedures.

Efforts to facilitate the development of better ways to authenticate consumers without burdening consumers or businesses—for example, multi-factor authentication or layered security—would go a long way toward preventing criminals from profiting from identity theft.

Hold Workshops on Authentication

- Engage academics, industry, entrepreneurs, and government experts on developing and promoting better ways to authenticate identity.
- Issue reports on workshop findings.

Develop a Comprehensive Record on Private Sector Use of SSNs

VICTIM RECOVERY: HELPING CONSUMERS REPAIR THEIR LIVES

Identity theft can be committed despite a consumer's best efforts at securing information. Consumers have a number of rights and resources available, but some surveys indicate that they are not as well-informed as they could be. Government agencies must work together to ensure that victims have the knowledge, tools, and assistance necessary to minimize the damage and begin the recovery process.

Provide Specialized Training About Victim Recovery to First Responders and Others Offering Direct Assistance to Identity Theft Victims

- Train law enforcement officers.

- Provide educational materials for first responders that can be used as a reference guide for identity theft victims.

- Create and distribute an ID Theft Victim Statement of Rights.

- Design nationwide training for victim assistance counselors.

Develop Avenues for Individualized Assistance to Identity Theft Victims

Amend Criminal Restitution Statutes to Ensure That Victims Recover the Value of Time Spent in Trying to Remediate the Harms Suffered

Assess Whether to Implement a National System That Allows Victims to Obtain an Identification Document for Authentication Purposes

Assess Efficacy of Tools Available to Victims

- Conduct assessment of FACT Act remedies under FCRA.

- Conduct assessment of state credit freeze laws.

LAW ENFORCEMENT: PROSECUTING AND PUNISHING IDENTITY THIEVES

Strong criminal law enforcement is necessary to punish and deter identity thieves. The increasing sophistication of identity thieves in recent years has meant that law enforcement agencies at all levels of government have had to increase the resources they devote to investigating related crimes. The investigations are labor-intensive and generally require a staff of detectives, agents, and analysts with multiple skill sets. When a suspected theft involves a large number of potential victims, investigative agencies often need additional personnel to handle victim-witness coordination.

Coordination and Information/Intelligence Sharing

Establish a National Identity Theft Law Enforcement Center

Develop and Promote the Use of a Universal Identity Theft Report Form

Enhance Information Sharing between Law Enforcement and the Private Sector

- Enhance ability of law enforcement to receive information from financial institutions

- Initiate discussions with financial services industry on countermeasures to identity theft

- Initiate discussions with credit reporting agencies on preventing identity theft

Coordination with Foreign Law Enforcement

Encourage Other Countries to Enact Suitable Domestic Legislation Criminalizing Identity Theft

Facilitate Investigation and Prosecution of International Identity Theft by Encouraging Other Nations to Accede to the Convention on Cybercrime

Identify the Nations That Provide Safe Havens for Identity Thieves and Use All Measures Available to Encourage Those Countries to Change Their Policies

Enhance the United States Government's Ability to Respond to Appropriate Foreign Requests for Evidence in Criminal Cases Involving Identity Theft

Assist, Train, and Support Foreign Law Enforcement

Prosecution Approaches and Initiatives

Increase Prosecutions of Identity Theft

- Designate an identity theft coordinator for each United States Attorney's Office to design a specific identity theft program for each district.

- Evaluate monetary thresholds for prosecution.

- Encourage state prosecution of identity theft.

- Create working groups and task forces.

Conduct Targeted Enforcement Initiatives

- Conduct enforcement initiatives focused on using unfair or deceptive means to make SSNs available for sale.

- Conduct enforcement initiatives focused on identity theft related to the health care system.

- Conduct enforcement initiatives focused on identity theft by illegal aliens.

Review Civil Monetary Penalty Programs

Gaps in Statutes Criminalizing Identity Theft

Close the Gaps in Federal Criminal Statutes Used to Prosecute Identity Theft–Related Offenses to Ensure Increased Federal Prosecution of These Crimes

- Amend the identity theft and aggravated identity theft statutes to ensure that identity thieves who misappropriate information belonging to corporations and organizations can be prosecuted.

- Add new crimes to the list of predicate offenses for aggravated identity theft offenses.

- Amend the statute that criminalizes the theft of electronic data by eliminating the current requirement that the information must have been stolen through interstate communications.

- Penalize creators and distributors of malicious spyware and key-loggers.

- Amend the cyber-extortion statute to cover additional, alternate types of cyber-extortion.

Ensure That an Identity Thief's Sentence Can Be Enhanced When the Criminal Conduct Affects More Than One Victim

Law Enforcement Training

Enhance Training for Law Enforcement Officers and Prosecutors

- Develop course at National Advocacy Center focused on investigation and prosecution of identity theft.

- Increase number of regional identity theft seminars.

- Increase resources for law enforcement on the Internet.

- Review curricula to enhance basic and advanced training on identity theft.

Measuring the Success of Law Enforcement

Enhance the Gathering of Statistical Data Impacting the Criminal Justice System's Response to Identity Theft

- Gather and analyze statistically reliable data from identity theft victims.

- Expand scope of national crime victimization survey.

- Review U.S. Sentencing Commission data.

- Track prosecutions of identity theft and resources spent.

- Conduct targeted surveys.

ABOUT THE AUTHOR

Cliff Roberson, LL.M., Ph.D, is Editor-in-Chief of *Professional Issues in Criminal Justice Journal* and a member of the core faculty, Graduate School of Criminal Justice, Kaplan University. Cliff is also a Professor Emeritus of Criminal Justice at Washburn University. He has authored or coauthored 47 books and texts.

Cliff's previous legal experiences include: Director of Programs, National College of District Attorneys; Professor of Criminology and Director of Justice Center, California State University, Fresno; Assistant Professor of Criminal Justice, St. Edwards University; U.S. Marine Corps service as an infantry officer, trial and defense counsel, and military judge as a marine judge advocate; and Director of the Military Law Branch, U.S. Marine Corps. Other legal employment experiences include Trial Supervisor, Office of State Counsel for Offenders, Texas Board of Criminal Justice and Judge ProTem in the California courts. Cliff is admitted to practice before the U.S. Supreme Court, U.S. Court of Military Appeals, U.S. Tax Court, federal courts in California and Texas, the Supreme Court of Texas, and the Supreme Court of California.

His educational background includes: Ph.D. in Human Behavior, U.S. International University; LL.M. in Criminal Law, Criminology, and Psychiatry, George Washington University; J.D., American University; B.A. in Political Science, University of Missouri; and one year of post-graduate study at the University of Virginia School of Law.

END NOTES

1. "Safeguard Your Personal Information." Pamphlet No. 280, Washington, D.C.: U.S. Postal Service. March 2005.

2. Graeme R. Newman and Megan M. McNally, "Identity Theft Literature Review," NCJRS Report No. 210459, page 14. Washington, D.C.: U.S. Dept. of Justice. July 2005.

3. President's Identity Theft Task Force. Combating Identity Theft Task Force Report, page 12. Washington, D.C.: Government Printing Office April 2007.

4. Graeme R. Newman, "Identity Theft." Problem-Oriented Guide for Police No. 25, U.S. Dept. of Justice, COPS and Center for Problem-Oriented Policing. June 2004. *www.popcenter. org/problems/indentity-theft.*

5. This table is a modification of the table presented in Newman, "Identity Theft," page 8.

6. Heith Copes and Lynne Vieraitis, "Identity Theft: Assessing Offenders' Strategies and Perceptions of Risk." NCJRS Report No. 219122. Washington, D.C.: U.S. Dept. of Justice. July 2007.

7. Graeme R. Newman and Megan M. McNally, page ix.

8. CALPIRG, "Nowhere to Turn: Victims Speak Out on Identity Theft." A CALPIRG/PRC Report. Sacramento: Privacy Rights Clearinghouse. May 2000.

9. Graeme R. Newman and Megan M. McNally, page x.

10. For a more detailed report on the Billings PD program, see *Police Chief Magazine*, April 2007, or visit the International Association of Police Chiefs at *www.policechiefmagazine.org.* In addi-

tion, the Billings Police Department website may be visited at *www.copshopsouth@ci.billings.mt.us.*

11. Graeme R. Newman, "Identity Theft." Problem-Oriented Guide for Police No. 25, U.S. Dept. of Justice, COPS and Center for Problem-Oriented Policing. June 2004. *www.popcenter.org/problems/indentity-theft.*

12. New Jersey Division of Consumer Affairs. "Credit Card Skimming: A Consumer Brief," at *www.njconsumeraffairs.gov,* accessed on October 14, 2007.

13. John Lelan, "Meth users, attuned to detail, add another habit: ID theft." *New York Times,* July 11, 2006. A-3.

14. United Nations Interregional Crime and Justice Research Institute. "Coalitions Against Trafficking in Human Beings in the Philippines." Research and Action Final Report: Anti-Human Trafficking Unit. Vienna, Austria: United Nations. 2003. Available online at *www.unodc.org/unodc/en/publications/publications.*

15. Norman Wilcox and Thomas Regan, "Identity Fraud: Providing a Solution," *Journal of Economic Crime Management,* vol. 1, issue 1, 2002.

16. Reported on CourtTV Website: *www.courttv.com/trials/soliah/olsonprofile_ctv.html.* Accessed on October 15, 2007.

17. As reported in the *Police Chief Magazine,* May 2007, vol. 74, no. 5.

18. Nicole van der Meulen, "The Spread of Identity Theft: Developments and Initiatives Within the European Union," *Police Chief Magazine.* May 2007, vol. 74, no. 5.

19. International Association of Police Chiefs, Training Key 534.

INDEX